Young People's Involvement in Sport

Those involved with the development of sport for young people will be aware that despite considerable interest in the topic, there is very little hard data on basic questions such as the 'who', 'what', 'why', 'where' and 'how' of participation. *Young People's Involvement in Sport* provides this information, based on data collected from 2,400 lengthy face-to-face interviews with children aged 7–16, 600 activity diaries, and focus groups with élite performers, coaches and parents. The book offers a comprehensive picture of young people's involvement in sport and physical activity in the 1990s and a benchmark against which development into the next millennium can be measured.

Set in the context of the literature on sport involvement and participation motivation, and accepting wider policy concerns, individual contributors have used the data to address a particular concern, including gender, age, school to club transition, personality, modelling the participation process, and sport policy concerns. Discussion is based on a range of methodological procedures, ranging from the psychometric and the quantitative, through to the purely qualitative. Written throughout in an accessible style, the book will be of considerable value to sport scientists, sports administrators, coaches, teachers and policy makers. It will also be welcomed by sport science, social science and psychology students with an interest in sport participation.

John Kremer and **Karen Trew** are in the School of Psychology, the Queen's University of Belfast. John Kremer's previous publications include *Psychology in Sport* (1994), with Deirdre Scully. **Shaun Ogle** is with the Sports Council for Northern Ireland.

Adolescence and Society

Series editor: John C. Coleman
The Trust for the Study of Adolescence

The general aim of the series is to make accessible to a wide readership the growing evidence relating to adolescent development. Much of this material is published in relatively inaccessible professional journals, and the goals of the books in this series will be to summarize, review and place in context current work in the field so as to interest and engage both an undergraduate and a professional audience.

The intention of the authors is to raise the profile of adolescent studies among professionals and in institutions of higher education. By publishing relatively short, readable books on interesting topics to do with youth and society, the series will make people more aware of the relevance of the subject of adolescence to a wide range of social concerns.

The books will not put forward any one theoretical viewpoint. The authors will outline the most prominent theories in the field and will include a balanced and critical assessment of each of these. Whilst some of the books may have a clinical or applied slant, the majority will concentrate on normal development.

The readership will rest primarily in two major areas: the undergraduate market, particularly in the fields of psychology, sociology and education; and the professional training market, with particular emphasis on social work, clinical and educational psychology, counselling, youth work, nursing and teacher training.

Young people's involvement in sport

Edited by John Kremer, Karen Trew
and Shaun Ogle

London and New York

First published 1997 by Routledge
11 New Fetter Lane, London EC4P 4EE

Simultaneously published in the USA and Canada
by Routledge
29 West 35th Street, New York, NY 10001

Reprinted in 2000

Routledge is an imprint of the Taylor & Francis Group

© 1997 Edited by John Kremer, Karen Trew, and Shaun Ogle

Typeset in Times by Pure Tech India Ltd, Pondicherry
Printed and bound in Great Britain by Creative Print and Design (Wales),
Ebbw Vale

British Library Cataloguing in Publication Data
A catalogue record for this book is available from the British Library

Library of Congress Cataloging in Publication Data
Young people's involvement in sport / edited by John Kremer, Karen
  Trew, and Shaun Ogle.
        p.   cm. – (Adolescence and society)
      Includes bibliographical references and indexes.
      ISBN 0–415–16649–7. – ISBN 0–415–16650–0 (pbk.)
      1. Sports–Northern Ireland. 2. Sports for children–Northern
      Ireland. 3. Recreational surveys–Northern Ireland.
      I. Kremer, John M.D. II. Trew, Karen J. III. Ogle, Shaun.
      IV. Series.
      GV605.5.Y68 1997
      796′.083′09416–dc21   97–1609
                                                          CIP

Contents

List of figures

List of tables

List of contributors

Walter Bleakley is Course Director of the Postgraduate Certificate in Education course at the University of Ulster at Jordanstown, where he lectures in physical education and research methods. His research interests, in particular, concern the role played by assessment within physical education.

Deirdre Brennan is Course Director for Sport and Leisure Studies at the University of Ulster at Jordanstown, where she also lectures on the sociology of sport, physical education and coaching studies. Her research is presently focused on the role of physical activity in the lives of young girls, and its potential as a medium for female agency and empowerment. She is also a national league basketball player and coach.

Garnet Busby is based in the School of Psychology at The Queen's University of Belfast where he is currently researching the relationship between exercise and psychological well-being among long term prisoners. Since 1994 he has been using this research to develop a multi-dimensional model of participation motivation with particular reference to sport and exercise.

Jacqueline Clarke is employed as a physical education teacher at St Oleans High School in Northern Ireland. Her research interests have focused on gender in sport, with particular reference to girl's socialisation.

Janthia Duncan lectures in communication and technology studies at Ravensbourne College of Design and Technology. She has developed a wide experience as a facilitator of focus group interviews and, in this capacity, has worked as a research associate with Research and Evaluation Services on a number of significant public and private sector projects over recent years.

Tony Gallagher is a Reader in the School of Education at The Queen's University of Belfast. Coming originally from a background in psychology, he has published extensively and has developed a considerable reputation in the area of community relations, education and equity policy in Northern Ireland.

John Kremer is a Reader in the School of Psychology at the Queen's University of Belfast where he lectures in applied social psychology. His research has ranged across sport and exercise psychology, dealing with both pure and applied concerns. Over the years he has been involved in the design and implementation of a large number of surveys, normally incorporating both qualitative and quantitative techniques.

Craig Mahoney is Head of the Sport Studies Department at Roehampton Institute in London. A former primary school teacher, he lectured for seven years in Northern Ireland, during which time he was involved with four major surveys of young people relating to fitness, attitudes and health. He has published widely in this field and also in relation to physical education, élite performance and motor learning.

Shaun Ogle is Senior Research Officer with the Sports Council for Northern Ireland, where he has been actively involved in sports research since 1988. His research interests centre on the performance measurement of public policy and he has initiated and managed several large-scale surveys connected with sport, including 'The Northern Ireland Health and Activity Survey', 'The Economic Impact of Sport in Northern Ireland', and 'Public Perceptions of Sport'.

Deirdre Scully is a Lecturer in the Department of Sport and Leisure Studies at the University of Ulster at Jordanstown. She obtained her first degree in physical education and her MSc and PhD in sport psychology from the University of Illinois. She has published widely on a variety of sport psychology topics and as an accredited sport psychologist she has worked with a number of sports including golf, athletics, swimming, ice skating and basketball. Recent publications include 'Psychology in Sport' with John Kremer.

Karen Trew is a Senior Lecturer in the School of Psychology at The Queen's University of Belfast, specialising in applied social psychology. She has published extensively in this field, with a particular emphasis on identity and development/education. Her previous research has utilised time diaries, both in the context of education and unemployment.

Peter Ward is Managing Director of Resarch and Evaluation Services (RES), a company which he founded in 1987. The Company specialises in academic and social policy research, and has managed a considerable number of large scale survey projects in the UK and Ireland. For this project, RES assisted with the technical design of the questionnaire, managed the survey itself and produced a fully validated dataset for subsequent analysis.

Anneke van Wersch qualified as physical education teacher before completing her psychology honours and masters degrees at Nijmegen University in The Netherlands. She completed her doctorate in sport and exercise psychology at Queen's University and subsequently has worked as a research psychologist on a range of projects related to health psychology.

Preface

From whatever background they come, whether as academics, practitioners or policy makers, those involved with the development of sport for young people will be aware that despite widespread interest in the topic, there is very little in the way of hard data to guide development. *Young People's Involvement in Sport* provides hard data for those charged with development, based on information collected from 2,400 lengthy face-to-face interviews with children aged 7–16, 600 four-day time diaries, and focus groups with élite performers, coaches and parents. The book offers a comprehensive picture of young people's involvement in sport and physical activity in the 1990s and a benchmark against which development in the last years of this millenium and the first decade of the new millennium can be measured.

While the survey took place in one small region of the United Kingdom, and local factors will have played some part in determining the profile of activity patterns, at the same time we feel the book has been able to make observations and raise issues which relate to young people wherever they engage in sport and physical activity. A scan across the chapter titles should confirm our intention to deal with issues of a universal nature, encompassing gender, age, school to club transition, individual differences, modelling the participation process and policy concerns, alongside an array of methodological procedures ranging from the psychometric and the quantitative, through to the purely qualititative. In turn, we sincerely hope, and planned, that this approach would mean that the book could offer something for everyone with an interest in young people and sport.

Set in the context of the literature on sport involvement and participation motivation, and accepting wider policy concerns, individual contributors were invited to use the data in whatever way they felt best in order to address a particular substantive concern. The authors specifically were asked to write not only for a local audience but with a wider international readership in mind and including sport scientists, sports administrators, coaches, teachers and policy makers, indeed anyone with an interest in the who, what, why and how of young people's involvement in sport. It may be that there are further issues which warrant investigation and we are keen to facilitate further analyses. For those who may wish to work with the data, the complete data set is to be lodged with the UK's Economic and Social Research Council Data Archive, or alternatively contact Dr Shaun Ogle at the Sports Council for Northern Ireland, House of Sport, Upper Malone Road, Belfast, for further information.

As editors, we are most grateful to the many people who have helped move the project through to its conclusion. Aside from the contributors to this volume, who volunteered their services so generously and who co-operated so readily throughout the editorial process, we would especially like to offer our sincere thanks to the various research officers who have been so valuable at different stages of the project. In particular, we would like to thank Anne McKee and Evelyn McCrum for their meticulous work with the main data set, Charlotte Russell and Jane Hale for all their invaluable work with the time diaries, and all the staff of Research and Evaluation Services for the professional execution of the fieldwork. Particular thanks are also due to the schools and children who co-operated and to the Sports Council for Northern Ireland who sponsored the research and made available the data for further consideration.

John Kremer, Karen Trew and Shaun Ogle

1   Introduction

John Kremer

Put the terms sport and young people together and almost inevitably questions about participation will spring to mind – who takes part, what do they do, where do they do it and why do they do it? As you may expect, of the four questions sport scientists have tended to busy themselves most with the last and most interesting, the why question, or the reasons or underlying motives behind involvement. An understanding of 'why' clearly is important but at the same time it can be argued that by artificially disentangling any single question, theme or area of concern, the totality of the picture or jigsaw which we call participation will be destroyed. For example, we may know a great deal about why young people like to take part in certain activities, and what turns them off other activities, but unless we know what is or has been available, and their opportunities for translating wishes into actions, then an understanding of underlying motives remains an artificial or academic enterprise.

It is to be hoped that the survey of young people which forms the mainstay to this book may go some way towards providing answers to a great many questions surrounding involvement in sport and physical activity, including the who, what, where and why. In aspiring towards that goal, the project joins a surprisingly small body of research which has tried to determine both the structural and the psychological determinants of sport and physical activity. The project itself has yielded four sets of data. The first set, which is the basis for the major part of this book, was derived from face-to-face interviews, the second from various psychometric measures administered to all young people who were interviewed (Chapter 3), the third from a series of focus groups with coaches, teachers, parents and élite performers (Chapter 8), and the fourth from weekly activity diaries completed by a subset of the sample (Chapter 7).

The face-to-face interviews were carried out with 2,400 young people, aged between 7 and 18 years, who were drawn from schools across Northern Ireland and who each had a unique biography of involvement in sport and physical activity. For each young person, a special set of circumstances have conspired together either to nurture or inhibit budding sporting potential. Unfortunately, there is not time to tell each of those stories. Instead, the intention here is to apply broader brush strokes across the data set, and so to identify trends across a discrete sample of young people, and from there to draw inferences which may be applicable to other samples.

From the outset of the project it was important to keep in mind key variables for subsequent analysis. The most significant of these have been afforded special attention in subsequent chapters, that is gender (Chapter 2), personality or individual differences (Chapter 3), community background (Chapter 6), and age (Chapter 5), alongside structural considerations such as the relationship between schools and clubs (Chapter 4).

Those familiar with previous surveys concerning socialisation and leisure may be surprised to learn that socio-economic class was not included as a primary variable. The reasons for this omission are twofold. First, at the time of survey a great many school principals in Northern Ireland refused to allow interviewers to gather information on parental occupations (given sensitivities over security force work); hence it was impossible to derive this variable through interviews. Second, selection at age 11 years has perpetuated the grammar/ secondary divide in post-primary schools in Northern Ireland, with those who attain certain academic standards being offered grammar school places. Inevitably, the middle classes tend to predominate in grammar schools and hence it was felt that this grammar/secondary divide could serve as a useful proxy for socio-economic class.

Chapter 9 stands apart from earlier chapters as it is a more overt attempt to tackle the more theoretical or 'why' question relating to participation. As such this chapter includes an innovative process model of sport participation which brings together a variety of structural, biographical, psychological and attitudinal components, set within the context of existing research, and tested against some of the key findings to emerge from the present survey.

PREVIOUS RESEARCH

Looking back at the history of work on young people's sporting lives, it is possible to identify at least three discrete areas of activity. First there is the psychological, where, generally speaking, sport and exercise psychologists have focused on either how competitive sport may impact on children's perception of sport and physical activity, or how models of intrinsic motivation (often derived from the wider world of education) can be operationalised in the world of sport. Second, there have been sport sociologists who have turned their attention towards socialisation, mainly during adolescence, and who look upon sport and leisure as an essential part of this process of socialisation. Third, there is a loose alliance of educationalists, developmentalists and medics who have endeavoured to chart children's physical activity, primarily but not exclusively against the backcloth of the school curriculum. Over the years then there have been contributions from a variety of disciplines, including psychology, sociology, anthropology, education and medicine, but in all honesty with very few exceptions there has been virtually no co-ordination or liaison between these disciplines. Regrettably, this has prevented the subject moving forward on a broad front, and has certainly made the task of integrating the literature no easier.

A scan across this disparate literature reveals four themes which tend to recur. Apart from records of physical activity itself (referred to as 'Activities'), there is concern with the factors which influence socialisation into sport itself ('Antecedents'), the factors which encourage either continued participation or drop-out ('Motivators and inhibitors'), and finally the consequences of participation in competitive sport ('Outcomes').

Major theoretical contributions are not spread evenly across this research landscape but have tended to cluster around very specific concerns in very specific ways. For example, internationally, the work on 'Activities' has almost inevitably been descriptive. There is a considerable literature charting physical education in schools and most especially in response to curricular changes (see Armstrong, 1990) but large-scale surveys or even estimates of activity rates outside the school curriculum are far from plentiful. In the USA, Martens (1988) drew on a variety of sources when estimating the number of young people between the ages of 6 and 18 years who were thought to be participating in sports away from school. He deduced that approximately 20 million or 44 per cent of America's 45 million youths were involved in non-school sport, a figure made up of 20.97 million boys (59 per cent) and 14.58 million girls (41 per cent). Softball was the most popular sport with both sexes (4.53 million), followed by baseball (4.53 million, including 3.91 million boys), swimming (3.93), soccer (3.9), bowling (3.57), basketball (3.35), tennis (2.59), gymnastics (2.25) and athletics (1.75).

In equivalent research in 1974, baseball (4.99 million) and softball (4.38) had topped the popularity charts, with soccer languishing in

4 *John Kremer*

11th place (1.24). The average age at which children had started to participate in sport was 11 years, although gymnasts (8 years) and baseball players (9 years) were both significantly younger, and ten-pin bowlers and tennis players (both 14 years) were older. Closer to home, the Sports Council (Great Britain) commissioned a survey of 4,437 young people and sport in England in 1994 (Mason, 1995), the report of which highlighted the interplay between school-based and extra-curricular sport in the lives of young people, and which has the potential to become a very valuable database for further analyses of physical activity.

Other research has considered physical activity in relation to health-related fitness (HRF), an area of research which briefly mushroomed in response to the now less vociferous call for HRF as part of the new National Curriculum in the UK in the late 1980s. Despite being generally atheoretical, this descriptive work has been useful in dis-proving one popular 'common-sense' theory or misconception: that young people somehow magically and mysteriously take exercise and as a consequence are naturally fit; plainly the majority do not exercise often enough or hard enough to enjoy cardiovascular benefits and hence are not fit (Sleap and Warburton, 1992), and that the trend is towards ever poorer fitness levels among the young (see Willis and Campbell, 1992). Research has concluded, for example, that British children 'have surprisingly low levels of habitual physical activity and that many children seldom experience the intensity and duration of physical activity associated with health related outcomes' (Armstrong and McManus, 1994, p.23). This same study also showed that primary (5–11 years) and post-primary (11–18 years) schools in the UK were devoting among the fewest hours to physical education of all European countries, on average approximately $1\frac{1}{2}$ hours per week.

Within Northern Ireland, the picture is not dissimilar. In 1991 the Sports Council for Northern Ireland (SCNI) sponsored a survey of post-primary schools which revealed that, on average, pupils in Year 8 (age 11–12 years, the first year of second-level education) received 114 minutes of curriculum-based physical education but this fell to 92 minutes for boys and only 85 minutes for girls by Year 12 (age 15–16 years, GCSE year) (Sutherland, 1992). In a similar vein, a survey of post-primary school children in 1989 revealed that approximately one-third admitted to not having taken exercise (defined as any activity that caused breathlessness) outside school in the seven days prior to the survey (Division of Physical and Health Education, Queen's University, 1990).

Beyond childhood and even adolescence, research shows that the picture does not become any rosier. By way of example, according to the Northern Ireland Health and Activity Survey, 'Of those aged 16–24, seven out of ten men and eight out of ten women were below the target threshold (of physical activity) likely to confer a benefit.' (Ogle and Kelly, 1994, p.18).

In contrast to 'Activities', when considering 'Motivators and inhibitors' (usually intrinsic and extrinsic motivation respectively) then a great many theoretical contributions spring to view. Bandura's self-efficacy theory, together with Harter's theory of perceived self-competence, Deci's cognitive evaluation theory and the work of Dweck, Maehr and Nicholls on achievement orientation, have all enjoyed prominence (for reviews, see Roberts, 1992; Weiss and Chaumeton, 1992). This work highlights how personal expectancies and values dominate the reasons why people take up sport, and how they can best be motivated to continue their involvement. Intrinsic motivation itself is now seen as multifaceted (Fortier *et al.*, 1995; Frederick and Ryan, 1995), and achievement goals likewise (Roberts and Treasure, 1995). Of the many conclusions drawn from this work, an important message is just how dangerous extrinsic rewards can be in taking away from an experience which may have been enjoyable in its own right, and long before the ubiquitous cup, medal or 'gong' makes its appearance.

Alongside these contributions, other psychologists have sought to list 'Antecedents' or motivational factors, and to develop scales which can be used to measure motivation. There is now general consensus that the most significant factors appear to be perceived self-competence, fitness, affiliation, teamwork, competition and fun. These are seen to act in concert, although the combination and significance of factors varies considerably by culture, age and gender. As regards drop-out, here the most significant inhibitors, and particularly for older children, have been found to be conflict of interests or simply other interests, followed by factors such as lack of fun, injury, lack of improvement, dislike of coach, competition and time pressure (Weiss and Chaumeton, 1992).

From a sociological perspective, attention has focused primarily on 'Antecedents' and 'Outcomes', with a weaker focus on 'Motivators' and 'Inhibitors' (Coleman, 1979; Hendry *et al.*, 1993). The psychological process of socialisation is set squarely against an elaborate socio-economic backcloth, highlighting the role of leisure in the world of adolescence. In addition, attention is placed on the interaction between demographic variables such as age, gender, class, family background and ethnicity in the determination of life chances and even sporting opportunities, and from there how factors interact in determining particular lifestyles or outcomes, with social position and material resource figuring large in a discussion of sporting chances. Implicitly at least, each approach reinforces the need to bring together contributions from various disciplines, operating at different levels of analysis from the individual to the socio-cultural. Unfortunately, concerted attempts at integration still remain thin on the ground but there have been encouraging signs of change. As one example, according to Greendorfer (1992), three principal clusters of factors combine to predict participation. These are personal attributes (including expectancies, values and attitudes), significant others (for example, family, peers, siblings, teachers, coaches and sporting role models) and socialisation situations (or opportunity sets). Of the three clusters, significant others has received the most attention, normally discussed in the context of social learning theories. Above all else, social learning theories have been instrumental in alerting us to children's great capacity for learning through observation, identification and imitation. For example, it has been shown repeatedly that the family, and particularly the father, has a considerable influence on whether or not a child becomes involved in sport (Lewko and Greendorfer, 1988). If a child is used to seeing his or her parents involved in sport, that is the child has been raised in a sporting family culture, then it is more likely that the child will see sport involvement as natural, in comparison with the child whose parents show no interest in sport. At the same time, a number of studies point to other influential factors contributing to this socialisation process, such as the mediating role played by teachers and coaches, the influence of siblings or peers, and the impact of socio-economic status on the opportunities for involvement in more costly sports (Hendry *et al.*, 1993; Greendorfer, 1992). Gender is also taken to be of significance in the sport socialisation process (Colley, Eglinton and Elliott, 1992), and numerous studies point to the different ways in which boys and girls are motivated by and respond to competitive sport, and how this reaction changes dramatically throughout adolescence (Fortier *et al.*, 1995), thus implicating age as a further significant variable.

Whichever factors are identified as significant, it is clear that an individual's motivation to take up sport will be influenced by both the reinforcement and the support which is offered. In turn, his or her continued involvement will hinge on the rewards (both intrinsic and extrinsic) which are seen to be associated with involvement, and hence satisfaction with the process. Here are the bare bones of a process model of participation, and it is variations on this theme which have become increasingly significant in attempts to understand why people take up and then continue sport and exercise. One example from the mid-1980s is the Exercise Behaviour Model (Noland and Feldman, 1984), which considered predisposing factors (for example, health, appearance and fitness), modifying factors (demographic, social, structural and physical variables) and cues to action (health, advice, role models and the media), all determining the likelihood of action but then mediated by perceived benefits and barriers before exercise itself is taken. More recently, researchers such as Sallis and Hovell (1990), Schmidt and Stein (1991), Scanlan *et al.* (1993) and Weiss and Chaumeton (1992) have each in their own way helped to refine the motivational process which ties together intentions, participation, commitment, rewards, satisfaction and motivation. However, as Chapter 9 endeavours to show, despite the growing complexity and sophistication of these process models, modelling participation in sport remains unfinished business.

THE INTERVIEW SURVEY

Details of the sample and the survey procedures can be found in Chapter 11. Briefly, the sample was school based, with the sampling scheme defined by two variables, school type and Education and Library Board area. The primary sampling units were schools in each stratum and the secondary units were pupils in each school, based on probability proportional to size, in order to achieve a self-balancing sample. The sample itself comprised 49 per cent girls and 51 per cent boys, drawn from Key Stage 2 (that is, primary school pupils in Years 5 to 7, normally aged 8 to 11 years; 42 per cent), Key Stage 3 (post-primary students in Years 8 to 10, aged 11 to 14 years; 30 per cent), Key Stage 4 (post-primary students in Years 11 and 12, aged 14 to 16 years; 20 per cent), and those in 'Sixth Form' (post-primary students who remain at school beyond Year 12, aged 16 to 18 years; 8 per cent). Of those in post-primary education (58 per cent of the sample), 47 per cent attended a grammar school.

Before offering some flavour of the survey data, it is important to define the terms of reference which were used during the research. So often these terms are merely taken as read and yet in reality it can be difficult to draw boundaries or ring-fence what are quite nebulous concepts. For example, it is necessary to define just what is meant by the term sport and physical activity – when does a walk become a ramble and when does that ramble constitute mountaineering? In turn, when is mountaineering recognisable as a competitive sporting activity? When does a 'kick-about' in the local park become a game of soccer? Is dance a sport or an art form?

These may seem futile diversions but without a clear idea of boundaries then it will be impossible to determine physical activity rates precisely. Having wrestled with the problem of classification for some time, it was eventually decided to revert to the list of accredited sports as recognised by the Sports Council for Northern Ireland at the time of survey. This is a very extensive list which includes 106 separate activities, and was seen to be appropriate given that it encompassed such a diverse range of physical activity; the problem of overinclusion was seen to be the lesser of two evils (see Table 1.1).

Within this list, a further distinction was made between mini- and full versions of particular sports (relevant sports being marked with an asterisk). To ascertain which version was actually being played, children were asked a series of questions about aspects of play. For example, if rugby was the chosen sport, then they were asked if there were line-outs. If the answer was no, then the sport was classified as mini-rugby.

Previous research has endeavoured to make a distinction between curricular and extra-curricular school sport but to young people themselves, these terms may mean little. Instead the interviewees were asked whether activities took place in school between 9.00 a.m. and 3.30 p.m. and, if they occurred beyond these times, whether these were school-based activities associated with teams, clubs which were open to all pupils, or were activities entirely separate from school.

To determine the level of attainment in each activity, it was eventually decided to rely on a universal three-tier classification system, as shown below.

- Basic: Family recreation; play; school clubs open to all; recreational; largely non-competitive; informal.
- Competitive: Competitive club level; selected school teams; for martial arts, all belts except black or equivalent.
- Élite: County; regionally and nationally recognised standard; black belt or equivalent.

Attention next turned to the interview schedule itself, a copy of which is included in the appendix to this book. To capture the diversity of young people's experience of physical activity, ranging from those enduring the minimum of compulsory school physical education through to those devoting hours of voluntary practice to their chosen sport, a three-part interview schedule was employed. The first part

Table 1.1 List of recognised sporting activities

Aerobics	Gymnastics	Rounders
Aikido	Handball	Rowing
Angling	Hang gliding	Rugby League*
Archery	Hockey (field)*	Rugby Union
Athletics	Hockey (ice)	Sailing
Badminton*	Hockey (roller)	Sand and land yachting
Ballooning	Hurling	Shinty
Baseball	Jogging	Shooting
Basketball*	Judo	Skateboarding
Bicycle Polo	Jujitsu	Skating (ice)
Bobsleigh	Karate	Skating (roller)
Bodybuilding	Keep fit	Skiing
Bowls	Kung fu	Soccer*
Boxing	Lacrosse*	Softball
Camogie*	Life saving	Squash rackets
Camping	Model aircraft flying	Sub aqua
Canoeing	Modern pentathlon	Surfing
Caving	Motor sport (flying)	Swimming
Chinese martial arts	Motor sport (hovering)	Table tennis
Cricket*	Motor sport (karting)	Tae kwondo
Croquet	Motor sport (motor cycling)	Ten-pin bowling
Cycling	Motor sport (power boating)	Tennis (lawn)*
Dancing (ballet)	Mountaineering	Tennis and rackets
Dancing (ballroom)	Netball*	Tobogganing
Dancing (contemporary)	Orienteering	Trampolining
Dancing (disco)	Parachuting	
Dancing (folk)	Parascending	Triathlon
Dancing (Irish)	Petanque	Tug of war
Dancing (Scottish)	Pool	Volleyball
Darts	Potholing	Water polo
Fencing	Powerlifting	Waterskiing
Fives	Quoiting	Weightlifting
Gaelic football*	Racquetball	Wildfowling
Gliding	Rambling	Windsurfing
Golf	Riding	Wrestling
	Rock climbing	Yoga

* Includes both full and mini-versions

(Section A) dealt with basic information including age, school type and educational attainment. The second part considered all the young person's experience of sport and physical activity, and gave an opportunity to list all sports which had ever been attempted. Information obtained here included a description of the activities themselves, levels of attainment, involvement and aspirations, reasons for involvement and drop-out, instruction and school involvement, as well as sports which they would like to try, sports which were available at their schools (past and present), their experience of watching live sport, their family's involvement in sport, their friends' interests in sport, paid part-time work and its impact on involvement, and their use of leisure centres. Finally, Section C focused on those who identified a 'top sport', that is the sport which was presently, or had been in the past, considered to be their most important or had been significant to them. This set of questions covered level of attainment, factors which had influenced their career in the sport, patterns of activity, types of practice instruction and competition, school, family and club involvement, and their attainments and goals.

Involvement was classified as active participant, administrator, coach, spectator or official, with each young person being asked to give details of their involvement with their 'top sport', and with all their 'attempted sports' (that is, all sports, past and present, which they had ever experienced). For all attempted sports, the numbers falling into each category are as shown in Table 1.2 (based on a usable sample of 2,295 replies).

Table 1.2 Attempted sports: patterns of activity

Active participant	13,827
Administrator	25
Coach	9
Spectator	1
Official	0
Total	13,862

When considering 'top sports', as anticipated not all young people were able to identify a 'top sport'. That is, apart from compulsory physical education at school there were those who were unable to name a sport which was important to them either now or in the past. Of the entire sample, 361 (16 per cent) fell into this category. As expected, the majority attended primary school (72 per cent) but the group included almost equal number of boys and girls (49 per cent vs. 51 per cent) from both Catholic and Protestant schools (43 per cent vs. 56 per cent).

THE SURVEY DATA: GENERAL TRENDS

To set the scene for the subsequent chapters, the remainder of this chapter offers a snapshot of the survey data, built around the four themes already introduced (namely, 'Activities'; 'Antecedents'; 'Motivators and inhibitors'; and finally, 'Outcomes'). In this way it is hoped to start the process of bringing together demographic, social, personal and structural factors towards an understanding of the who, what, where and why of young people's participation in sport and physical recreation.

The 'Activities'

As mentioned earlier, interviewees had the opportunity to select from a list of 106 sports but in reality the number which was actually mentioned was surprisingly small. Indeed, 20 sports accounted for 85 per cent of all the 'top sports'. Two sports (soccer and swimming) alone accounted for 41 per cent of all 'top sports', and four (soccer, swimming, netball and Gaelic football) accounted for over half (53 per cent). Only 31 sports had been tried by over 100 young people (or 4 per cent of the sample) and a further 41 sports had each been attempted by fewer than 50 or 2 per cent. These included what would be regarded as high-profile sports such as (in descending order of popularity) judo, handball, boxing, skiing, water polo, sailing and rowing.

Table 1.3 summarises this breakdown, showing the number of young people who named a particular activity as their top sport, the number who had ever attempted that particular sport, as well as the ratio of top sport (first column) to attempted sport (second column), represented as a percentage. By way of example, 8 per cent of the sample had attempted horse riding, and 73 of these young people (42 per cent of all those who had tried horse riding) still regarded it as their 'top sport' at the time of interview. In contrast, although 627 (27 per cent) had experience of playing basketball, only 42 of these young people (7 per cent of those who had experience of basketball) subsequently described it as their 'top sport'.

In terms of popularity, soccer headed the list, with 23 per cent of the entire sample having named soccer as their most important sport, including 39 per cent of all boys interviewed. In contrast, 17 per cent of girls mentioned swimming, 11 per cent netball, but only 6 per cent cited soccer. Soccer topped the popularity lists for both grammar and secondary schools, and for each of Protestant, Catholic and integrated schools.

Looking at the entire list of attempted sports, the usable sample of 2,295 young people recorded 13,827 sports which they had tried at some time. Only eight sports had been experienced by at least 20 per cent of the sample as a whole, these being swimming (79 per cent of the sample had swum), soccer (58 per cent), netball (29 per cent),

Table 1.3 'Top sports' and attempted sports

	Top sport	Attempted sport	% top sport to attempted sport
Soccer	529	1,323	40
Swimming	256	1,824	14
Netball	129	665	19
Gaelic football	127	447	28
Athletics	90	570	16
Horse riding	73	175	42
Field hockey	69	533	13
Badminton	52	601	9
Cycling	44	545	8
Basketball	42	627	7
Camogie	42	133	32
Irish dancing	40	261	15
Rugby union	36	144	25
Golf	35	307	11
Lawn tennis	31	451	7
Gymnastics	27	342	8
Rounders	23	381	6
Aerobics	21	159	13
Ice skating	20	252	8
Tennis and rackets	19	265	7
Others	229		
None	368		
Total	2,295	13,827	

basketball (27 per cent), badminton (26 per cent), athletics (25 per cent), cycling (24 per cent) and field hockey (23 per cent).

When considering whether indoor or outdoor activities were more prevalent, 53 per cent (1,244) took part predominantly in outdoor sports and 30 per cent (696) in indoor sports. Interestingly, the gender breakdown for indoor sports was 74 per cent female to 26 per cent male, yet for outdoor sports it was 66 per cent male to 34 per cent female.

It would also appear that mini-sports are aptly named for they appeared to remain minority activities. Across the whole sample, surprisingly only 19 young people said that they had taken part in mini-versions of games such as basketball, hockey, netball, rugby or soccer.

Time devoted to sport

Of those who named a 'top sport', it was surprising that only 19 per cent maintained that they spent more than one hour per week

Table 1.4 Hours per week on 'top sport' (outside school)

Hours per week	N	%
0	218	9
1	355	15
2–5	920	40
6–10	293	13
11–20	126	5
21+	17	1

during school hours on their favourite sport, and only 5 per cent said they spent more than one hour with school beyond 9.00 a.m. and 3.30 p.m. Away from school, 75 per cent of the sample devoted more than one hour per week to their 'top sport', with several reporting considerably more time, as shown in Table 1.4. On average, 57 minutes were spent on their 'top sport' in school hours, 27 minutes outside of school hours, but 238 minutes away from school per week.

When asked how often they received instruction, practised or actually competed in their chosen or 'top sport', 1,672 (73 per cent of the sample) said they practised once a week or more and 1,236 (54 per cent) stated that they received instruction at least once a week. However, in contrast to these reports of high levels of instruction and practice, only 550 (24 per cent) stated that they competed weekly, and surprisingly 832 said they never actually competed in their top sport at all (representing 36 per cent of the entire sample).

As regards their preference for spending more or less time, 43 per cent said they would prefer to spend much more time, 32 per cent a bit more time and 23 per cent the same amount of time. Only 1 per cent would choose to spend less time. In addition, when asked how easy or difficult it had been to find time for their chosen sport, 35 per cent said 'very easy', 34 per cent said 'quite easy', 16 per cent 'quite difficult' and 3 per cent 'very difficult'.

Level of attainment

Table 1.5 indicates that over half the sample either had not played at a competitive level or had no involvement with sport. At the other extreme, only 52 young people (2 per cent) had performed at an élite level in their top sport. Over half of the boys who named a 'top sport' (51 per cent) had experience at either competitive or élite level, in comparison with only 33 per cent of girls.

Table 1.5 'Top sport' and level of attainment

Basic	1,112	49%
Competitive	771	34%
Élite	52	2%
No 'top sport'	360	15%
Sample	2,295	100%

When asked if they felt they had the potential to play to a certain standard in their chosen 'top sport', then a different picture is revealed: 504 (26 per cent of those naming a 'top sport') felt they had the potential to perform at an élite level. The level of performance also varied considerably between sports, as the following tables demonstrate. Table 1.6 shows the percentage of participants at each level of attainment in their chosen top sport.

Table 1.6 Level of attainment by 'top sport'

	Basic %	Competitive %	Élite %	N
Soccer	56	42	1	526
Swimming	82	18	0	256
Netball	56	43	2	129
Gaelic football	34	65	1	127
Athletics	67	30	3	90
Horse riding	49	51	0	73
Field hockey	43	52	3	69
Badminton	77	21	2	52
Cycling	86	14	0	44
Camogie	31	60	10	42
Basketball	79	19	2	42
Irish dancing	63	35	3	40
Rugby Union	39	58	3	36
Golf	43	51	6	35
Lawn tennis	71	26	3	31
Gymnastics	67	22	11	27
Rounders	68	32	0	22
Aerobics	95	5	0	21
Ice skating	80	15	5	20
Tennis and rackets	84	16	0	19

The 20 most popular attempted sports are next presented in terms of the percentage of basic, competitive and élite performers, as well the percentage who believed they had the ability to perform at élite level (Table 1.7).

Table 1.7 Level of attainment by attempted sport

	Basic %	Competitive %	Élite %	Élite potential? %	N
Swimming	91	9	0	1	1,816
Soccer	67	32	1	8	1,314
Netball	63	36	1	5	659
Basketball	88	12	0	1	627
Badminton	85	15	0	2	599
Athletics	78	21	2	8	565
Cycling	99	2	0	1	543
Field hockey	73	27	0	3	531
Lawn tennis	92	8	0	2	450
Gaelic football	44	55	1	15	445
Rounders	95	5	0	1	379
Gymnastics	89	10	1	2	342
Billiards/snooker	95	5	0	1	328
Golf	86	13	0	5	307
Tennis/rackets	98	2	0	0	262
Irish dancing	53	44	3	9	261
Ice skating	98	1	0	1	252
Cricket	76	23	0	7	223
Ten-pin bowling	97	3	0	0	220
Volleyball	93	7	0	1	191

When asked when they felt they had achieved their highest standard, of those who answered, 84 per cent (1,250) felt this had been either in the last year or at present. In response to the question, 'What standard would you like to have achieved?', 28 per cent said basic, 48 per cent competitive and 20 per cent élite (with 4 per cent 'don't know'). A further question asked what standard they felt they had the potential to achieve. Replies did not vary substantially from the previous question, with 23 per cent saying basic, 46 per cent competitive and 26 per cent élite.

Focusing attention on those 2 per cent who were performing at an élite level, 14 were sixth formers, 21 were at Key Stage 4, 15 were at Key Stage 3 and only two were at Key Stage 2. Most often the élite performers had become involved in their chosen sport early in life, with 40 per cent between the ages of 6 and 9 and around one-quarter (27 per cent) as early as 5 years old. As regards their close friends' sporting activities, it was uncommon to find friends also competing at élite level. Of 52 élite athletes in the sample, only 10 (19 per cent) named at least one of their two closest friends as also being an élite performer, and of these only six were competing at this level in the same sport.

Not surprisingly, those who were competing at an élite level were most often those devoting the greatest amount of time to their chosen sport. For example, 63 per cent of the élite performers maintained they were spending at least 20 hours per week outside school, and a further 33 per cent stated that they were spending between 16 and 20 hours. Further, 45 of the 52 (87 per cent) maintained that they practised at least twice a week, and 98 per cent received instruction either twice a week (65 per cent) or once a week (33 per cent). As regards competition, 27 per cent competed at least twice a week, 31 per cent once a week, 29 per cent once a month and 14 per cent only occasionally.

Overall, the opportunities for youth competition in a great many sports appeared to be limited. It is also interesting that when looking at all attempted sports, only a small number (perhaps realistically) saw themselves as having the potential to be élite performers, but their prevalence in each sport seemed to depend not on the overall numbers who took part in that sport but instead on whether there were opportunities for competition, that is the percentage who had played at a competitive level.

School and club sports

On average, four sports were cited as being made available at school. At their present school, soccer was most frequently mentioned (47 per cent), followed by swimming (46 per cent), netball (35 per cent), athletics (32 per cent) and basketball (29 per cent), hockey (28 per cent), badminton (22 per cent) and Gaelic football (20 per cent). Looking at primary schools alone, soccer, swimming and rounders headed the list. It was generally true that favourite or 'top sports' were more readily available at primary (55 per cent) rather than post-primary (43 per cent) school, although with soccer heading the list of sports available at primary school (followed by swimming) this finding is predictable.

For clubs, 835 (36 per cent of the entire sample) were members of a club which played that sport, whether specifically a sport club or even a church or youth group. A remarkable total of 588 clubs was mentioned, but the availability of club membership in relation to sports was far from even (see Chapter 4). For example, 89 per cent of those naming Gaelic football as their 'top sport' (and 48 per cent of those naming soccer) were members of a club, whereas only 16 per cent of swimmers, 18 per cent of netball players and 28 per cent of track and field athletes enjoyed club membership. These variations across the sport spectrum are considerable and obviously have considerable policy implications (see Chapter 10).

When asked who looked after club training sessions, parents were mentioned relatively infrequently, by only 3 per cent of those who attended clubs. In contrast, 29 per cent mentioned a coach, 9 per cent a club member and 9 per cent a youth leader. In describing the form of instruction given, many forms of help were mentioned including practice games (by 35 per cent of club members), help with skills (37 per cent), generally managing the team (25 per cent), talking tactics (27 per cent) and organising transport (24 per cent).

When asked to list the places where they practised their top sport, schools were mentioned by 61 per cent of young people, public parks or the street by 24 per cent, youth clubs by 14 per cent, and sports clubs (including leisure centres) by 26 per cent. As regards instruction, schools again were mentioned most often (50 per cent), followed by sports clubs (26 per cent) and youth clubs (18 per cent).

Watching sport

A total of 1,251 (55 per cent) had seen at least one live soccer match, with 382 (17 per cent) having seen 10 or more games. Gaelic football was the next most popular spectator sport, with 553 young people (24 per cent) having attended one game or more and 231 (10 per cent) spectating at 10 or more matches. Other sports, including Rugby Union (7 per cent of the sample had seen one match or more), hurling (5 per cent), netball (4 per cent), hockey (4 per cent), athletics (4 per cent), riding (3 per cent), basketball (3 per cent), camogie (3 per cent), swimming (3 per cent), cricket (3 per cent), boxing (3 per cent) and wrestling (3 per cent), had each failed to attract more than 10 per cent of the sample to a single competition.

The 'Antecedents'

As to the age at which involvement had begun, no particular age band was most common, with roughly equal numbers spread between the ages of 5 and 12. At the same time, 60 per cent of those surveyed had some experience of at least one sport before the age of 9, and of those naming a 'top sport', 68 per cent had experience of that sport by that age.

When asked why they had attempted sports, 'because of school' was mentioned most frequently (31 per cent), followed by 'because of friends' (20 per cent), 'because of father' (10 per cent), 'because of mother' (7 per cent), 'something to do' (7 per cent) and 'because of elder brother or sister' (6 per cent). Focusing attention only on their 'top sport', a similar profile was revealed. School was mentioned most often (26 per cent), followed by friends (21 per cent), father (19 per cent), mother (10 per cent) and brother or sister (8 per cent). When asked which person was most important in continuing to maintain their interest and involvement, fathers were mentioned by 21 per cent of those with a 'top sport', with PE teacher (12 per cent), mother (10 per cent) and brother/sister (8 per cent) once more featuring. However, 17 per cent said that nobody was significant.

Despite the fact that 50 per cent of attempted sports were based outside school, when comparing different sports, the availability of the sport at school was highly significant. For example, 'because of school' was the factor mentioned most often in relation to swimming (30 per cent), netball (88 per cent), basketball (57 per cent), badminton (41 per cent), athletics (69 per cent), hockey (75 per cent), Gaelic football (28 per cent), rounders (69 per cent), gymnastics (52 per cent), cricket (34 per cent) and volleyball (61 per cent).

Looking at other socialising agents, when asked who else in the family was involved in sport, 64 per cent of the sample named their father but only 34 per cent mentioned their mother. In a similar vein, 1,477 brothers and 529 uncles were said to take part in at least one sport but only 1,045 sisters and 134 aunts. Fathers' three most popular sports were soccer (34 per cent), golf (17 per cent) and Gaelic football (14 per cent), while mothers' were swimming (24 per cent), keep fit (19 per cent) and aerobics (15 per cent). Brothers' three most often named sports were soccer (56 per cent), Gaelic football (23 per cent) and swimming (10 per cent), and sisters' were swimming (22 per cent), netball (18 per cent) and hockey (14 per cent). Clearly both gender and age have a significant impact on relatives' sporting activities.

As regards the match between the young people's chosen sports and those of their relatives, of the 1,340 relatives who were said to have played soccer, 600 (44 per cent) of their young relatives (that is, the sample) also played. Similarly, of the 626 relatives associated with Gaelic football, 233 (37 per cent) had young footballers following in their footsteps, as was true to a lesser extent of swimming (28 per cent), camogie (25 per cent), athletics (22 per cent), Rugby Union (21 per cent) and hockey (19 per cent). However, other popular sports such as golf (15 per cent), netball (14 per cent), badminton (14 per cent) and cycling (4 per cent) appeared to be less frequently characterised by family ties.

Of those who were members of clubs, most mentioned that friends (40 per cent), parents (31 per cent), brothers and sisters (10 per cent), or other relatives (6 per cent) had introduced them to the club, but when asked who now took them to their club, 'no-one' headed the list (34 per cent), followed by father (21 per cent), mother (20 per cent) or both parents (10 per cent). Those young people who mentioned a top sport were also asked how often their relatives came to watch them play or perform. Over two-thirds of parents (76 per cent of mothers and 64 per cent of fathers) were said to watch never or rarely, and only 5 per cent of mothers and 8 per cent of fathers always attended.

The young people were also asked to name their two closest friends and then to give some indication of their friends' involvement in sport. Replies indicated a close concordance of interest in certain sports, these usually being the more popular sports. For example, of those who cited soccer as their 'top sport' and also listed their two closest friends' activities, soccer was named as their friends' 'top sport' by 63 per cent. Relatively high rates of coincidence were also found for horse riding (57 per cent), Gaelic football (46 per cent) and camogie (47 per cent), but not for sports such as basketball (15 per cent), cycling (19 per cent), gymnastics (19 per cent) and tennis (16 per cent). With very few exceptions, however, the young people had more friends associated with their own sport than with any other.

The 'motivators and inhibitors'

In general, findings here match closely with those obtained from previous research, emphasising once more the importance of intrinsic motivators. For example, when asked to rate the importance of factors which had made them more keen about their chosen sport, only one-third (33 per cent) said that winning was very important, one-quarter (25 per cent) mentioned trophies and only 11 per cent cited perks such as money or equipment. In contrast, the majority said intrinsic factors such as getting better (78 per cent), enjoyment (69 per cent), feeling good (67 per cent), keeping fit (65 per cent), making friends (63 per cent), and the excitement of the sport (63 per cent) were very important. Meeting people (32 per cent) and various forms of encouragement (for example, from school, family, older players) were also not seen as being particularly important, an interesting contrast with adult surveys where the social opportunities associated with sport figure large. Finally, boys appeared to place somewhat greater emphasis on winning than girls, with 38 per cent of boys saying this was very important in contrast with 26 per cent of girls, but overall, gender differences were not large.

In terms of factors which had made them less keen, losing (8 per cent), cost (8 per cent) and time (10 per cent) were rarely seen as very important whereas lack of enjoyment (35 per cent), lack of family support and injuries (28 per cent) were mentioned more frequently.

Considering the role played by the school in fostering interest, of those who named a 'top sport', 56 per cent were unable to say how the school had helped or encouraged them with that sport. Of the remainder, various replies were offered but only 'provides coaching/guidance' (16 per cent) was cited by more than 10 per cent of respondents. When asked how the school hindered their sport, 88 per cent were unable to identify a single factor but 4 per cent mentioned that there was not enough sport and 4 per cent mentioned that their chosen activity was not on the curriculum.

When asked to name sports which they would like to see being made available at school, it may come as no surprise to learn that 88 boys mentioned soccer but more interestingly, 119 girls. At the same time, only 189 girls (17 per cent) stated that soccer was currently available at their school and these were predominantly primary school pupils. Other sports which featured significantly on the 'wish list' included rugby (68 boys, 13 girls), snooker (53 boys, 9 girls) and golf (63 boys, 12 girls).

In more general terms, when asked about sports which they would like to try, an extremely wide ranging 'wish list' was generated, headed by ice skating (mentioned by 11 per cent of the entire sample), ice hockey (10 per cent), parachuting (9 per cent), water skiing (8 per cent), skiing (7 per cent), gymnastics (7 per cent), basketball (6 per cent), karate (6 per cent), canoeing (5 per cent), golf (5 per cent), surfing (5 per cent), hang gliding (4 per cent) and sailboarding (5 per cent). The 2,091 (91 per cent) who said they wanted to try another sport mentioned in total 4,881 sports, an average of 2.3 sports per respondent. Five reasons for wanting to try a particular sport predominated: 'It looks like fun' (48 per cent); 'I have seen it on the TV/films/video' (33 per cent); 'It looks exciting' (39 per cent); 'It looks like a challenge' (24 per cent); and 'I like to learn new skills' (22 per cent). Factors such as the interest of parents (2 per cent), siblings (3 per cent) or friends (7 per cent) were of far less importance.

As to why the sport had not been attempted, the single most popular reason given was lack of opportunity or knowledge, 'I don't know how to start' (51 per cent), followed by 'I don't know anyone who is involved' (39 per cent); 'I don't have the equipment (24 per cent); and 'I'm too young' (12 per cent). Factors such as cost, danger and lack of expertise or approval were mentioned relatively infrequently.

Previous research is thought to have exaggerated the extent of complete drop-out from sport, and the survey would tend to confirm this speculation. The incidence of drop-out across the sample was low. For example, of those who had ever attempted a sport, only 17 per cent stated that they had discontinued that sport completely and for the majority this was after 12 years of age. Similarly when looking at 'top sports', only 86 (4 per cent of those who named a top sport) had dropped out, the majority between the ages of 10 and 15. The reasons cited for quitting were many and varied, the most common being 'lack of interest' (34 per cent), 'not available at school' (16 per cent), 'school commitments' (9 per cent), 'starting another sport' (6 per cent), 'too time consuming' (4 per cent) and 'because friends had stopped' (4 per cent). Other factors such as injury, expense and lack of encouragement were rarely mentioned. Of the few who had retired from their top sport, lack of interest (18 per cent) and school commitments (22 per cent) were the two factors cited most often.

When asked to name the ways in which their families had helped them with their chosen sport, most interviewees were at a loss to identify specifically how support had been given (that is, 'don't know' was cited by 32 per cent). This most frequent reply was followed by 'encouragement' (24 per cent), 'supply equipment' (13 per cent), 'provide training' (13 per cent) and 'provide transport' (10 per cent). When asked how their family had hindered them, only a small minority (5 per cent) could think of anything. When asked if parents ever provided instruction, 56 per cent said 'never' and only 18 per cent said either 'all the time' or 'quite often'.

Finally, 409 (18 per cent of the sample) had part-time jobs, including 218 boys and 191 girls. Of these, 381 (93 per cent) were actively involved in a sport at present, and in fact 18 (4 per cent) were competing at an élite level in a wide range of sports (a slightly higher percentage than for the sample as a whole). When asked how this part-time work impacted on finding time for sport, the majority said there was not a problem. This was despite the fact that 332 (81 per cent) had to work on a Saturday, and 244 (60 per cent) after school; 57 per cent said that they found making time for sport was either very easy (22 per cent) or quite easy (35 per cent), but 25 per cent did find making time quite difficult and 6 per cent very difficult.

The 'Outcomes'

When considering what the young people felt they had derived from their involvement in sport, most were positive. In an open-ended question, those who named a 'top sport' were asked to identify the two most important things which they had gained from their sport. From a wide ranging list, fitness (47 per cent of those naming a top sport), enjoyment (34 per cent), improving co-ordination (21 per cent), making friends (18 per cent), experiencing sport itself (17 per cent) and developing self-confidence (14 per cent) were mentioned most often. As to their feelings towards their 'top sport' over the last year, 51 per cent maintained they had become 'a lot more keen', 26 per cent 'a bit more keen', 18 per cent had not changed and only 5 per cent had become less keen.

When asked whether they felt the time they had spent on their chosen sport had been worthwhile, 77 per cent said very worthwhile and 18 per cent said quite worthwhile. Finally, in response to the question 'Will you continue to play your "top sport" when you leave school?', it was pleasing to find that 61 per cent said definitely, 18 per cent probably, 9 per cent possibly and only 7 per cent replied no. Clearly, whatever their experiences so far, these young people had derived enjoyment from their experience and had every intention of continuing their sporting careers.

CONCLUSIONS

At the risk of pre-empting later discussions, this overview of the results paints a picture of young people who are able to experience a number of sports, and particularly after primary school age, but who appear to be most attracted to a small number of activities, headed by soccer and swimming. To maintain their involvement in a 'top sport', many young people must look beyond opportunities available at school and have been prepared to make a more active commitment to their sport, a commitment which does not appear to diminish with age to the extent that previous research may have suggested. Instead, the opportunities for involvement in preferred activities may be limited, and these structural reasons for discontinuation may warrant closer investigation.

In terms of the antecedents to involvement, the role played by schools appears to be most significant, followed by friends and family. While the family plays a role in young people's involvement in sport, it is not perhaps so crucial a role as some previous commentators may have suggested. Nevertheless, parental support was acknowledged as significant in maintaining an involvement in sport, and the primary motivators were seen to be intrinsic, in keeping with earlier work. Overall, the data reveal a population who appear keen to continue their involvement with sport beyond the school years on a voluntary basis. Clearly this finding does not tally with adult surveys of physical activity, and raises interesting questions about the post-school years. Do attitudes to sport change, or does it become increasingly difficult to continue to be involved? Only longitudinal research will be able to throw light on these questions and that must remain business for another day. In the mean while it would be pleasing to end by drawing comparisons between this sample and young people surveyed elsewhere. However, to return to the point made earlier, this is not possible because substantial, comparative data are not yet available elsewhere. It is to be hoped that this situation will change, for the sake of research, for sport and for young people alike, and if this project is able to play some small part in beginning this process of data generation then those involved in the project will consider it to have been a success.

REFERENCES

Armstrong, N. (1990). *New Directions in Physical Education, Volume One.* Champaign, IL: Human Kinetics.

Armstrong, N. and McManus, A. (1994). Children's fitness and physical activity – A challenge for physical education. *The British Journal of Physical Education, Spring,* 20–26.

Coleman, J. (1979). *The School Years.* London: Methuen.

Colley, A., Eglinton, E. and Elliott, E. (1992). Sport participation in middle childhood: Association with styles of play and parental participation. *International Journal of Sport Psychology,* 23, 193–206.

Division of Physical and Health Education, Queen's University of Belfast (1990). *The Fitness, Physical Activity, Attitudes and Lifestyles of Northern Ireland Post-Primary Schoolchildren.* Belfast: Queen's University.

Fortier, M.S., Vallerand, R.J., Briere, N.M. and Provencher, P.J. (1995). Competitive and recreational sport structures and gender: A test of their relationship with sport motivation. *International Journal of Sport Psychology,* 26, 24–39.

Frederick, C.M. and Ryan, R.M. (1995). Self-determination in sport: A review using cognitive evaluation theory. *International Journal of Sport Psychology,* 26, 5–23.

Greendorfer, S.L. (1992). Sport socialization. In T.S. Horn (ed.) *Advances in Sport Psychology.* Champaign, IL: Human Kinetics.

Hendry, L.B., Shucksmith, J., Love, J.G. and Glendinning, A. (1993). *Young People's Leisure and Lifestyles.* London: Routledge.

Lewko, J.H. and Greendorfer, S.L. (1988). Family influences in sport socialization of children and adolescents. In F.L. Smoll, R.A. Magill and M.A. Ash (eds) *Children in Sport, 3rd Edition*. Champaign, IL: Human Kinetics.

Martens, R. (1988). Youth sport in the USA. In F.L. Smoll, R.A. Magill and M.A. Ash (eds) *Children in Sport, 3rd Edition*. Champaign, IL: Human Kinetics.

Mason, V. (1995). *Young People and Sport in England, 1994: A National Survey*. London: Sports Council.

Noland, M.P. and Feldman, R.H.L. (1984). Factors related to the leisure exercise behavior of returning women college students. *Health Education, 15(2)*, 32–36.

Ogle, S. and Kelly, F. (1994). *Northern Ireland Health and Activity Survey: Main Findings*. Belfast: Sports Council for Northern Ireland.

Roberts, G.C. (1992). *Motivation in Sport and Exercise*. Champaign, IL: Human Kinetics.

Roberts, G.C. and Treasure, D.C. (1995). Achievement goals, motivational climate and achievement strategies and behaviors in sport. *International Journal of Sport Psychology, 26*, 64–80.

Sallis, J.F. and Hovell, M.F. (1990). Determinants of exercise behavior. *Exercise and Sport Science Reviews, 18*, 307–330.

Scanlan, T.K., Carpenter, P.J., Schmidt, G.W., Simons, J.P. and Keeler, B. (1993). An introduction to the sport commitment model. *Journal of Sport and Exercise Psychology, 15*, 1–15.

Schmidt, G.W. and Stein, G.L. (1991). Sport commitment: A model integrating enjoyment, dropout and burnout. *Journal of Sport and Exercise Psychology, 8*, 254–265.

Sleap, M. and Warburton, P. (1992). Physical activity levels of 5–11 year old children in England as determined by continuous observation. *Research Quarterly for Exercise and Sport, 63(3)*, 238–245.

Sutherland, A. (1992). *Physical Education and Games in Post-Primary Schools in 1991*. Belfast: Sports Council for Northern Ireland.

Weiss, M.R. and Chaumeton, N. (1992). Motivational orientations in sport. In T.S. Horn (ed.) *Advances in Sport Psychology*. Champaign, IL: Human Kinetics.

Willis, J.D. and Campbell, L.F. (1992). *Exercise Psychology*. Champaign, IL: Human Kinetics.

2 Gender issues in sport participation

Deirdre Scully and Jackie Clarke

INTRODUCTION

Despite the highlighting of gender issues across recent publications in sport and physical education (see Evans, 1993; Costa and Guthrie, 1994) we have yet to see a coherent research strategy which can offer practical guidance for those dealing with gender issues or, at a theoretical level, which can advance our understanding of the role played by gender in sport. Common criticisms of research on gender include discussion of biases which either exaggerate (*the alpha bias*) or minimise/dismiss (*the beta bias*) gender differences in sport (Oglesby and Hill, 1993). In addition, it has been suggested that research must reach out to encompass the diversity of sport participants beyond the élite, and to consider the processes as well as the outcomes of involvement (Gill, 1994). In fact, arguments have recently been made for the development of a 'feminist biopsychosocial perspective on women's sport and exercise to guide research and serve participants.' (Gill, 1994, p.278).

While it is not within the scope of this chapter to move such proposals forward, we hope that this analysis will at least add fuel to the ongoing debate, by examining hard empirical data derived from the SCNI survey in relation to contemporary discussions in the fields of sociology, social psychology and education. Since very little data currently exist, either specifically in relation to gender or more generally with regard to all young people's sporting activities, there is great benefit to be had from both profiling the contemporary situation and analysing those factors which may influence and motivate young men and women to participate in sport. In particular, the chapter will focus on gender similarities and differences in four key areas: choice of sport and level of participation; amount of exposure to sport; external influences on involvement in sport; and finally, motivation, expectations and factors influencing drop-out from sport.

CHOICE OF SPORT AND LEVEL OF PARTICIPATION

The 20 most popular sports were given 'top 20' status for girls and for boys (see Table 2.1). Of these 20 sports, 11 were common to both girls and boys, leaving a number of sports which were almost exclusively male or female. For example, netball, camogie, rounders and aerobics each attracted over 95 per cent of female participants, while the sports of Gaelic football, Rugby Union and golf showed male participation rates over 94 per cent. In a similar vein, when male and female data were considered separately a number of other sports were also heavily gender biased. For example, in a listing of the 20 most popular sports for boys, hurling, cricket, motor cycling, billiards and snooker, angling and Rugby League are also exclusively male. Conversely, in a 'top 20' listing for girls, only two additional sports alter the general listing slightly, both being forms of dance – ballet and disco (Irish dancing appears in the common 'top twenty' list).

Table 2.1 Percentages of male and female participants in top 20 sports

Sport	Male %	Female %
Association football	46.0	7.0
Swimming	7.0	19.8
Netball*	0.6	13.2
Gaelic football[†]	11.8	0.9
Athletics	2.6	6.8
Riding	1.0	6.8
Field hockey	0.9	6.4
Badminton	1.3	4.2
Cycling	1.6	3.0
Basketball	2.9	1.4
Camogie*		4.5
Irish dancing	0.5	3.8
Rugby Union[†]	3.5	0.1
Golf[†]	3.3	0.2
Lawn tennis	0.7	2.6
Gymnastics	0.3	2.6
Rounders*	0.1	2.4
Aerobics*		2.3
Ice skating	0.5	1.6
Tennis and rackets	0.4	1.6
Cutout sports	14.9	8.5
N	1,002	927

* Females account for ⩾95 per cent of participants
[†] Males account for ⩾94 per cent of participants

It is also noteworthy that the total participation rate varies by gender, with males having a higher participation rate than females, a finding which echoes similar surveys in the USA (Martens, 1988; Ewing and Seefeldt, 1989), Canada (Valeriote and Hansen, 1988) and England (Mason, 1995). One likely explanation for the variation in participation rates by gender is related to what society defines as gender-appropriate behaviour. Children are exposed to gender-role stereotypes associated with masculine and feminine behaviour from an early age and these come to 'exert a powerful influence on their lives' (Northern Ireland Curriculum Council, 1993, p.3). The literature (Leaman, 1986; Lopez, 1987) suggests a close connection between masculinity and physical activity, and hence sport tends to attract males in large numbers as they see it as an arena in which to prove or reinforce their masculinity.

The results of this survey show not only that more males than females are participating in a chosen or 'top' sport, but that the majority (58 per cent) are involved with stereotypically masculine sports such as soccer and Gaelic football. At the same time there is a consensus within the literature that the cultivation of femininity places limitations on the participation rates and choices of females (Scraton, 1986; Brown, Frankel and Fennell, 1989). Those who do take part tend to do so in sports which society considers to be more acceptable for females, for example gymnastics, ice skating and dance. While the results of this survey generally support this hypothesis, it is interesting to note that 8 per cent of the young women identified soccer and Gaelic football as their 'top sport' which may suggest that traditional sex-role stereotyping may be becoming less constraining for girls.

Activity patterns appear to be differentiated between boys and girls not only in terms of the proportion of active participants in each sport but also in the type of activity chosen. For example, 66 per cent of boys identified a team activity as their top sport while only 19 per cent claimed an individual activity. Girls, on the other hand, seemed to show a preference for individual activities, with 55 per cent identifying an individual-based 'top sport', in comparison with only 36 per cent who said their 'top sport' was team based. In analysing the difference between boys' and girls' play, Adler, Kless and Adler (1992) concluded that boys enjoyed games which were highly complex, competitive, rule infused, large and goal directed. In contrast, girls enjoyed small intimate groups, engaging in similar independent activities which focused on enjoyment rather than winning. Similarly, Williams (1988) has highlighted a marked gender difference in preference for team sports, with boys showing a clear preference for team sports while girls appear to shy away from team situations. Results from research on Canadian youth sport also support this notion, with male participation rates in team sports estimated to be twice as great as for females, but female participation in individual sports being 50 per cent greater than that for males (Valeriote and Hansen, 1988).

The clear differences in activity preferences shown by respondents in the SCNI survey lend credence to the belief that team sports are more attractive to males than females. Colley *et al.* (1987) conclude that it is sex-stereotyped attitudes which have established this trend among female participants. Sports, they note, vary in their acceptability for girls and as the more acceptable sports for young women are individual in nature it is to be expected that more of them will attempt these sports. This survey supports this view by showing that despite the lower overall participation rates of females there are larger numbers of girls participating in a number of individual 'top 20' sports, primarily swimming, athletics, riding, badminton, cycling, tennis, gymnastics and ice skating.

Relationship between identified 'top sport' and sex of school

In attempting to understand the effect of gender on participation rates in some of the above sports it was felt important to examine 'top sport' in relation to school type. For example, it could be hypothesised that a mixed-sex school has the potential to broaden opportunities for girls and boys in terms of their exposure to a greater variety of sports. Certainly, the survey data suggest that for boys at least this may be true. Table 2.2 shows that the sports of field hockey, lawn tennis, netball, ice skating and gymnastics are only identified as 'top sports' by boys attending mixed-sex schools. For girls the picture is less clear cut but there were small but consistent numbers of girls attending mixed-sex schools who identified a greater number of sports from the full range. At the same time it is interesting that a greater percentage (9 per cent) of girls from single-sex schools identified soccer as their 'top sport', in comparison with 6 per cent of girls from mixed-sex schools, while field hockey is nominated by 9 per cent of girls attending mixed-sex schools but only 1 per cent from girls-only schools. The provision of a sex-differentiated PE curriculum in mixed-sex institutions may provide an explanation for the difference in 'top sport' identified by girls in co-educational schools and those in girls-only schools. Talbot (1990; 1993) warns that a sex-differentiated curriculum policy is often based on stereotypical

Table 2.2 Relationship between identified 'top sport' and sex of school

Sport	Mixed-sex school Male %	Mixed-sex school Female %	Girls only %	Boys only %
Association football	48.6	6.1	9.3	34.6
Swimming	6.8	18.3	23.9	7.9
Netball	0.7	13.7	12.0	
Gaelic football	8.4	1.0		26.2
Athletics	2.6	5.8	9.3	2.6
Horse riding	0.9	6.4	7.7	1.6
Field hockey	1.0	8.6	0.8	
Badminton	1.2	4.3	3.5	1.6
Cycling	1.7	3.1	2.7	1.0
Basketball	2.7	1.3	1.5	3.6
Camogie		4.2	5.4	
Irish dancing	0.5	4.5	1.9	0.5
Rugby Union	3.6	0.1		3.1
Golf	3.5	0.1	0.4	2.6
Lawn tennis	0.9	2.4	3.0	
Gymnastics	0.4	2.7	2.3	
Rounders	0.1	1.8	3.9	
Aerobics		2.8	0.8	
Ice skating	0.6	1.9	0.8	
Other racket sports	0.1	1.8	1.2	1.6
Other sports	15.5	8.2	9.3	13.0
N	809	671	259	191

Column percentages total 100

constructs of femininity and masculinity, and consequently may actually contribute to the perpetuation of inequality.

One could argue that a sex-differentiated curriculum disregards the underlying egalitarian principle of the National Curriculum, supposedly designed to provide equality of access to educational opportunities for all pupils. Legislation fails to challenge such inequality, for while sex discrimination is unlawful, treating the sexes as equal but different is legally permissible, providing no disadvantage accrues to either sex. Clearly therefore, schools can legally provide pupils with a sex-differentiated PE curriculum such as field hockey for girls and soccer for boys. The only proviso must be that the relative merits of different sports are sufficiently similar to ensure no disadvantage accrues to either sex by not being afforded the opportunity to participate in one or the other. While the relative merits of field hockey and soccer may be sufficiently similar to permit them equal status as curriculum sports, one cannot disregard the fact that in terms of the value which society places upon them, they are certainly of unequal status.

The literature suggests that early adolescence is characterised by an intensification of gender-related expectations, with subsequent constraints placed upon participation patterns being more intense for boys than girls (Griffen, 1984; Talbot, 1986; Lawrie and Brown, 1992). Certainly the single-sex boys' schools appeared to encourage gender stereotyping of sport, an approach which the NICC (1993, p.4) warns can 'close doors for individuals and inhibit many of them from pursuing subjects and interests which they would find enjoyable and rewarding'. The large proportion (61 per cent) of boys attending single-sex schools identified the stereotypically masculine sports of soccer and Gaelic football as their top sports, while failing to recognise activities such as gymnastics and ice skating which have been traditionally viewed as stereotypically feminine activities. Single-sex girls' schools, on the other hand, have made a small but encouraging breach into the traditionally male-dominated sport of soccer with 9 per cent of their student body identifying this as their top sport. Although this breakthrough does not, as yet, extend to Gaelic football and rugby, one could tentatively surmise that single-sex girls' schools are making a greater effort to challenge traditional gender biases than are their male counterparts.

Level of attainment in 'top sport'

When asked about level of attainment in their chosen or 'top sport', 15 per cent of the sample said they had no top sport. Of the remainder the breakdown across basic, competitive, élite and retired levels is shown in Table 2.3. The majority of the sample were participants at the basic level only, with 40 per cent being involved competitively, and a small percentage (2.7 per cent) competing at the élite level. The breakdown by gender shows that at the basic level a higher percentage of those participating were girls (56 per cent) than boys (44 per cent). This trend is reversed for the competitive level (64 per cent boys; 36 per cent girls). However, it is noteworthy that the élite-level group comprises a higher percentage of girls (54 per cent) than boys (46 per cent). This finding contradicts recent findings in the national survey of young people in sport in England (Mason, 1995) which shows a higher percentage of males in all categories of participation.

One possible explanation for this unexpected finding may be the definitions set by the survey both in terms of sport and level of attainment. For example, it could be argued that various forms of

Table 2.3 Level of attainment in 'top sport'

Level	Total %	Male %	Female %
Basic	57.4	48.9	66.8
Competitive	39.8	48.7	30.0
Élite	2.7	2.4	3.0
N	1,937	1,003	929

dance are not typically defined as sport. Arnold (1988) has maintained that a clear distinction should be made between dance as an art form, activities such as gymnastics or ice skating which are 'partly aesthetic' sports, and more conventional sports activities which he categorises as 'purposive' sport. If dance is excluded from Tables 2.4 and 2.5 we reduce the proportion of élite female 'sport' performers by slightly more than a third. Therefore, in order to consider trends by individual sports, Table 2.4 illustrates the breakdown of attainment level by both sport and gender.

Table 2.4 Level of attainment in 'top sport' by sport and gender

Top 20 Sports	Basic Male %	Basic Female %	Competitive Male %	Competitive Female %	Élite Male %	Élite Female %	N Male	N Female
Soccer	52.4	67.1	46.3	24.3	1.3		462	70
Swimming	80.0	93.0	18.6	7.0	1.4		70	186
Netball	50.0	46.3	50.0	51.2		2.4	6	123
Gaelic football	7.6	42.8	89.8	57.1	2.5		118	7
Athletics	38.5	73.4	53.8	25.4	7.7	3.2	26	63
Horse riding	70.0	54.0	30.0	46.0			10	63
Field hockey	44.4	35.0	55.5	60.0		5.0	9	60
Badminton	30.8	79.5	69.2	20.5			13	39
Cycling	75.0	92.9	25.0	7.1			16	28
Camogie		23.8		61.9		11.9	0	41
Basketball	79.3	91.7	20.7	8.3			29	12
Irish dancing		17.1	80.0	60.0	20.0	22.9	5	35
Rugby Union	25.7	100.0	74.3				35	1
Golf	33.3	50.0	66.6	50.0			33	2
Lawn tennis	42.9	83.3	42.9	16.6	14.3		7	24
Gymnastics	66.6	54.2	33.3	37.5		8.3	3	24
Rounders	100.0	72.7		27.3			1	22
Aerobics		100.0					0	21
Ice skating	100.0	86.7		6.6		6.6	5	15
Other racket sports	100.0	100.0					4	15

Row percentages total 100, by gender

Table 2.4 highlights the point that sex bias or stereotyping in choice of sport carries over and possibly has an effect on the level attained in an individual's chosen sport. For example, at the élite level it can be seen that girls excel in the stereotypically female sports of dance, gymnastics and ice skating. Furthermore, despite the large proportion of basic level or recreational swimmers, there were no élite female swimmers in this sample. On the other hand, while males have a much prominently percentage of participants at the competitive level overall it would appear from Tables 2.3 and 2.4 that they do not feature so highly at the élite level. However, again this result may be skewed by the inclusion of dance which accounts for almost a third of élite females (see Table 2.5 which presents specific sports identified at élite level) and the fact that male élite sports include eight sports which do not appear on the 'top 20' list. Even in sports which are not stereotypically male (for example, badminton, Irish dancing, lawn tennis), we see a high proportion of the male sample participating at a competitive level. Such results support the literature suggesting that boys tend to demonstrate competitiveness and winning goal orientations (Gill, 1988) and therefore possibly seek out sports and opportunities in which competition is available. Conversely, it has been

Table 2.5 Male and female élite performers and their sports

Élite sports	Male	Female
Soccer	6	
Athletics	2	2
Boxing	1	
Camogie		5
Gaelic football	3	
Hurling	4	
Gymnastics		2
Field hockey		3
Judo	1	
Lawn tennis	1	2
Karting (motor sport)	1	
Power boating	1	
Netball		3
Ice skating		1
Swimming	1	
Table tennis	1	
Contemporary dancing		2
Irish dancing	1	8
Tae kwon do	1	
N	24	28

suggested that females tend to be more concerned with task mastery orientations, the achievement of personal goals and non-competitive activity (Weinberg and Ragan, 1979; Gill, 1988) and therefore may be happy to participate at a basic level in sports which do not have an overtly competitive structure (for example, ice skating, aerobics, cycling and recreational swimming).

EXPOSURE TO SPORT

How much time do young people devote to sport?

Those who named a top sport were asked how many hours per week they devoted to that sport. Table 2.6 shows the number of hours these young people claimed to be actively involved in their 'top sport' in school between 9.30 a.m. and 3.30 p.m., in school but outside these hours, and in the community separate from school. A high percentage of young people (45 per cent) claim that no time was spent participating in their top sport during a normal school day, while almost 32 per cent claimed only one hour was spent in this pursuit. This finding may be partly due to the National Curriculum providing children with a broader physical education experience and therefore forcing many schools to extend their PE curriculum beyond the traditional games/ sports of individual institutions.

Such a suggestion is credible given that respondents named 81 sports and 11 mini-sports as being available in schools. The breakdown by gender, at first glance, appears even more damning in demonstrating that the majority of girls (52 per cent) receive no time in school on their favourite or 'top sport' compared with 39 per cent of boys who made a similar claim. However, this statistic may be somewhat misleading as it should be remembered that there is a greater spread of females across the range of 'top sports' whereas the majority of males (58 per cent) are concentrated in soccer and Gaelic football. Given the greater spread of females across 'top sports' this may not be surprising.

Although more boys than girls claimed they spent one hour participating in their 'top sport' during regulation school hours, boys certainly seem to benefit from a longer exposure time with almost 32 per cent of boys compared with under 12 per cent of girls claiming they spent more than one hour on their favourite sport in school hours. On average it was found that only 57 minutes were spent on their 'top sport' in school hours, with boys benefiting from 74 minutes whereas girls only received 40 minutes. Furthermore, when one considers that on average only 27 minutes per week (36 minutes for

34   *Deirdre Scully and Jackie Clarke*

Table 2.6 Number of hours per week involved in 'top sport'

Hours per week	In school hours			Out of school hours			Not with school		
	Total %	Male %	Female %	Total %	Male %	Female %	Total %	Male %	Female %
0	45.3	39.4	51.9	77.5	72.3	83.2	11.2	6.5	16.4
1	31.9	28.4	35.8	11.5	13.8	9.0	18.3	12.4	24.7
2–5	21.7	30.9	11.6	9.3	11.7	4.5	46.9	50.3	43.0
6–10	0.7	1.0	0.3	1.0	0.8	0.5	15.1	19.9	10.1
11–20							6.5	9.2	3.6
21+							0.9	1.2	0.5
Don't know							1.0	0.7	1.3
N	1,941	1,004	932	1,941	1,004	932	1,941	1,004	932

Column percentages total 100

boys and 19 minutes for girls) were reportedly spent on their 'top sport' in school outside of regulation hours, one could perhaps argue that extra-curricular activities in the schools are in a poor state, both in terms of the amount of extra-curricular provision and in terms of the type of provision. If, on average, only 27 minutes per week is spent on a young person's 'top sport' in school outside regulation hours, perhaps PE departments are not addressing students' needs but are merely providing traditional activities after school hours. The majority of pupils (78 per cent) claimed they spent no time on their 'top sport' at school outside regulation hours, and only 10 per cent claimed that more than one hour was spent on their sport. The gender breakdown reveals a similar pattern to 'in-school' findings, with more girls (83 per cent) than boys (73 per cent) claiming they spent no time on their 'top sport' outside regulation hours. Only 7 per cent of girls in comparison with 13 per cent of boys spent more than one hour per week on their 'top sport'. These findings tend to support the rather bleak prognosis regarding extra-curricular sport, as identified by the 1991 Northern Ireland survey of physical education and games in post-primary schools (Sutherland, 1992). In that survey it was shown that the opportunities for girls' involvement in extra-curricular activities were considerably fewer than for boys. The 1991 survey also warned that the situation regarding extra-curricular sport was likely to worsen as teachers freely admitted that personal and professional circumstances made contributing to extra-curricular programmes increasingly difficult.

Involvement away from school shows a much healthier picture, with only 7 per cent of boys and 16 per cent of girls claiming that they spent no time actively involved in their 'top sport'. Most encouraging was that 69 per cent of young people maintained that they spent more than one hour per week on this sport away from school. The pattern of higher rates of participation among males is continued away from school. A similar observation was made by Williams (1988) on investigating participation patterns in physical activity outside of school. In the present study, 81 per cent of boys, as compared with 57 per cent of girls, claimed they devoted more than one hour per week to their top sport away from school. This gender difference may be linked to the fact that more girls (23 per cent) than boys (17 per cent) reported finding it quite difficult to find time to devote to their chosen sport. Nevertheless, the majority of both boys (72 per cent) and girls (67 per cent) found it relatively easy to find time for their sport and even more encouraging is the fact that the vast majority of respondents (95 per cent of boys and 96 per cent of girls) stated that the time spent on their sport was very worthwhile.

It could be argued that these results present an optimistic picture for those concerned with health-related fitness, as it would appear that the majority of young people are taking part with sufficient frequency to enhance fitness levels. However, it should be cautioned that the data do not allow us to establish the intensity of activity and therefore such suggestions fall into the realms of speculation.

When looking at 'attempted sports' rather than 'top sport', respondents indicated very few sports which were played more than once a week (see Table 2.7). Once again, the picture for boys would appear slightly healthier with boys more often active in aerobic sports such as football, Rugby Union, cycling and even tennis (see Table 2.1). Although we know little about the intensity of participation it is possible to surmise that the health-related fitness benefits of participating more than twice a week in rugby, soccer or cycling for even 30

Table 2.7 Percentage participating at least twice weekly in an attempted sport

Sport	Males		Females	
	%	N	%	N
Soccer	74.7	(1,011)	48.1	(308)
Gaelic football	57.4	(408)		
Cycling	77.1	(297)	64.0	(247)
Billiards/snooker	41.2	(289)		
Rugby Union	45.3	(137)		
Racket sports	42.0	(143)		
Roller skating			53.3	(107)

minutes a session will outweigh the fitness benefits of participating only once a week in the other sports identified.

How much time is devoted to practice, instruction and competition?

Scrutiny of how much time boys and girls choose to devote to their 'top sport' in practice, instruction and competition also highlights gender differences. Table 2.8 shows that young people practise and receive instruction on a regular basis, with 86 per cent of the sample claiming to practise once a week or more and a further 64 per cent receiving instruction on one or two occasions weekly. The breakdown by gender revealed no marked differences in terms of practising and receiving instruction on a weekly basis, although boys tended to practise more and to receive more instruction. This trend is confirmed by the gender breakdown of frequency of play/competition at various locations. This reveals that more boys participated in their top sport more frequently in all the named locations than girls. In contrast to the high levels of reported practice and instruction, only 28 per cent stated they competed on a weekly basis. The breakdown by gender is revealing insofar as girls compete in sport to a significantly lesser degree than boys; only 16 per cent of girls, compared with 40 per cent of boys, claimed they competed on a weekly basis, while the majority of girls (52 per cent) claimed they never actually competed in their 'top sport' (in comparison with 34 per cent of boys).

In interpreting these results we should consider not only Gill's (1988) suggestions about gendered goal orientations in relation to sport but also applied research conducted on school age children which shows that the genders value very different outcomes from

Table 2.8 Frequency of practice, instruction and competition

How often?	Practice			Instructed			Play/compete		
	Tot. %	Male %	Fem. %	Tot. %	Male %	Fem. %	Tot. %	Male %	Fem. %
Twice a week +	52.2	62.2	41.2	20.0	22.9	16.8	8.2	12.2	4.0
Once a week +	34.0	26.3	42.4	43.7	39.9	47.7	20.1	27.3	12.3
Once a month +	1.2	0.9	1.6	4.9	6.6	3.2	11.4	10.4	12.4
Very ocasionally	3.6	2.8	4.5	14.0	13.4	14.6	9.7	7.6	12.0
Never	6.3	4.6	8.3	14.8	14.2	15.6	42.9	34.2	52.4
Don't know	2.7	3.3	2.0	2.6	3.0	2.1	7.7	8.5	6.9
N	1,941	1,004	932	1,941	1,004	932	1,941	1,004	932

Column percentages total 100

physical activity. Studies by Williams (1988) and Stockard and John-son (1977) have shown that a marked gender difference exists between the sexes in terms of preference for competitive activity. Boys were found to thrive on competitiveness, while girls disliked being put in competitive situations and failed to feel motivated when required to display competitive behaviour. The SCNI survey has shown that girls actually compete to a significantly lesser degree or they choose sports which afford few opportunities for competition (for example, ice skating and gymnastics). Furthermore, the majority of girls who participate in a 'top sport' never actually enter the competitive struc-ture of that sport. The difference in how boys and girls spend their time on chosen activities, as evidenced by this survey, lends support to the belief that competitive situations are not of primary interest to many girls, the majority of whom participate at the basic level only.

The SCNI survey reveals that boys compete more frequently than girls. Such a finding clearly has implications for curriculum sport especially in mixed-sex schools operating a co-educational PE pro-gramme. If a competitive ethos is anathema to some pupils, especially females, and motivating to others, especially males, problems may lie in store. Clarke's (1995) research highlights this compatibility problem in mixed-sex PE classes with the majority of girls (74 per cent) claim-ing boys were too competitive, and the majority of boys (59 per cent) claiming girls were not competitive enough. She concludes that such compatibility problems raise the question of which strategy for group-ing the sexes during PE best provides equal physical educational opportunities.

EXTERNAL INFLUENCES ON INVOLVEMENT

Significant others and choice of sport

In trying to understand the amount of time children devote to their 'top sport' it may be useful to examine the factors which influence initial involvement and motivate continued participation in a chosen sport. The first three columns in Table 2.9 list the significant others whom young people felt were important in introducing them to their top sport. The second set of columns shows those individuals who were seen as important in maintaining interest. Despite the fact that 45 per cent of the young people interviewed claimed that no time was spent on their 'top sport' during school hours, the same young people rated school as the most important 'significant other' in introducing them to their 'top sport'. Williams (1988, p.23) notes: 'the school

Table 2.9 Influence of significant others on starting and maintaining interest in 'top sport'

Significant others	In starting a sport			In maintaining interest		
	Total %	Male %	Female %	Total %	Male %	Female %
School	26.4	16.5	37.0			
Father	19.2	26.4	11.4	20.7	28.3	12.3
Mother	9.8	3.9	16.2	9.9	4.9	15.3
Brother/sister	8.3	11.2	5.4	8.3	9.1	7.5
Other relative	3.8	4.7	2.9	3.8	4.9	2.6
By yourself	5.7	7.6	3.6			
Youth/church club	2.6	1.6	3.6			
Tried on holiday	0.2	0.1	0.2			
Through friends	20.5	23.9	16.7			
PE teacher				12.1	0.9	15.9
Other teacher				4.5	3.2	5.9
Coach				8.2	8.7	7.6
Nobody				17.4	15.7	19.2
Other	3.5	4.2	2.9	15.1	16.6	13.6
N	1,941	1,004	932	1,941	1,004	932

physical educational curriculum is seen by many as a major promotor of and initiator into active lifestyles'. Significant gender differences exist, however, concerning the extent to which boys and girls consider school fosters an interest in sport.

In terms of initial involvement in a top sport the school represents a significantly greater influential factor for females (37 per cent) than males (17 per cent). Indeed if one looks at the top 19 sports available at the school attended at the time of survey (1994), it equates more readily with the top 20 female sports than the top 20 male sports. Young people also rate friends as important in becoming involved in a sport. However, one can observe that this peer influence is a more significant factor for boys (24 per cent) than girls (17 per cent) in encouraging initial involvement. These findings show a slightly different trend to research conducted in the USA. Lewko and Greendorfer (1988) reviewed various factors implicated in children's sport socialisation and found that school represented a more influential factor for boys than girls. In a more recent review Greendorfer (1992) cites various studies which indicate that the family is more influential than peers or school as a socialising agent into sport. However, she does go on to point out that many studies which claim to examine socialisation into sport are in fact examining factors which influence maintenance of involvement in sport. For this reason alone the present study is valuable in contributing distinct data on both socialisation and maintenance factors. Also, as Chapter 5 indicates, the retrospective nature of this question may be significant in the determination of responses. What were actually the most significant influences at the time, and what were perceived to have been the most significant influences with hindsight, may not always correspond closely.

That aside, on average, the father was identified by 19 per cent of young people as the most important significant other in introducing them to their favourite or 'top' sport. Once more a marked gender difference is observable here with a greater percentage of boys (26 per cent) than girls (11 per cent) citing the importance of their father in initially encouraging participation. While only 10 per cent cite their mother as the most important significant other in commencing a sport, one can again observe a marked gender difference with 16 per cent of girls but only 4 per cent of boys claiming their mother was the most important significant other in starting a sport. This trend of the father being rated highly, especially by boys, and the mother, while ranking quite low, having a greater impact upon boys, is continued when one looks at which person(s) young people considered to be important in maintaining involvement in their top sport. Over a fifth (21 per cent) believed their father was the most important factor in their continued involvement in their 'top sport'. The gender breakdown again shows a greater dependence upon fathers by sons (28 per cent) than daughters (12 per cent) in maintaining interest. Although only 10 per cent of young people claimed their mother was responsible for maintaining their interest in their chosen sport, this was more important for girls (16 per cent) than boys (5 per cent). The PE teacher was cited by 12 per cent as the most significant other in maintaining interest. The gender dimension here is interesting with 16 per cent of females compared with only 1 per cent of males citing the importance of the PE teacher in the maintenance of interest. Next to fathers, however, it would appear that sustained involvement reflects more on self-motivation, with a greater reliance on self by males (17 per cent) than females (14 per cent).

The present results support previous studies which have identified the father as being the most influential significant other within the family, although most other studies fail to identify any differential influence for boys and girls (Greendorfer and Ewing, 1981; Lewko and Greendorfer, 1988). A small number of studies looking at the development of play and motor skills in infancy have shown that fathers tend to encourage vigorous play and 'roughhousing' with boys (Lewis, 1972; Power and Parke, 1982). Differential treatment of the sexes is even more apparent in early childhood, with fathers actively involved in teaching gross motor skills to sons but not daughters, and girls in general being given no systematic instruction in motor skills by either parent, in fact even being punished for vigorous physical activity (Tasch, 1952; Fagot, 1978; Tauber, 1979; Langlois and Downs, 1980; Lewko and Greendorfer, 1980). However, Greendorfer (1992) argues that it is difficult to separate the influence of significant others from general social learning in terms of the messages that parents and adults convey to children about appropriate or inappropriate behaviour. Although the present survey does not explore the early years it is worth noting that research has shown that from a very early age (0–3 years), boys are encouraged to explore and interact with their environments whereas young girls are more likely to be picked up or restricted in their exploration of the physical world (Lewko and Greendorfer, 1988).

The findings of the SCNI survey could offer support to the hypothesis that this trend continues throughout childhood, resulting in conscious or unconscious gender-role stereotyping. Hence young boys may grow up believing that physical play and sport is associated with being male, and with being successful (Langlois and Downs, 1980; Lewko and Greendorfer, 1980), while young girls may have more ambivalent attitudes. These subtle socialising influences may influence girls into believing that quiet, less physical and non-competitive play is more appropriate for girls. By early adolescence girls have learned that engaging in contact sports which require strength and power can jeopardise their popularity as a female and as a consequence, sport may assume a low priority in their lives (Coakley, 1992).

Significant others and instruction in 'top sport'

It may prove interesting to see if the same significant others who young people felt had influenced their taking up of a sport and motivated their continued interest were also concerned in instructing young people in their chosen sport. When asked about who had instructed them in their 'top sport' and who had given the most important help, 15 per cent of the sample said they had no 'top sport', 12 per cent said they had never received instruction and 2 per cent replied that they did not know. Of the remainder the breakdown of instruction received from significant others is shown in the first three columns of Table 2.10, the others indicating those people who had given the most help with their 'top sport'.

Table 2.10 Significant others and 'top sport' instruction

Instructor	Who instructs			Who gives most important help?		
	Total %	Male %	Female %	Total %	Male %	Female %
Mother	3.9	1.8	7.1	3.2	1.3	5.3
Father	14.1	17.4	9.4	13.0	18.2	6.6
PE teacher	22.6	21.1	24.6	23.8	19.2	29.0
Other teacher	9.7	10.1	9.1	6.8	6.2	7.6
Qualified coach	28.0	25.1	32.2	35.2	33.8	36.5
Friends	8.2	9.7	6.1	4.7	6.3	3.0
Brother/sister	5.9	6.4	5.4	4.4	5.0	3.7
Other relatives	4.3	5.5	2.7	2.7	4	1.3
Other	2.9	2.8	3.3	6.2	6	6.4
N	3,046	1,773	1,263	1,649	860	784

Looking at the first part of Table 2.10 it appears that the person from whom young people received the most instruction was a qualified coach, with 32 per cent of girls and 25 per cent of boys receiving instruction from this source. Almost 23 per cent said they received instruction in their chosen sport from their PE teacher. Again one can see the trend of greater female dependence upon the school/PE teacher with 25 per cent of girls compared with only 8 per cent of boys claiming this type of instruction. While family members rank low as sport instructors, the previous trend of greater involvement by fathers, especially for sons, is continued; 14 per cent of respondents said their father instructed them in their top sport with more boys (17 per cent) than girls (9 per cent) receiving instruction. Only 4 per cent claimed they received instruction from their mother but yet again a gender dimension can be detected here, with 7 per cent of females and only 2 per cent of males saying they had received instruction from this source.

From the second part of Table 2.10 it can be seen that again the qualified coach (35 per cent) and PE teacher (24 per cent) rank highest in terms of who gives the most important help. While no major gender differences are observable concerning the coach, it can be seen that girls rank the importance of the PE teacher higher than boys, with 29 per cent of girls recognising the importance of this help, compared with 19 per cent of boys. Again the results indicate that respondents rank the help given by family members as quite low, especially mothers. A similar trend is evident when we consider attempted sports. The majority of children had received instruction in their attempted sport and when young people were instructed it was generally in school. Of the female respondents 42 per cent, compared with 30 per cent of male respondents, claim instruction in school, which illustrates once again the greater dependence upon the school as a sports provider for females rather than males. These results highlight the importance of both the school and PE teachers as influential factors in girls' participation in sport.

However, a more worrying finding is the number intending to play (or not to play) their 'top sport' after leaving school (see Table 2.11). Not surprisingly, more boys (69 per cent) than girls (54 per cent) are definite about their intentions to continue playing their sport, but it is disappointing to find that a significantly greater number of girls (12 per cent compared with only 4 per cent of boys) can already state that they do not intend to play their top sport after they leave school. It is difficult to speculate at this stage as to why so many girls do not intend to continue with their sport. Could it be that they are already aware of the many documented barriers to women participating in sport and so they anticipate difficulties in trying to fit sport into their lives, or have 'chill factors' already begun to discourage sport participation?

Table 2.11 'Will you still play your "top sport" after you leave school?'

	Boys %	Girls %
Yes, definitely	68.6	53.6
Yes, probably	15.9	20.0
Yes, possibly	8.5	12.8
No	3.9	12.0
Don't know	3.1	1.6
N	1,004	932

It would be unrealistic to expect the school PE programme to cater exclusively for the development of all top or chosen sport; clearly the PE curriculum has a broader remit. A direct consequence of the Education Reform (NI) Order 1989 was the introduction of the Common Curriculum into schools in Northern Ireland. The Common Curriculum represented a major break with traditional school-based methods for defining the curriculum as it specified the subject content which pupils were to follow at each stage of their education. The Common Curriculum, through its insistence on schools following the programmes of study for PE, has enormous potential for providing all pupils up to the age of 16 with a broad and balanced PE experience. How extensively a PE department can now legitimately afford to devote time to the development of a 'top sport' must be limited given that so many elements of the programme of study, including athletics, games, dance, swimming and gymnastics, must be catered for. Therefore, policy makers should perhaps take particular note of these findings as, when set in the context of little in-school provision and declining extra-curricular exposure for 'top sports', they indicate that sports clubs will have to take responsibility not only for attracting girls into private/voluntary clubs but of finding ways to cater for their different goals and aspirations within sport.

Sports clubs and 'top sport' participation

Perhaps surprisingly, of the 1,941 young people who named a 'top sport', only 43 per cent were members of a club which played that sport. For boys, most club members were found in the sports of soccer (43 per cent club members) and Gaelic football (21 per cent club members) with fewer club members reported for golf (27), swimming (15), badminton (11), athletics (10), and indeed the remainder of male top sports included fewer than 10 club members per sport.

For girls, the breakdown of membership was spread thinly across a greater number of sports, with largest club membership in the sports of riding (34), camogie (32), Irish dancing (30) and somewhat encouragingly, soccer (30), with swimming (25) and netball (23) receiving slightly fewer counts. Next followed a range of activities with counts between 13 and 15, these including athletics, badminton, gymnastics, field hockey and aerobics. Obviously, with so few young people involved in club sport at present, there is room for improving youth development infrastructures, particularly with regard to recruiting procedures, if clubs are to become more influential in nurturing 'top sports'. It is interesting that in the developing sport of girls' soccer there is a relatively large club membership in comparison with some of the more traditional female sports.

In order to examine the clubs' influence, the young people were asked in which two ways their club had helped them with their sport. Little difference existed between what boys and girls felt were the most important ways, with both sexes in agreement that clubs helped most with training (33 per cent of boys; 32 per cent of girls) and improving technique (29 per cent and 27 per cent for boys and girls respectively). Possibly more important information may be gleaned from data

Table 2.12 Ways clubs hinder participation in sport

Ways clubs hinder	Whole valid %	Male valid %	Female valid %
Club disputes	1.0	1.8	
Unfriendly instruction	7.1	8.8	4.9
Restricted time	23.5	28.1	7.1
Unfit yet made to play	1.0		2.4
More attention to improving	3.1	1.8	4.9
Overtraining/overtired	8.2	8.8	7.3
Taken off team	1.0	1.8	
Others not as advanced	1.0		2.4
Poor team selection	3.1	3.5	2.4
People fouling	2.0	1.8	2.4
Poor facilities	5.1	5.3	4.9
Leaders too strict	3.1	3.5	2.4
Not enough events	14.3	8.8	22.0
Others' bad language	1.0	1.8	
Closed due to lack of numbers	1.0	1.8	
Poor coaching	9.2	5.3	14.6
Poor leader communication	3.1	3.5	2.4
Not enough instruction	2.0	3.5	
Age limits	2.0	3.5	
Can't use own bike	1.0	1.8	
Golf course too easy	1.0	1.8	
Lack of transport	1.0		
Injury risk high	2.0	1.8	2.4
Club is impersonal	1.0		2.4
Grass is too black!	1.0	1.8	
N	98	57	41

generated by asking subjects for two ways in which they were hindered by their club. Table 2.12 shows the responses to both questions amalgamated. Unfortunately, the information which it can provide is restricted as only 86 (10 per cent) club members answered the first question and 12 (1 per cent) responded to the second of these questions.

Almost a quarter (24 per cent) of those who replied claimed that their club hindered sports participation most by not spending enough time on a sport. Boys (28 per cent) felt that restricted time affected them to a greater extent than girls (7 per cent). Not having enough events also ranked highly (14 per cent) as a factor which hindered sport participation. On this occasion it was girls (22 per cent) more than boys (9 per cent) who felt this was true, with boys also citing unfriendly instruction and overtraining an equal number of times (9 per cent respectively). Unfortunately, although the survey does not allow us to speculate as to precisely what kinds of events may be more desirable for both genders, it is noteworthy that the word event is used rather than competition, which may imply that it is not always competition *per se* which is sought. Nevertheless, policy makers may wish to examine the gender differences highlighted by the survey and perhaps probe further exactly what is desirable for both sexes, and particularly if sports clubs are to assume an increasingly important position in the provision of sport.

MOTIVATION, EXPECTATIONS AND FACTORS INFLUENCING DROP-OUT FROM SPORT

Beginning sport

Table 2.13 shows the ages at which both attempted sports and 'top sports' were started. In terms of attempted sport there appears to be no predominant age band when involvement began with roughly equal numbers between the ages of 5 and 12. However, 60 per cent had attempted a sport before the age of 9 and boys tend to become involved in sport at a younger age. For example, by the age of 9, 65 per cent of boys compared with 55 per cent of girls had attempted a sport. A greater percentage of girls (22 per cent) than boys (15 per cent), however, tend to attempt sport after the age of 12 years. For 'top sports' these trends are even more accentuated, with the majority of boys (42 per cent) having started their involvement between the ages of 5 and 7 but the starting ages for girls spread more evenly across the three middle age bands of 5–7 years (27 per cent), 8–9 years (22 per cent) and 10–11 years (24 per cent) and a sizeable proportion of girls (17 per cent) not starting their top sport until after 12 years. Although comparative data with a gender breakdown are difficult to find, both American and Canadian studies (Martens, 1988; Valeriote and Hansen, 1988) show similar trends with the mean age of entry to top sports reported as 11 years and 10.5 years respectively. However, related American research also suggests that children's sport participation peaks around 12 years of age (Ewing and Seefeldt, 1989). Therefore, it may be speculated that to be only starting involvement at 12 years or older may not bode well for adherence statistics, given that drop-out rates from organised sports programmes are estimated to be in the region of 35 per cent in any given year (Gould and Petlichkoff, 1988).

Table 2.13 Age started in sports (attempted and 'top')

	Attempted sports			Top sports		
	Total	Male	Female	Total	Male	Female
Age	%	%	%	%	%	%
4 years	7.3	8.0	6.5	13.2	16.4	10.0
5–7 years	29.0	31.8	25.7	34.8	42.3	27.2
8–9 years	23.8	24.8	22.7	15.1	18.2	12.1
10–11 years	21.7	20.5	23.0	19.1	13.9	24.3
12+ years	18.2	14.9	22.0	12.9	9.3	16.5
N	13,808	7,329	6,479	1,941	1,004	934

What motivates children to attempt sport?

In trying to understand young people's involvement in sport it is important to examine what motivates young people to attempt a sport initially. Table 2.14 summarises the responses made when the young people were asked why they had attempted certain sports.

The most popular reasons selected by young people as to why they attempted a sport were 'because of school' and 'because of friends', accounting for 31 per cent and 20 per cent of responses respectively. It

Table 2.14 Reasons for attempting sports

Reasons for starting	% of total responses	% of male responses	% of female responses
Because of school	31.3	23.9	39.8
Because of friends	20.3	23.4	16.8
Because of father	10.2	13.6	6.4
Because of mother	7.3	5.0	10.0
Something to do	6.5	7.0	6.0
Older brother/sister	5.8	6.1	5.4
Seemed interesting	3.9	3.7	4.1
Thought it would be good	2.9	3.3	2.5
To keep fit	2.0	2.2	1.8
To learn new skills	1.8	1.8	1.8
Saw it on television	1.8	2.9	0.7
Seemed a challenge	1.1	1.2	0.9
To practise skill	0.6	0.8	0.4
Saw a game live	0.1	0.2	
Don't know	0.5	0.5	0.5
Other reason	3.7	4.4	3.1
N	13,864	7,339	6,489

Column percentages total 100

would appear that girls' initial participation in an attempted sport depends more crucially upon school involvement, with almost 40 per cent of girls citing school as the most influential motivating factor, compared with almost 24 per cent of boys. This finding supports previous suggestions regarding the important influence exerted by schools in selection of top sports. Peer influence or 'because of friends' was a stronger motivating force for males (23 per cent) than females (17 per cent). Siblings did not rank particularly highly as motivating factors in attempting a sport, although 'older brother/sister' sometimes featured. The father appears to be a greater motivating force in general, although when considering the gender breakdown, in terms of female involvement, the mother rates as more influential than the father.

In order to gain a clearer picture of what influences young people to become involved in particular sports, the top 20 listed sports were examined by gender. Table 2.15 highlights the top two rated influences for each sport for boys and girls (although in a number of cases the data apply only to one sex). It is clear from this table that involvement in specific sports is influenced by different factors. More importantly, perhaps, is the implication that both boys and girls are similarly influenced to participate in many sports. For example, school appears to be a key influence for both sexes in all traditional team sports, namely Rugby Union, netball and hockey. However, sports such as golf, horse riding, cycling, dancing and skating rely more heavily on parental influence and these also appear to adhere to traditional stereotyped choices, that is golf for boys, ice skating for girls, cycling for both. Interestingly, both boys and girls cite their mother as a key influence for swimming. Girls also cite mothers as the primary influence for ice skating, Irish dancing and cycling, although fathers are equally influential for the latter and are also influential for horse riding. Boys cite their father as a key influence in the sports of golf, cycling and Gaelic football, although both boys and girls appear to be primarily influenced by friends (rather than schools) in participating in soccer. Friends also appear to be a significant influence on participation in the additional 'male-only' sports of snooker, cricket and archery and the school is also cited as influencing participation in hurling and cricket, whereas fathers are a major influence on taking up angling.

By presenting the motivating factors for attempting sports in this way, the extremely influential role played by schools and parents is made explicit. In some ways it is not surprising that schools, friends and parents emerge as the most influential factors in selecting sports, as these young people spend most of their waking hours either in

Table 2.15 Relationship of two key influences in attempting specific sports

Sport	School Male %	School Fem. %	Friends Male %	Friends Fem. %	Father Male %	Father Fem. %	Mother Male %	Mother Fem. %	Other Male %	Other Fem %
Soccer			36.6	**31.8**	12.3					21.8
Swimming	**30.1**	30.5					23.5	**31.6**		
Netball		**89.2**								
Gaelic football	**29.6**		24.4							
Athletics	**62.1**	**74.8**							9.4	
Horse riding				**26.6**		14.1				
Field hockey	**59.3**	**83.1**	14.0	6.4						
Badminton	**29.4**	**49.6**	29.4	18.9			6.7			
Cycling			13.1		**37.5**	20.2		**21.5**		
Basketball	**57.1**	**56.1**	17.3	16.6						
Camogie		**39.7**		23.7						
Irish dance				24.1				**39.8**		
Rugby	**53.6**		21.0							
Golf			28.6		**36.3**					
Lawn tennis		**22.9**	**26.1**	22.0					12.8	
Rounders	**62.3**	**72.3**	22.9							
Gymnastics		**46.2**	17.5							
Aerobics		**42.5**								20.3
Ice skating			**35.0**					10.7		
Racket sports	**34.3**	**28.9**							21.0	12.4

Numbers in **bold** indicate primary influence; numbers in light face indicate secondary influence

school or in the company of family and friends. However, in the context of these seemingly overriding influences we should also consider the recent research highlighting the distinct differences in girls' and boys' motives and goal orientations towards sport. While it may seem fortunate that both sexes seem influenced in generally similar ways, caution should also be voiced when one considers recent psychological research which indicates that quite different dispositional variables can predict level of involvement in sport for males and females (Ryckman and Hamel, 1995). In a study of 154 high school students it was found that hypercompetitiveness (defined as the indiscriminate need to compete and win at any cost) was the strongest and only predictor of male involvement in sport whereas this predisposition was unrelated to female sports' involvement. Hypercompetitiveness was found to be unrelated to sports' involvement for females but girls involved in sport were found to have stronger competitive attitudes towards personal development than those with lower levels of involvement.

Policy makers need to consider research of this nature which draws attention to the extent to which girls' experience in sport may be quite different to boys'. If we are to expand the numbers of girls becoming involved in sport at all levels we must heed the importance of studies which suggest that the sporting environment must cater for the aspirations and expectations of all involved. Parents and schools could also help by emphasising the personal and social facets of competitive sports rather than only the competition.

In looking at what motivates children to attempt a sport initially it may prove interesting to look at the top 20 sports for males and females separately, to compare the number of young people who named a particular activity as their top sport and the number who had claimed they had attempted that sport. The third column in each of the following tables shows the ratio of top sport to attempted sport, represented as a percentage. This ratio may represent an index of the attractiveness of a particular activity; for example, of the 1,011 boys who had ever played soccer, 46 per cent still regarded it as their top sport at the time of interview (Table 2.16). In contrast, although 909

Table 2.16 Ratio of 'top sport' to attempted sport: males

Top 20 male sports	Top sport	Attempted sport	% top sport to attempted sport
Soccer	462	1,011	45.7
Gaelic football	118	409	28.9
Swimming	70	909	7.7
Rugby Union	35	138	25.4
Golf	33	260	12.7
Basketball	29	462	6.3
Athletics	26	257	10.1
Karate	17	74	23.0
Cycling	16	297	5.4
Hurling	16	169	9.5
Badminton	13	252	5.2
Cricket	11	190	5.8
Motor cycling	11	33	33.3
Horse riding	10	47	21.3
Billiards/snooker	9	289	3.1
Field hockey	9	172	5.2
Angling	7	93	7.5
Lawn tennis	7	203	3.4
Rugby League	7	47	14.9
Netball	6	32	18.8
Other sports	90	1,627	5.5
N	1,002	6,971	

males had swum, only 8 per cent regarded it as their 'top sport'. Interestingly though, if we refer back to Table 2.4 we see that despite the fairly small percentage who regard swimming as their 'top sport' almost a fifth participate at competitive level. In contrast, a higher proportion of girls (20 per cent) regard swimming as a 'top sport' yet the majority (93 per cent; see Table 2.1) participate at a recreational or basic level.

Referring to Table 2.17, the most popular attempted sport among girls was swimming, with 912 (76 per cent) claiming they had attempted this sport, and at the time of interview 20 per cent felt it was their 'top sport'. In contrast, although 163 had played basketball, only 8 per cent (13) maintained it was their 'top sport'.

Table 2.17 Ratio of 'top sport' to attempted sport: females

Top 20 female sports	Top sport	Attempted sport	% top sport to attempted sport
Swimming	185	912	20.3
Netball	123	631	19.5
Soccer	65	308	21.1
Athletics	63	309	20.1
Horse riding	63	128	49.2
Field hockey	60	360	16.7
Camogie	42	131	32.1
Badminton	39	349	11.2
Irish dancing	35	241	14.5
Cycling	28	247	11.3
Gymnastics	24	251	9.6
Lawn tennis	24	245	9.8
Rounders	22	242	9.1
Aerobics	21	154	13.7
Ice skating	15	177	8.5
Racket sports	15	121	12.4
Basketball	13	163	8.0
Disco dancing	10	105	9.6
Ballet dancing	10	71	14.1
Gaelic football	8	37	21.7
Other sports	62	1,191	5.2
N	927	6,373	

Dropping out of sport

The incidence of drop-out across the sample was pleasingly low, with only 17 per cent of those who had ever attempted any sport stating that they had discontinued that sport completely. Furthermore, within 'top sports' the drop-out rate was extremely low indeed with 98 per

Table 2.18 Age of drop-out from attempted sports and 'top sports'

Age	Attempted sports			Top sports		
	Total	Male	Female	Total	Male	Female
4– years	0.0	0.0	0.0	0.0	0.0	0.0
5–7 years	1.0	0.7	1.3	0.0	0.0	0.1
8–9 years	1.8	1.3	2.4	0.3	0.2	0.4
10–11 years	3.6	2.8	4.6	0.9	0.4	1.4
12+ years	10.2	6.9	13.8	3.3	1.6	4.9
n/a	83.4	88.3	77.8	95.5	97.8	93.2
N	13,866	7,340	6,490			

cent of boys and 93 per cent of girls still involved in their sport. Although the incidence of drop-out was low, one can see from Table 2.18 that across the age bands, the female drop-out rate was greater than the male rate with a marked difference occurring after age 12 years, particularly in relation to attempted sports. As was previously mentioned, early adolescence is characterised by an intensification of gender-related role expectations. The cultivation of masculinity encourages continued sports participation, as sport is traditionally viewed as an arena in which to prove one's masculinity. The cultivation of femininity on the other hand places limitations upon female participation rates. Brown, Frankel and Fennell (1989, p.397) note: 'sex-role stereotypes of gender appropriate behaviour continue to define involvement in sport past the childhood years as being inconsistent with the female role', and this may help to explain these gender differences in atttrition rates.

Results from this study show that early adolescence is marked with a slightly greater drop-out rate for females than males although drop-out from 'top sports' is still very low. However, it is rather disappointing to put these results in the context of Table 2.11, which highlights that 12 per cent of girls said they would cease involvement in their 'top sport' after school. Nevertheless, it must also be pointed out that ceasing involvement in a favourite sport may not necessarily mean dropping out of sport permanently. A number of studies (Gould, *et al.* 1982; Klint and Weiss, 1986; Gould and Petchlikoff, 1988) have highlighted the importance of distinguishing between sport-specific withdrawal (withdrawing from one sport to become or stay involved in another) and general drop-out (dropping out of all competitive sport permanently). It is hoped that the girls intending to cease involvement in their current 'top sport' will still stay involved in some form of sport or leisure after leaving school.

Although the incidence of drop-out from sport is quite low within the SCNI survey, it may be worth considering the answers which young people gave to the survey questions concerned with participation motivation and attrition. Such information may prove valuable for policy initiatives aimed at increasing the level of participation for both sexes. The reasons given for dropping out of sport were many and varied, but the most frequently cited reason for quitting both top and attempted sport was 'lack of interest'. There was virtually no difference between boys and girls with slightly over a third of each group giving this as their major reason. The other major reasons given for dropping out were 'school commitments' and 'sport not played at school'. Again, these reasons were cited equally often by both males and females. It would appear, therefore, that when it comes to dropping out there is very little difference between boys and girls – both seem to experience similar forms of dissatisfaction leading them to quit their sport. Other studies which have examined the issue of drop-out also cite lack of fun, lack of interest and other commitments as the main reasons for cessation of a sport (Gould *et al.*, 1982; Gould and Horn, 1984; Gould and Petchlikoff, 1988).

Owing to the fact that there were few data generated concerning drop-out, it was considered important to probe the issue a little further by examining any gender differences evident when respondents were asked to rate factors which would make them more keen or less keen to participate in their sport. Again, very few gender differences were found with over 60 per cent of male and female respondents rating the following factors as very important in making them more keen on their sport over time: enjoying taking part, being with friends, keeping fit, excitement of the sport, feeling good about performing well, getting better as a player. Family encouragement was also rated as very important by boys (54 per cent) and girls (57 per cent) with school encouragement being highly rated by fewer individuals (36 per cent of boys, 35 per cent of girls). However, sex differences do appear to exist in relation to feelings about winning. Results seem to support previous suggestions about male/female differences in competitive goal orientations. It would appear that boys tend to see winning (39 per cent) as a more important motivating factor than do girls (26 per cent) with more girls (46 per cent) than boys (33 per cent) stating that winning is not important. In a similar vein, more girls (56 per cent) than boys (41 per cent) rate trophies and medals as not important with 41 per cent and 54 per cent respectively rating them as quite or very important. Such findings generally support the speculations raised earlier about male and females differences in attitudes to competition and winning.

In examining the factors which make participants less keen over time, again there are some noteworthy similarities between the sexes. For example, both boys (31 per cent) and girls (39 per cent) rate lack of enjoyment as the most important factor. Only two other factors received 'very important' ratings and these were lack of support from family (35 per cent for girls, 28 per cent for boys) and injuries/getting hurt (31 per cent for girls, 25 per cent for boys). However, it should also be noted that for both sexes a number of factors were rated as not being important in making participants less keen over time. These included the impact of losing, cost of sport, time taken, lack of support from school and the weather/getting cold.

SUMMARY

This chapter has examined gender differences across four main areas, as identified in the introduction, and has referenced the particular problems which must be addressed when endeavouring to encourage greater female participation in sport. In general, a number of gender differences emerged in the data but the chapter concludes on a rather optimistic view of the future of sport for both sexes in Northern Ireland. Both boys and girls are motivated by roughly equivalent forces, and both appear to derive pleasure from their involvement in sport, with boys showing keener interest in team sports and girls more inclined towards individual activities, and often those with a less overt competitive element.

The key differences identified between boys and girls were in terms of choice and level of involvement in sport and exposure to sport. The survey revealed that more boys than girls participate in sport and this gender difference carries over into choice of sporting activity and level of participation. Furthermore the survey reveals that boys receive greater exposure to sport, both within and outside of school. This difference was also found to translate into greater time being devoted to practice, instruction and competition. These results were discussed in terms of both motivational forces and implications for school curriculum and club policy. Different external influences were also identified by boys and girls for becoming started in sports, although both sexes concurred in identifying family influences as important factors in maintaining their interest in sport. The main difference between the sexes in terms of motivational variables appears to be the hypercompetitive trait previously identified for males, with girls expressing greater interest in participating for reasons of personal development. However, no differences were found for factors

54   *Deirdre Scully and Jackie Clarke*

influencing drop-out, and to end on an upbeat note, the majority of boys and girls showed little inclination to leave their sporting careers at the school gates. Whether these aspirations translate into healthy adult participation profiles must remain a topic for future research.

REFERENCES

Adler, P.A., Kless, S.J. and Adler, P. (1992). Socialization to gender roles: Popularity among elementary school boys and girls. *Sociology of Education*, *65*, 169–187.

Arnold, P.J. (1988). *Education, Movement and the Curriculum*. London: Falmer Press.

Brown, B.A., Frankel, B.G. and Fennell, M.P. (1989). Hugs and shrugs: Parental and peer influence on continuity of involvement in sport by female adolescents. *Sex Roles*, *20*, *(7/8)*, 397–409.

Clarke, J. (1995). Organisational strategies: Pupil perspectives on class grouping and their impact upon physical educational opportunities. Unpublished MEd. Dissertation, University of Ulster at Jordanstown.

Coakley, J. (1992). Burnout among adolescent athletes: A personal failure or a social problem? *Sociology of Sport Journal*, *9*, 271–285.

Colley, A., Nash, J., O'Donnell, L. and Restorick, L. (1987). Attitudes to the female sex role and sex-typing of physical activities. *International Journal of Sport Psychology*, *18*, 19–29.

Costa, D.M. and Guthrie, S.R. (eds) (1994). *Women and Sport*. Champaign, IL: Human Kinetics.

Evans, J. (ed.) (1993). *Equality, Education and Physical Education*. London: Falmer Press.

Ewing, M. and Seefeldt, V. (1989). *Participation and Attrition Patterns in American Agency-Sponsored and Interscholastic Sports: An Executive Summary. Final Report*. North Palm Beach, FL: Sporting Goods Manufacturer's Association.

Fagot, B.I. (1978). The influence of sex of child on parental reaction. *Developmental Psychology*, *10*, 554–558.

Gill, D. (1988). Gender differences in competitive orientation and sport participation. *International Journal of Sport Psychology*, *19*, 145–159.

Gill, D. (1994). Psychological perspectives on women in sport and exercise. In D. M. Costa and S.R. Guthrie (eds) *Women and Sport*. Champaign, IL: Human Kinetics.

Gould, D. and Horn, T. (1984). Participation motivation in young athletes. In J.M. Silva III and R.S.Weinberg (eds) *Psychological Foundations of Sport*. Champaign, IL: Human Kinetics.

Gould, D. and Petlichkoff, L. (1988). Participation motivation and attrition in young athletes. In F. Smoll, R. Magill, and M. Ash (eds) *Children in Sport, 3rd Edition*. Champaign, IL: Human Kinetics.

Gould, D., Feltz, D., Horn, T. and Weiss, M.R. (1982). Reasons for discontinuing involvement in competitive youth swimming. *Journal of Sport Behavior*, *5*, 155–165.

Greendorfer, S. (1992). Sport socialisation. In T. Horn (ed.) *Advances in Sport Psychology*. Champaign, IL: Human Kinetics.

Greendorfer, S.L. and Ewing, M.E. (1981). Race and gender differences in children's socialisation into sport. *Research Quarterly for Exercise and Sport*, *52*, 301–310.

Griffen, P. (1984). Co-educational physical education: Problems and promises. *Journal of Physical Education Recreation and Dance*, *55(6)*, 36–37.

Klint, K. and Weiss, M.R. (1986). Dropping in and dropping out: Participation motives of current and former youth gymnasts. *Canadian Journal of Applied Sport Sciences*, *11(2)*, 106–114.

Langlois, J. H. and Downs, A.C. (1980). Mothers, fathers and peers as socialization agents of sex-typed play behaviors in young children. *Child Development*, *51*, 1237–1247.

Lawrie, L and Brown, R. (1992). Sex-stereotypes, school subject preference and career aspirations as a function of single/mixed sex schooling and presence/absence of an opposite sex sibling. *British Journal of Educational Psychology*, *62(1)*, 132–137.

Leaman, O. (1986). Physical education and sex differentiation. *The British Journal of Physical Education*, *17,(4)*, 123–124.

Lewis, M. (1972). State as an infant-environment interaction: An analysis of mother-infant behavior as a function of sex. *Merrill-Palmer Quarterly*, *18*, 95–121.

Lewko, J.H. and Greendorfer, S.L. (1980). Family influence and sex differences in children's socialization into sport: A review. In R.A. Magill, M.J. Ash, and F.L. Smoll (eds) *Children in Sport, 2nd Edition*. Champaign, IL: Human Kinetics.

Lewko, J.H. and Greendorfer, S.L. (1988). Family influences in sport socialization of children and adolescents. In F.L. Smoll, R.A. Magill, and M.J. Ash (eds) *Children in Sport, 3rd Edition*. Champaign, IL: Human Kinetics.

Lopez, S. (1987). Mixed-sex groups in physical education – Some problems and possibilities. *The Bulletin of Physical Education*, *23(1)*, 19–22.

Martens, R. (1988). Youth sport in the USA. In F.L. Smoll, R.A. Magill, and M.J. Ash (eds) *Children in Sport, 3rd Edition*. Champaign, IL: Human Kinetics.

Mason, V. (1995). *Young People and Sport in England, 1994: A National Survey*. Sports Council: London.

Northern Ireland Curriculum Council (NICC) (1993). *Equal Opportunities Northern Ireland Curriculum: Gender Equality (Post-Primary) Guidance Materials*. Belfast: HMSO.

Oglesby, C.A. and Hill, K.L. (1993). Gender and sport. In R. Singer, M. Murphey and L. Tennant (eds) *Handbook of Research in Sport Psychology*. New York: Macmillan.

Power, T.G. and Parke, R.D. (1982). Play as a context for early learning: Lab. and home analyses. In I.E. Siegel and L.M. Asosa (eds) *The Family as a Learning Environment*. New York: Plenum.

Ryckman, R. and Hamel, J. (1995). Male and female adolescents' motives related to involvement in organized team sports. *International Journal of Sport Psychology*, *26*, 383–397.

Scraton, S.J. (1986). Gender and girls' physical education. *The British Journal of Physical Education*, *17*, *(4)*, 145–147.

Stockard, J. and Johnson, M.M. (1977). *Sex-Role Development and Sex Discrimination* London: Houghton-Miflin.

Sutherland, A. (1992). *Physical Education and Games in Post-Primary Schools in 1991*. Belfast: Sports Council Northern Ireland.

Talbot, M. (1986). Gender and physical education. *The British Journal of Physical Education, 17(4)*, 82–90.

Talbot, M. (1990). Equal opportunities and physical education. In N. Armstrong (ed.) *New Directions In Physical Education*. Champaign, IL: Human Kinetics.

Talbot, M. (1993). A gendered physical education: Equality and sexism. In J. Evans (ed.) *Equality, Education and Physical Education*. London: Falmer Press.

Tasch, R.G. (1952). The role of the father in the family. *Journal of Experimental Education, 20*, 319–361.

Tauber, M.A. (1979). Parental socialization techniques and sex differences in children's play. *Child Development, 50*, 225–234.

Valeriote, T.A. and Hansen, L. (1988). Youth sport in Canada. In F.L. Smoll, R.A. Magill, and M.J. Ash (eds) *Children in Sport, 3rd Edition*. Champaign, IL: Human Kinetics.

Weinberg, R.S. and Ragan, J. (1979). Effects of competition, success/failure, and sex on intrinsic motivation. *Research Quarterly, 50*, 503–510.

Williams, A. (1988). Physical activity patterns among adolescents – Some curriculum implications. *Physical Education Review, 11(1)*, 28–39.

3 Individual differences and intrinsic motivations for sport participation

Anneke van Wersch

INTRODUCTION

Over recent years, two significant developments have served to give physical exercise and sporting activities greater recognition and significance in the public eye. First, there has been a growing appreciation of the value of exercise for promoting health and general well-being; and second, in a period when leisure time is on the increase, sporting activities have come to be seen as a meaningful way of occupying non-working hours. These developments have their consequences for young people's sport, or as Martens (1980) has written:

> Improving the quality of youth sports programs is not a panacea to the nation's problems: it will not significantly reduce crime, inflation, poverty or disease. But we do know that sports are an important part of many children's lives, helping influence their socialization into adulthood. If we can help youngsters know the joy of sports, the benefits of a physically active life, and come to know themselves as worthy human beings, we may indeed be making a significant contribution to preventive medicine.
>
> (p.385)

Creating appropriate opportunities and conditions should help encourage children to engage in physical exercise and sporting activities at an early age, and to continue for many years thereafter. Yet, while the rate at which children enter sport seems to grow, their subsequent drop-out, particularly during adolescence, may frustrate the long-term advantages which may be gained. Research which has looked at why young people drop out (cf. Roberts, 1984) has found that the reasons which are most often mentioned include an overemphasis on winning in sport, and having other interests (for example, other commitments at school, part-time employment), as well as more nebulous yet intrinsic constructs which are central to this chapter, namely lack of enjoyment and lack of interest.

Over the last 20 years, sport and exercise psychologists have shown great interest in the intrinsic motives which underlie participation and, as Chapter 9 demonstrates, have made great strides towards determining the mechanisms by which intrinsic motives such as interest, enjoyment and challenge may impact on participation rates. As Frederick and Ryan (1995, p.5) conclude, 'the most salient motives for sport participation (outside of the professional sphere) are of an intrinsic nature', and it is a consideration of the significance of these intrinsic motives which forms the backbone of this chapter, operationalised through the work of Susan Harter on perceived self-competence.

MOTIVATION AND COMPETENCE

As already mentioned, sport and exercise psychologists have paid considerable attention to the question of why people do or do not exercise or take part in sport. Research has tended to focus on either personality traits or the process of motivation. The former approach has been criticised on several grounds, for example because it is not based on any a priori hypotheses concerning relationships between personality and sport participation, or because many of the personality measures used have no face validity in the specific context of sport (cf. Gill et al., 1988; Kremer and Scully, 1994).

The present chapter has opted for a motivational approach but at the same time aims to consider the role which individual differences may play in shaping motivation. From the many psychological models and theories of motivation available, the one employed here is that developed by Harter (Harter, 1981a; 1981b; Harter and Connell, 1984). Harter's model is attractive because it focuses on the motivations of young people of different ages and in different educational settings, and because it adopts a multifaceted view of self. Rather than concentrating on just one aspect of motivation, as is true for many models, it makes an explicit distinction between cognitive, social and physical domains, a distinction which in turn has been empirically validated. Although the physical domain has been rather underplayed in Harter's own empirical research, this categorisation of motives has been picked up with enthusiasm by those interested in sport and physical education (Feltz and Petlichkoff, 1983; Gould, 1984; Gilbert and van Wersch, 1989).

Harter's original model was proposed to refine and extend White's (1959) concept of 'competence'. White saw 'competence' as the most important determinant of human motivation. In all achievement-oriented contexts, motivation impels an individual to engage in mastering the relevant task. White assumed that this need to exercise mastery over the environment was intrinsic; its gratification would produce inherent pleasure. Harter took these ideas further by, inter alia, operationalising the concepts in terms of a set of measuring instruments, elucidating the domain specificity of competence, and making a distinction between intrinsic and extrinsic motivation. Extrinsic motivation rests on such rewards as winning the approval of others or obtaining good marks at school, whereas, put simply, intrinsic motivation is about feeling good or feeling competent about performance.

'Competence' and related concepts have been used in a number of research studies of young people's sporting activities. For example, it has been found that perceived physical competence is the best predictor of boys' satisfaction with their performance in games (Kimiecik, Allison and Duda, 1986). Several other studies have shown the positive influence of participation in sport on self-confidence and self-esteem (for example, Gould, Weiss and Weinberg, 1981; Roberts, 1984; Underwood, 1987) and research has also found that sport participants perceive themselves as more physically competent than either non-participants or drop-outs (for example, Burton and Martens, 1986), and young people even drop out of sport when their self-perceived physical ability is threatened. In terms of individual differences, gender plays a significant role; boys' perception of their physical competence seems generally to be higher than that of girls – for pre-adolescent and adolescent children as well as college students (see Fox, Corbin and Couldry, 1985; Granleese, Turner and Trew, 1989; Cairns, 1990).

The distinction between intrinsic and extrinsic motivation is clearly significant in terms of physical activity and participation, and the juxtapositioning of the two sets of motives forms the basis of the measures of competence operationalised in the SCNI survey. Empirically, extrinsic motivation has been found to derive from the anticipation of awards or approval (winning, prizes), avoidance of disapproval and improving one's sporting skills in order to please others. In contrast, intrinsic values applicable to sporting activities include the experience of mastering sporting skills, satisfaction in the pursuit of challenge, bettering oneself rather than beating an opponent, and feeling good through improved fitness. Generally, it is these intrinsic motives which have been shown to be the more powerful predictors of future participation and satisfaction (Weiss and Chaumeton, 1992).

MEASURING MOTIVATION FOR SPORT

In a precursor to the present study (Gilbert and van Wersch, 1989; van Wersch, 1990), a set of scales were constructed to measure five dimensions of intrinsic and extrinsic motivation in the physical domain. The first three (1–3 below) paralleled existing dimensions used by Harter for measuring competence in the cognitive domain, while the last two (4–5) were specifially designed for use in the context of sport and physical exercise. The five bi-polar scales (with the pole of intrinsic motivation expressed first) are:

1 'Preference for challenge' vs. 'Preference for easy work': Young people's intrinsic motivation is seen as their willingness to work hard at physical exercise and sporting activities, wanting to learn, and to practise and improve in different areas of sport. Extrinsic motivation involves a preference to take things easy and to be satisfied with existing skills and familiar sports.

2 'Curiosity' vs. 'Pleasing the teacher and getting good marks': Here, the contrast is between young people's motivation to engage in sport in order to satisfy their own 'Curiosity', as opposed to wishing to satisfy the teacher, obtain good marks or win.

3 'Succeed against oneself' vs. 'Compete against others': This scale measures the degree to which young people undertake sporting activities in order to improve their performance levels rather than to become better than, or beat, others.

4 'Independent mastery' vs. 'Dependence on others': In this case, intrinsic motivation is represented by young people's preference to practise sport on their own and extrinsic motivation by their relying on others for their sporting activities.

5 'Fitness for its own sake' vs. 'Fitness for appearance in the eyes of others': Here, young people are seen as undertaking sporting activities either because it makes them feel good to be fit and healthy or because they think that being fit makes them look good.

In addition to the above, a number of other scales have been used by the author (van Wersch, 1990) to measure aspects of young people's self-perception, particularly with regard to their feelings of competence. Four of these scales, derived directly from Harter's (1986) self-perception profile for adolescents, were included in the present study:

6 'Scholastic competence': The degree to which adolescents perceive themselves as being good at their schoolwork.

7 'Athletic competence': The degree to which adolescents perceive themselves as being athletic and good at all kinds of sporting and athletic activities.
8 'Physical appearance': Adolescents' satisfaction with their own body and the way they look.
9 'Self-worth': Adolescents' perception of themselves as being satisfied with the way they are and the way they behave.

The 50 questionnaire items which made up these nine scales required young people to apply to themselves one of two oppositely formulated statements which represented either an aspect of intrinsic or extrinsic motivation (scales 1–5), or the degree of their self-perceived competence (scales 6–9). The items were presented in a separate questionnaire to all the post-primary young people who participated in the interview survey. Technical details about the scales (number and wording of items, response format, method of administration and reliability) can be found in van Wersch (1990) or Gilbert and van Wersch (1989), or may be obtained directly from the author of this chapter.

PREVIOUS RESEARCH

The application of the scales in the present research was intended to facilitate a better understanding of the motivations underlying young people's participation in sport and of the way in which their self-perception related to that participation. For example, whether there were variations in motivation or self-perception according to young people's age, gender or type of education.

An earlier study in Northern Ireland (van Wersch, 1990; van Wersch, Turner and Trew, 1992), which used a very similar rationale and design to examine interest in physical education (PE) of 3,344 11–18-year-old boys and girls in grammar and secondary schools, did find considerable variations. Of the motivational variables, 'Preference for challenge' and 'Curiosity' showed the strongest associations with interest in PE, even more so in the case of girls than boys. However, there tended to be a shift from intrinsic to extrinsic motivation on these two scales as young people grew older, and particularly after age 16. This was a trend which Harter had earlier (1981a) noted in relation to the cognitive domain. This shift was also found in the case of 'Fitness for its own sake'. The older pupils were progressively more concerned with becoming fit in the eyes of others rather than for its own sake, with the exception of grammar school boys who became more concerned with fitness for its own sake.

'Athletic competence' was more important for boys' than for girls' interest in PE, more so for the younger than for the older boys, and even more so for the younger boys at grammar school. In addition, at all ages boys perceived themselves to be more competent in sporting and athletic activities than girls. There was also a decline with age in girls' perceived 'Athletic competence' (cf. van Wersch, Trew and Turner, 1990).

The general association which was found between 'Athletic competence' and the motivational variables – in particular, 'Preference for challenge' and 'Curiosity' – is in line with a central hypothesis of Harter (1981a), namely

> motivational orientation and perceived competence should be related such that children with an intrinsic orientation in a given domain would have higher perceived competence in that domain; conversely, that children with an extrinsic orientation would have lower feelings of competence.

(p.301).

A more marked relationship between 'Athletic competence' and the other three motivational variables was found in the case of girls than boys.

RESEARCH FINDINGS FROM THE SCNI SURVEY

Competitive and non-competitive sport

The earlier study measured 'Interest in PE' by means of a questionnaire consisting of five sub-scales, each with seven items. In the present research, a simpler analogue for 'Interest in sport' was used, namely the level of the young person's participation in their 'top sport', wherever applicable. All but 7 per cent of post-primary students in the survey reported having a 'top sport', with half of those who had a 'top sport' (38 per cent of boys and 62 per cent of girls) participating at a 'basic' level (family recreation; play; school clubs open to all; recreational; largely non-competitive; informal). Of the others, 58 per cent of boys and 34 per cent of girls played 'competitively' (competitive club level; selected school teams; all belts, or equivalent, except black), and 4 per cent each of boys and girls at an élite level (county, regionally or nationally recognised standard; black belt, or equivalent).

On three of the five motivational scales, a significant difference was found in the scores of pupils participating in their 'top sport' at these

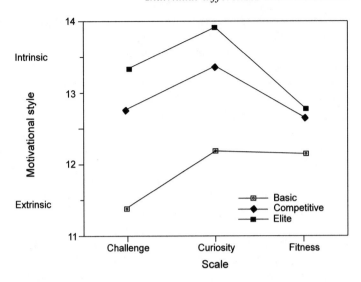

Figure 3.1 Motivation by level of attainment in top sport

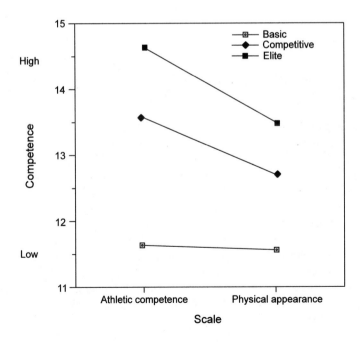

Figure 3.2 Perceived self-competence by level of attainment

different levels (see Figure 3.1). 'Basic' participators had the lowest mean score for 'Preference for challenge', 'Curiosity' and 'Fitness for its own sake', while 'élite' participants had the highest. The difference between the two groups in the case of 'Fitness for its own sake' was much less than in the case of the other two variables. In the case of all three variables, the mean score of the 'competitive' participants was noticeably closer to that of the 'élite' than of the 'basic' participants. In sum, the 'basic' participants showed a markedly lower intrinsic motivation for their sporting activities than did their 'competitive' or 'élite' peers.

The difference for 'Athletic competence' was even more marked than for the motivation variables (though 'Athletic competence' did have a relatively high positive correlation with both 'Preference for challenge' and 'Curiosity'). There were also statistically significant, though less marked, differences between the three groups on 'Physical appearance'. For both these self-profile variables (see Figure 3.2), the pattern was the same as for the motivational variables; the mean score of 'basic' participants was the lowest, and the mean score of 'élite' participants was the highest. Once again, the mean scores of 'competitive' participants were consistently closer to those of 'élite' than of 'basic' participants.

Girls and boys

Although there were very clear differences in the intrinsic–extrinsic motivation of young people participating in sport at the three levels, and in their self-profiles, these differences were even greater when boys' and girls' scores were compared (see Figure 3.3).

Boys scored higher than girls on all variables except 'Succeed against oneself'. There were highly significant differences on all the scales, with the exception of 'Scholastic competence', on which the difference only just reached significant, and on 'Fitness for its own sake', on which the difference was not significant. The (descending) order of magnitude of these differences was as follows: 'Physical appearance', 'Athletic competence', 'Preference for challenge', 'Self-worth', 'Independent mastery', 'Curiosity', 'Succeed against oneself' and 'Scholastic competence'. Boys clearly had a heightened perception of their own competence or adequacy in the domains measured, as well as a higher intrinsic motivation for all aspects of sporting activities except with regard to 'Succeed against oneself' and 'Fitness for its own sake'.

No significant interactions were found between young people's gender and the level of their 'top sport' participation in relation to

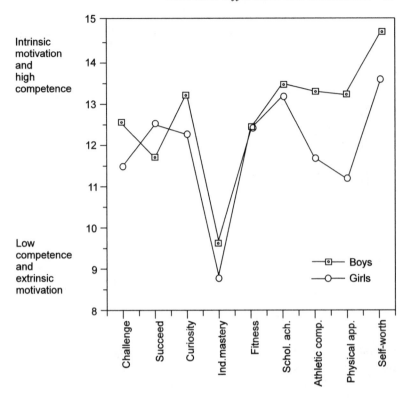

Figure 3.3 Gender and competence/motivation

motivation. In other words, the mean scores of, respectively, the girls and the 'basic' participants, and the boys and the 'competitive/élite' participants, tended to be closer to one another than to the other two gender/participation groups. This is not surprising in view of the fact that significantly more boys than girls participated at a competitive level.

Age

Variation in scores between the various age-groups (13 years or younger, 14, 15, 16, 17, 18 years or older) was smaller than the gender differences, and no differences in age or school-type were found on any of the competence scales. Significant, but not particularly marked, age differences were found on four of the five motivational scales – the exception being 'Independent mastery' (see Figure 3.4). In order of

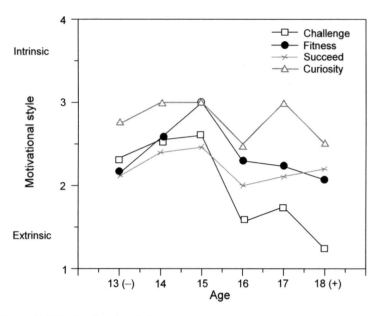

Figure 3.4 Motivational style by age

magnitude, these involved 'Preference for challenge', 'Fitness for its own sake', 'Succeed against oneself' and 'Curiosity'. On 'Preference for challenge', mean scores declined sharply after 15 years of age. 'Fitness for its own sake' showed a rise at ages 14 and 15 years and thereafter a fall, with the youngest and oldest respondents having comparable mean scores. On the other two scales – 'Succeed against oneself' and 'Curiosity' – there was no evidence of linear progression in the scores with age. However, in both cases, the mean scores of those aged 15 years and younger were in general higher than those of the older respondents.

Significant interactions between gender and age were found in the case of three scales, echoing earlier findings (van Wersch, 1990), with the strongest association being with interest in physical education (see Figure 3.5).

In order of magnitude, interaction effects were found for 'Curiosity', 'Athletic competence' and 'Preference for challenge'. For 'Curiosity', although the difference in mean scores between boys and girls tended to increase with age, girls showed a clearer decrease in intrinsic motivation over time than did boys. As already noted, there was no significant difference between the various age groups in terms of 'Athletic competence'. However, while boys scored significantly

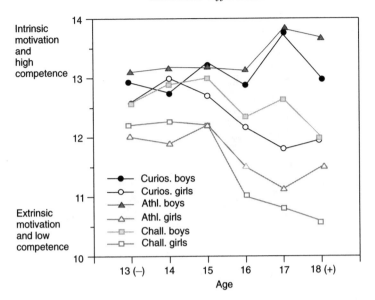

Figure 3.5 Gender and age by 'Curiosity', 'Athletic competence' and 'Preference for challenge'

higher in all age bands this perception of themselves as being physically competent at sport was more marked among the older pupils, but the opposite was the case for the girls. Finally, with respect to 'Preference for challenge', boys scored higher than girls in every age group, and the difference tended to increase with age, particularly after age 15.

'Athletic competence' showed a strong relationship with the motivation variables (see Figure 3.6), especially in the case of 'Preference for challenge' and 'Curiosity'. This finding is in line with earlier research and with Harter's original predictions. For 'Succeed against oneself', 'Independent mastery' and 'Fitness for its own sake', this relationship was somewhat stronger for girls than for boys.

School type

There were differences between those from grammar and secondary schools on only three scales (in descending order of magnitude), 'Preference for challenge', 'Scholastic competence' and 'Succeed against oneself', though they were more marked than the age differences noted above. In the case of 'Scholastic competence' and

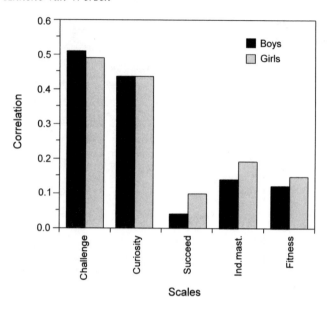

Figure 3.6 Correlations between athletic competence and motivation

'Succeed against oneself', grammar school students scored higher than those in secondary school. On 'Preference for challenge', the reverse was true. On the 'Scholastic competence' scale, there was an interaction between school type and gender, with the difference in scores between those from grammar and secondary schools being three times as great for boys as for girls.

MOTIVATIONAL FACTORS

Although motivation and competence were measured by means of nine separate scales, in practice there was a degree of overlap or correlation between scales. For this reason, the nine scales can legitimately be reduced to a smaller number of 'factors', each of which is defined by the number of scales which are closely related to one another. Analysis of the data revealed three underlying factors. The differences between categories of pupils which have so far been observed can be re-expressed, more economically, in terms of these three factors.

The group of scales which were most closely interrelated, and therefore carry most weight in statistical terms, consists of (in descending order of the size of their contribution to the factor) 'Preference for challenge', 'Athletic competence', 'Curiosity' and 'Independent mastery'. This factor accounted for somewhat more of the variance in the data than did the other two factors together. One of these factors was defined by 'Self-worth', 'Physical appearance' and 'Scholastic competence', the other by 'Succeed against oneself' and 'Fitness for its own sake'. There were, thus, two motivational factors and one competence factor. Intrinsic motivation was differentiated between, on the one hand, a desire to extend oneself in exercising and practising sporting skills, independently of the wishes or participation of others, and on the other hand, a desire to gain a sense of personal sporting achievement and physical fitness, rather than to compete successfully against, and impress, others. As far as competence was concerned, a feeling of 'Athletic competence' was more closely related to the first of the motivations for sporting activities than to general, physical or scholastic competence.

On all three factors, there was a highly significant difference between boys and girls, with boys appearing to have a higher score in terms of intrinsic motivation and self-perceived competence than girls. In the case of the first factor – the primary aspect of motivation for sport – this gender difference decreased with age. There was also a significant difference between the three 'top sport' participating groups, in favour of the élite group, on the first and third factors though on the third factor ('Succeed against oneself' and 'Fitness for its own sake') it is only just significant. However, the latter factor reveals the strongest age effect, with lower scores being found at ages 16 and 17. With respect to school type, it was the second (competence) factor which distinguished between those who were attending either grammar or secondary school. The former had significantly higher mean factor scores for self-perceived competence.

DISCUSSION

In the author's earlier study in Northern Ireland, van Wersch (1990) developed a socio-psychological model of young people's interest in physical education (PE), and considered that interest at the three levels of society, school and self. At the level of self, the present study found that 'Athletic competence' and the motivation variables 'Preference for challenge' and 'Curiosity' were the most important predictors of the level of post-primary students' participation in their 'top sport'. This finding corresponds with the findings of the earlier study with respect to interest in PE. However, according to Harter's theory of self, in isolation, perceptions of high or low competence provide an insufficient understanding of young people's interest in PE; they are complementary variables which act in combination with aspects of motivation. That is precisely what was found in the SCNI survey with respect to 'Athletic competence'. This variable was found to have strong associations with three of the measures of intrinsic motivation for physical exercise and sport.

The fact that young people who participate in their 'top sport' at either a competitive or élite level show a greater degree of intrinsic rather than extrinsic motivation (in comparison with those participating at a basic level) has important implications for the development of young people's sport. The survey indicates that many young people do not have an opportunity to participate at a competitive level. Simply creating a greater number of concrete opportunities may help to develop a healthier motivational profile but is unlikely to provide the whole solution without careful control over the actual experience of sport or competition. For example, it is possible that those who aspire to competitive participation have inappropriate self-perceptions and motivations. We know, at least, that they perceive themselves to be less competent athletically, and have less intrinsic motivation than those who are already participating at a competitive or élite level. There is, in principle, no limit to the number of young people who could take part competitively in sporting activities. At the same time, their satisfaction from doing so may depend on their gaining a realistic appreciation of their current level of competence and their understanding that intrinsic motivation may be more helpful to them than extrinsic motivation. Their more 'competitive' peers already find self-improvement, as opposed to winning, more important than they do, and those who aspire towards that level of participation may require assistance along that particular path.

A similar point may be made with respect to those who felt that they had an unrealised potential to perform at an élite level, as opposed to the very small number who performed at that level (see Chapter 1). Obviously, there are practical as well as definitional limits to the numbers who can participate in an élite context, and those who aspire towards élite performance may also need encouragement to be more pragmatic and realistic in their attitude and approach.

At the level of the school, possible variations in sports' motivation and self-perception can be examined by comparing young people in grammar and secondary schools, and young people of different ages. While the former comparison may be self-evident at the level of the school, the latter needs some justification. Age is, after all, an individual characteristic. However, the decline in intrinsic motivation with age, which has been observed in several previous studies, has been attributed to the effects of the school system. For example, as Harter (1981a) has suggested, school systems may progressively smother young people's interest in what they are required to do at school. They may be subjected to a process of adaptation to the demands of the school culture, a culture which reinforces a relatively extrinsic motivation.

Differences in the mean scores of grammar (selective) and second-ary (non-selective) school students, independent of gender, were found on three of the nine motivation and perceived competence scales. Grammar school students had lower scores on 'Preference for chal-lenge', and higher scores on 'Succeed against oneself' and 'Scholastic competence'. Between the age groups, somewhat smaller differences were found on four scales, namely 'Preference for challenge', 'Fitness for its own sake', 'Succeed against oneself' and 'Curiosity'. There was evidence of an increase, with age, in extrinsic motivation. Overall, on all these scales, those younger than 16 years tended to show higher intrinsic motivation – as was found in the earlier research. A progres-sion towards a more extrinsic motivation with age was clearest for 'Preference for challenge' and 'Fitness for its own sake'. All these age differences (with respect to school type and age) appeared to operate independently of gender. The observed decline of intrinsic motivation in the physical domain with age, both in the present and earlier research, must be disappointing in relation to Harter's (1981a) pro-position that

> Though it would appear that one's motivation to perform in school is becoming less intrinsic with age, one's motivation in other domains may not show this trend. The child may be channeling intrinsic interest into other areas of his or her life (e.g. social relationships, sports, and other extra-curricular activities).
>
> (p.310)

In future research it would be interesting to consider differences in the decline in intrinsic motivation between the cognitive and physical domains during the school years. The results of van Wersch's earlier study (which showed more of a decline in 'Preference for challenge' in the physical domain at grammar than at secondary schools) suggest that, because of the challenge which young people probably experi-ence in academic work at grammar school, they may prefer to 'take it easy' with regard to physical activities. At the same time, while the decline in intrinsic motivation in the physical domain may be greater in grammar than in secondary schools, it is overshadowed by gender and age differences and by the interaction between the two.

Van Wersch (1990) found that both intrinsic motivation and interest in PE declined significantly with age, and more so in the case of girls than boys. She also found that 'Athletic competence' was more important for boys' than for girls' interest in PE, and more important for younger than for older boys' interest. The boys' perception of their own 'Athletic competence' was higher than that of girls, in all age groups. The decline in girls' perception of their 'Athletic competence' with age was striking. Harter (1986) has suggested that perceptions of competence are largely a function of how well young people see themselves perform, when achievement is called for, and when significant others are aware of their performance.

When interpreting the results of the earlier study in Northern Ireland, considerable emphasis was placed on the masculine connotation of sport. Not only did an interest in PE appear to suffer because of the decline with age in individuals' intrinsic motivation and because of the low status of PE as a school subject, but also the male bias of sport was found to be reproduced at the levels of self and school. Thus, boys were not only more interested in PE than were girls but they were also more satisfied with a games-oriented and competitive PE curriculum, and saw PE as a higher-status subject.

Girls' dissatisfaction with the PE curriculum, and their view of PE as a low-status subject at school, intensified with age, notably after 14 years of age. Their greater preference for keep-fit, individual physical activities and recreational rather than competitive sport is understandable in terms of these social connotations. Older girls generally have higher academic competence and are not particularly interested in seeking popularity with their peers through 'Athletic competence'. This may predispose them to view PE as a school subject with low status.

The SCNI survey would tend to confirm that it is exactly this male bias in sport which is the major stumbling block facing attempts to encourage more young women to participate in sport and to continue to do so after they leave school. In other words, young women, in particular, are more likely to drop out of sport (Butcher, 1985). While at school, girls perceived themselves to be less athletically competent than boys, as also found in the earlier study. Moreover, in both studies, one can observe a stronger relationship between 'Athletic competence', 'Interest in PE' and level of participation in sport, for boys than for girls. In both studies, 'Athletic competence' is positively related to all the motivational variables, especially to 'Preference for challenge' and 'Curiosity'. However, in the case of 'Succeed against oneself', 'Independent mastery' and 'Fitness for its own sake', this relationship is somewhat stronger for girls than boys. The same was true in the earlier study, suggesting that these three aspects of motivation may be more important for girls' than for boys' sporting activities.

It is interesting to note that the only motivation scale on which there were no gender differences was 'Fitness for its own sake'. On this scale, the difference between 'basic' and 'competitive/élite' participants was relatively small, though statistically significant, and there was an age effect, whereby the motivation of 'Fitness for its own sake', decreases steadily until age 16, especially in the case of girls, and thereafter rises quite sharply. These two scales, 'Succeed against oneself' and 'Fitness for its own sake' form a distinctive, though minor, cluster – the third of the factors referred to above. It seems as though this aspect of motivation is one which could be built upon in encouraging girls' sporting activities. It is relatively independent of 'competitive' participation in sport, which seems to be less attractive to girls, though it does have varying implications for young people of different ages – with an apparent breakpoint around age 15.

In passing, it is worth drawing attention to the possible significance of the distinction between biological gender and sexual identity. Only the former variable has been used in this discussion. The survey collected no data on sexual identity, nor on psychological masculinity and femininity. However, if the assumptions made here are valid, it seems likely that a number of the girls who participated at a competitive or élite level were more than generally able to accept the masculine connotations of such sport. Correspondingly, a number of the minority of boys who did not participate at that level may have had some difficulty in accepting aspects of that connotation. To ensure that as many young people as possible enjoy participation in sport and physical activity, special opportunities may need to be offered to schoolboys, as well as to schoolgirls, to engage in activities which do not carry the traditional male bias.

The fact that pupils who participate in their 'top sport' at a competitive or élite level show a greater degree of intrinsic than extrinsic motivation, in comparison with those participating at a basic level, may have important implications for the encouragement of young people's sport. Participation in competitive and élite sport is certainly determined by factors at the levels of school and society, as well as at the level of self. The SCNI survey has suggested that many young people miss an opportunity to participate at a competitive level. However, simply creating a greater number of concrete opportunities may not provide the whole solution. It is possible that those who aspire to competitive participation have inappropriate self-perceptions and motivations. We know, at least, that they perceive themselves as less competent athletically, and have less intrinsic motivation than those who are already participating at a competitive or élite level. There is, in principle, no limit to the number of young people who could take part competitively in sporting activities. However, their satisfaction from doing so may depend on their gaining a realistic appreciation of their current level of competence and on their understanding that intrinsic motivation may be more helpful to them than extrinsic motivation. Their more 'competitive' peers do seem to find self-improvement, as opposed to winning, more important than they do.

A similar point may be made with respect to those who felt that they had an unrealised potential to perform at the élite level, as opposed to the very small number who actually did so (see Chapter 1). Obviously, there are practical, as well as definitional, limits to the numbers who can participate in an élite context. However, given that those who do participate in such a context show the highest levels of intrinsic motivation and perceived self-competence, aspirant élite participants, just as aspirant competitors, may also need encouragement to change their attitude and approach.

The survey found that more than three times as many girls as boys nominated an indoor sport as their 'top sport'. Moreover, those girls whose 'top sport' was an outdoor one showed relatively lower intrinsic motivation than did boys whose 'top sport' took place outdoors. Although outdoor sports can involve extreme temperature, climate or uncontrolled exposure to spectators, which we know are factors unattractive to many young women, there are aspects of these sports themselves which may make them more or less acceptable, especially in relation to competition. As long ago as 1978, Mathes pointed out that those activities which include body contact with an opponent, the application of force to some heavy object, or projecting the body through space over long distances, do not enhance culturally feminine qualities and hence are less appealing to a great many women. On the other hand, forms of sport which involve the presentation of the body in an aesthetically pleasing pattern, rely on artificial devices to facilitate bodily movement, use lightweight implements (for example, a racket) or maintain a spatial distance from the opponent are likely to be much more acceptable to women.

Social approval can also play a role. Outdoor sports such as golf and tennis are more socially approved for women than, for example, field hockey and track athletics, while indoors, basketball and volleyball are less approved of than swimming and gymnastics (cf. Anthrop and Allison, 1983). One difference between these two sets of sports is that the less socially approved tend to be team sports. Across all 20 of the 'top sports' most frequently nominated in the survey, girls engaged in many more 'individual' or non-team sports than did boys. Not surprisingly, this tendency overlapped with a much lower participation in competitive sport on the part of girls than boys. Nonetheless, those girls whose 'top sport' was a team game did have a quite distinctive pattern of intrinsic motivation (characterised by 'Curiosity', 'Athletic competence' and 'Preference for challenge'), in comparison with non-team players.

However, the provision of more indoor facilities for girls' sporting activities (which are in any case already relatively well catered for in Northern Ireland), or greater opportunities for 'individual' or non-team sport, is probably not in itself the solution to the problem of diminishing participation in sport by young women in adolescence and thereafter. More active participation in sport by young people seems to require enhanced intrinsic motivation and more positive self-evaluation associated with sport participation, for which current patterns of female socialisation still give insufficient rewards. Organising sporting activities in such a way that intrinsic rewards are emphasised may be the more productive way forward.

Overall, this analysis has served to demonstrate yet again the linkages between sport, competition and perceived self-competence. Those who have been afforded opportunities to take part in their chosen activitity on a regular basis clearly derive psychological benefit in terms of enhanced self-esteem, and are intrinsically motivated to continue to perform. Those who miss these opportunities appear to fail to generate a 'success circle', perhaps because they have no yardsticks by which to gauge their worth accurately. For those involved in formulating sport policy, and for those who, in a more general sense, are simply concerned for the physical and psychological well-being of young people, the messages to emerge from this analysis should be hard to ignore. Once involved in sport of their choosing and deriving personal satisfaction from that experience then young people will continue to maintain an interest, irrespective of the availability of more obvious extrinsic rewards. The challenge remains to provide those opportunities and to allow young people to grow in sport.

REFERENCES

Anthrop, J. and Allison, M.T. (1983). Role conflict and the high school female athlete. *Research Quarterly for Exercise and Sport*, *54*, 104–111.

Burton, D. and Martens, R. (1986). Pinned by their own goals: An exploratory investigation into why kids drop out of wrestling. *Journal of Sport Psychology*, *8*, 183–197.

Butcher, J. (1985). Longitudinal analysis of adolescent girls' participation in physical activity. *Sociology of Sport Journal*, *2*, 130–143.

Cairns, E. (1990). The relationship between adolescent perceived self-competence and attendance at single sex secondary schools. *British Journal of Educational Psychology*, *60*, 207–211.

Feltz, D.L. and Petlichkoff, L. (1983). Perceived competence among interscholastic sports participants and drop-outs. *Canadian Journal of Applied Sport Science*, *8*, 231–235.

Fox, K.R., Corbin, C.B. and Couldry, W.H. (1985). Female physical estimation and attraction to physical activity. *Journal of Sport Psychology*, *7*, 125–136.

Frederick, C.M. and Ryan, R.M. (1995). Self-determination in sport: A review using cognitive evaluation theory. *International Journal of Sport Psychology*, *26*, 5–23.

Gilbert, R. and van Wersch, A. (1989). Motivating children to participate in sport. In J. Kremer and W. Crawford (eds), *The Psychology of Sport: Theory and Practice*. Leicester: British Psychological Society.

Gill, D.L., Dzewaltowski, D.A. and Deeter, T.E. (1988). The relationship of competitiveness and achievement orientation to participation in sport and nonsport activities. *Journal of Sport and Exercise Psychology*, *10*, 139–150.

Gould, D. (1984). Psychosocial development and children's sport. In J.R. Thomas (ed.) *Motor Development during Adulthood and Adolescence*. Minneapolis: Burgess.

Gould, D., Weiss, M. and Weinberg, R.S. (1981). Psychological characteristics of successful and non-successful big ten wrestlers. *Journal of Sport Psychology*, *3*, 69–81.

Granleese, J., Turner, I. and Trew, K. (1989). Teachers' and boys' and girls' perceptions of competence in the primary school: The importance of physical competence. *British Journal of Educational Psychology*, *59*, 31–37.

Harter, S. (1981a). A new self-report scale of intrinsic versus extrinsic orientation in the classroom: Motivational and informational components. *Developmental Psychology*, *17*, 300–312.

Harter, S. (1981b). The development of competence motivation in the mastery of cognitive and physical skills: Is there still a place for joy? In G.C Roberts and D.M. Landers (eds), *Psychology of Motor Behavior and Sport – 1980*. Champaign, IL: Human Kinetics.

Harter, S. (1986). *Self-Perception Profile for Adolescents*. University of Denver, Colorado.

Harter, S. and Connell, J.P (1984). A model of children's achievement and related self-perceptions of competence, control and motivational achievement. In J. Nicholls (ed.) *Advances in Motivation and Achievement*, *3*. Greenwich, CT: JAI Press.

Kimiecik, J.C., Allison, M.T. and Duda, J.L. (1986). Performance satisfaction, perceived competence and game outcome: The competitive experience of boys' club youth. *International Journal of Sport Psychology*, *17*, 255–268.

Kremer, J. and Scully, D. (1994). *Psychology in Sport*. London: Taylor and Francis.

Martens, R. (1980). The uniqueness of the young athlete: Psychological considerations. *American Journal of Sports Medicine, 8,* 382–385.

Mathes, S. (1978). Body image and stereotyping. In C. A. Oglesby (ed.) *Women and Sport: From Myth to Reality.* Philadelphia: Lea and Febiger.

Roberts, G.C. (1984). Achievement motivation in children's sport. *Advances in Motivation and Achievement, 3,* 251–281.

Underwood, M. (1987). Teaching strategies and young people's social development in physical education. *Research Papers in Education, 2,* 200–233.

van Wersch, A. (1990). A social-psychological model of interest in physical education: Age, gender and school-type differences. Unpublished PhD thesis, The Queen's University of Belfast.

van Wersch, A., Trew, K. and Turner, I. (1990). Young people's perceived competence and its implications for the new PE curriculum. *British Journal of Physical Education, 7,* 1–5.

van Wersch, A., Turner, I. and Trew, K. (1992). Post-primary school young people's interest in Physical Education: Age and gender differences. *British Journal of Educational Psychology, 62,* 56–72.

Weiss, M.R. and Chaumeton, N. (1992). Motivational orientations in sport. In T.S. Horn (ed.) *Advances in Sport Psychology.* Champaign, IL: Human Kinetics.

White, R. (1959). Motivation reconsidered: The concept of competence. *Psychological Review, 66,* 297–323.

4 Predictors, patterns and policies for post-school participation

Deirdre Brennan and E. Walter Bleakley

INTRODUCTION

There is wide consensus across the sports' constituency that involving young people in both organised and independent physical activity is beneficial to their long-term development. However, processes that could facilitate the transition from involvement in compulsory school-based physical activity to voluntary physical activity remain poorly understood. The fall in numbers of participants from school-based physical activity to physical activity in post-school life is one issue that current sport policies and strategies seem to have failed to address. Unquestionably, there is an abundance of knowledge, derived from diversified sources including physiology, psychology, sociology, education, health promoters, medical science, which reinforces the value of habitual physical activity but at the same time there has been a shortage of positive actions for translating such theory into practice. Educating young people so that they know why and how they should be physically active appears not to be the nub of the problem. While physical education specialists, sports coaches and various agencies are all aware of the sensitive and crucial process of adolescence and how this can threaten regular involvement in physical recreation, actually encouraging young people to be more active remains unfinished business.

Although this chapter is concerned with sport beyond the school gates, attention must first turn towards the antecedents to participation, as these factors will later impact on willingness to take up voluntary activity. Recent innovations in the field of physical education will come into focus as an attempt is made to interpret how these antecedents affect patterns of participation outside school. There will be a particular focus on defining the characteristics of the adolescent process, as it is during this highly volatile stage in the life-cycle that many young people re-evaluate, reprioritise and re-think the value of various life-domains, including sport. Common attitudinal changes to participation that are translated into behaviour will then be analysed through the patterns of participation found in this study. An attempt will also be made to interpret these patterns so that remedial action can be designed, and exemplars of good practice highlighted.

TO PLAY OR NOT TO PLAY, THAT IS THE QUESTION!

It would be difficult not to agree with Roberts (1996) when he suggests that participation in activities across the physical recreation continuum seems unlikely to reach a level where no-one will find cause to appeal for more. 'A highly active minority' among a majority of inactive people is how Roberts and Brodie (1992), cited in Green (1995), describe the sporting population. Roberts (1996) draws attention to the fact that recent investigations provide evidence to disarm fears of a decline in participation levels. Participation levels, he asserts, now exceed those recorded in the 1950s and 1960s, with the 1990s having a larger 'highly active minority' than any other age. However, despite the increase in numbers involved in sports participation, it is still the case that participation levels for health benefits alone are sub-optimal for the majority of the population. Also, the achievement of excellence at individual, local, national and international levels is still restricted by the numbers participating in a committed manner. The question of how to inculcate mass participation at commitment levels which are sufficient to address health needs, alongside participation in sport that may eventually lead to performance at the élite level, still remains to be answered fully. With this in mind, what factors set the scene for future participation?

ANTECEDENTS TO PARTICIPATION

Participation in sport and physical activity is a complex issue. Culture, gender, age, race and individual differences in ability are ascribed factors that can determine the activity type, level of attainment and motivation to participate. Many social agencies are also routinely identified as influencing both the uptake and drop-out of sport and physical activity. The family and the formal education system are taken to occupy poll positions in the formative years, with friends and peers playing important roles as children move from adolescence to adulthood. The degree of impact that each agent achieves is not fixed in time but constrained by the ebbs and flows of interests which change with age.

To explain how individuals' highly flexible attitudes and behaviours shift over time, Coleman (1979) developed focal theory, in which he proposed that particular sorts of relationships come into prominence at different ages, owing to adjustments of both a psychological and sociological nature. More recently, Hendry *et al.* (1993) have utilised this approach to help explain patterns of involvement in various activities across the life-cycle. Beginning with childhood, it was found that participation tends to be initiated in organised, traditional and conformist activities (for example, team games, boys and girls brigade) reflecting the influence in the early years of parents, the church and formal education. As children move towards mid-adolescence, more casual, peer-led, low-cost activities (for example, hanging about, meeting friends, visiting friends) take prominence, a time when friendships become an integral and vital part of adolescent life. Finally, the post-school years of late adolescence are characterised by a graduation to more commercial-based pursuits (discos, night-clubs, pubs, cinema) that reinforce various elements of youth culture, promoted specifically through the mass media.

Even accepting that attitudinal changes are inherent in this process of socialisation and maturation, research has indicated that an active lifestyle in adulthood is more likely if physical activity is engaged in during childhood and adolescence (Cale and Harris, 1993; Armstrong and McManus, 1994). This is based on the premise that it is at this time in a young person's life that basic attitudes are developed and that learned habits come to influence lifestyles. Not surprisingly therefore a family culture that values participation in physical recreation is considered conducive to the development of lifelong exercise habits.

PARENT POWER

Hendry *et al.* (1993) maintain that parental influence cannot be over-estimated. Although the latter has been found to decline with age their studies found that continued need for parental aid in terms of finance and transport bears testimony to parents' level of influence as pre-dictors of participation. In the SCNI survey, parental and family support appear and reappear as prominent socialising agents. For example, 39 per cent of young people mentioned family members as being most important in maintaining their interest and involvement, with the father being the most influential figure of all (21 per cent). A further 65 per cent recognised parental support, in terms of finance, transport and encouragement, as being vital to their participation. Hendry *et al.* (1993) also assert that parental participation in physical activities acts as a positive influencing factor, with children on sports' teams more likely to have fathers that play also.

In the SCNI survey, 64 per cent of young people recorded active participation by their father and 34 per cent by their mother. Lenskyi (1991) suggests that it is quite probable that the differences in father–mother participation rates are reflective of the restrictions on sport options available to women as compared with men. What is more, there was a definite relationship between sports played by family and close relatives and those played by the young people themselves. Soccer achieved prominence with the boys' fathers and brothers, and swimming with the mothers and sisters of girls who were interviewed. In addition 48 per cent mentioned the family as their source of introduction to an organised club and 61 per cent depicted parents as their main means of attending the club. Although only 17 per cent of the sample indicated that parental influence had been the most significant factor in their decision to take up sport, this type of influence was still portrayed as an important antecedent to participation, and was also vital to the continuance of that activity.

Moving beyond the data and beyond organised sport, and anticipating practices that could stimulate early interest in sport by siblings, then activities such as active play with parents encouraging their offspring to throw, catch, target, strike, run, jump, balance, etc., may all serve to awaken developing motor abilities which could eventually lead to skilful techniques executed in a variety of movement contexts. Equally, the opportunity to watch parents play sport would appear to be a positive factor in influencing eventual participation by children. Overall, the age-old adage, 'active parents appear to have active children', would appear to be supported in this survey.

EDUCATION

If induction to physical activity does not take place in the family setting school normally serves as the first point of introduction to sport for children. It is widely recognised that the school, and in particular the physical education department, plays a prominent role in formulating positive attitudes towards habitual physical activity, whether at a basic, competitive or élite level. Participation rates in curriculum-based physical education are healthy, not least because it now has compulsory status on the curriculum. However, Hendry (1978) and Roberts (1983) have found that the impact of formal education on leisure pursuits may be more limited. More recently Mason (1995) found that there was no linear relationship between

the importance that teachers attached to sport and their pupils' levels
of participation outside school. According to Roberts,

> Shakespeare and religion have not soared as popular leisure pas-
> times through their promotion in schools. Competitive team games
> are likely to fare similarly whatever governments pronounce and
> schools promote.
>
> (Roberts, 1996, p.56)

The degree of influence of physical education has quite probably been
hampered by the ongoing debates over the meaning and practices of
physical education. These debates, which have been well documented
over the years (Singer, 1976; Almond 1989; Kirk, 1992; Talbot, 1994),
along with recent government initiatives, have served yet again to
remind us that physical education continues to be influenced by
different discourses.

> Despite the apparent rise to prominence of HRE [health-related
> education]... the health related lobby continues to vie with those
> favouring a heightening emphasis on team games for occupation of
> the ideological high ground in physical education.
>
> (Green, 1995, p.27)

Green goes on to suggest that in recent times the encouragement of
lifelong participation in physical activity has emerged as a common
goal within the physical education profession. The creation of a
climate promoting extended participation through the establishment
of a sound pyramidic base of team and individual activities is now
expected to be the norm. Schultz *et al.* (1985) purport that it is widely
supported that it is the quality of physical education experiences,
coupled with the range of experiences offered, that may have a huge
bearing on whether the motivation to participate in the first instance,
and to continue to participate in the second, will persist. Lloyd and
Fox (1992) state that

> The challenge still remains, however, for physical education to find
> the most effective methods of promoting physical activity in chil-
> dren that is likely to carry over into adulthood.
>
> (p.13)

It is implicit in what the authors say, along with many others, that
physical education teachers are still held primarily responsible for
educating 'the physical'. This is a task that is constrained and compounded by the fact that education for leisure is but one of physical
education's overall objectives.

The SCNI survey supports the significance of the school as an important antecedent to participation. 'Because of school' (31 per cent) was ranked as the most influential factor in the uptake of sport; 26 per cent of the young people noted that their school was responsible for kindling their interest in their top sport. In all, 91 per cent of boys and 84 per cent of girls recorded that they had experienced their top sport by the age of 11, and 71 per cent of boys by age 8. It seems likely that the school will have played a large part in this early introduction, given that only 17 per cent recorded their parents as the biggest factor in their decision to take up sport.

As few as 20 from the list of 106 sports accounted for 85 per cent of all the 'top sports' mentioned in this study, and of these, 16 are traditionally offered on physical education programmes across the province. No fewer than 11 of these activities appeared to depend crucially on a school introduction: for example, swimming (30 per cent), netball (88 per cent), basketball (57 per cent), badminton (41 per cent), athletics (69 per cent), hockey (75 per cent), Gaelic football (28 per cent), rounders (69 per cent), gymnastics (52 per cent), cricket (34 per cent) and volleyball (61 per cent). All the activities listed have traditionally featured as prominent in the physical education curriculum in schools before and after the 1989 Education Reform Act (Northern Ireland Order). Such a pattern would therefore suggest the continuing prominence of the physical education curriculum as a primary motivating source facilitating pupils into active participation in sport.

Hendry (1976) has shown that most post-school competitors had been involved competitively in schools. This supports the proposal that fostering favourable attitudes towards participation through the teaching of physical education pays dividends. Sallis and Patrick (1994) feel that if a habit of physical activity is positively developed in adolescence it is more likely to remain in adulthood and this will be enhanced if young people are given the choice of activity they most enjoy and prefer. However, in 1992 they warned that a hidden curriculum of overcompetitiveness can in fact hasten departure from sport for some children, and perhaps especially girls (see Chapter 2). Evans (1989), Talbot (1994) and Hargreaves (1995) also note that physical education is often inequitable with programmes designed and delivered in favour of the motor élite and achievement-oriented pupils.

This elitism is subsequently extended into and reinforced by extra-curricular programmes that provide competitive opportunities for the select few. Whether extra-curricular sport is offered for all or just for the best is often determined by more than just the teacher's philosophy. The school ethos, teaching and coaching expertise, facilities and resources also have a huge bearing on what can and cannot be offered and achieved. One way or the other, these after-school experiences are considered a crucial link in the chain of participation. Clough, Thorpe and Traill (1995) and Hendry *et al.* (1993) found that this may in fact be even more so for girls than boys, as young women's sports participation and competitive experiences are based around the school. This may indicate that there is a shortage of organised sport for girls in the community, or simply that girls are constrained by male designs of sport (again, see Chapter 2).

The school was in fact the most popular site for the practice of sport for both girls (34 per cent) and boys (48 per cent) in the SCNI Survey, followed by the home (29 per cent and 44 per cent), and then the street or park for boys (33 per cent) and the swimming pool for girls (17 per cent). However, over half the girls (52 per cent) replied that they were never involved competitively in sport, compared with 34 per cent of boys. Nevertheless, it is reassuring to see that 67 per cent of sixth form respondents, and 64 per cent of those from Key Stage 4, recorded participation in some form of sport. Indeed participation rates in competitive play were higher in the older age groups prior to leaving school. However, the hours devoted to 'top sports' were greatest at Key Stage 2. These hours markedly decreased with age, with sixth formers recording the lowest level of time commitment to their 'top sport'. The greater time spent in sport by the younger age groups could perhaps be accounted for by fewer responsibilities and commitments at this age and their stage of skill acquisition. The less time devoted to sport in the latter years of full-time education may reflect a commitment to study, or a change in priorities, with young adolescents taking part-time jobs to boost their developing consumer desires, although evidence from this survey would suggest that these other commitments are not as significant as many would imagine (see Chapters 1 and 7).

Therefore educational, social and economic factors, and their commensurate time demands, have the potential to clash directly with the emerging sporting ambitions of the adolescent. At the same time, sport itself could be becoming more formal and organised as the young person becomes older, demanding a greater time commitment. All these influences are potentially incompatible leaving the young person with difficult choices. Moreover, decisions affecting sport participation have to be made at a time when the young person could also be confirming career choices, largely determined by examination performance. The picture emerges of the young person under pressure to take crucial decisions about the pattern of their future. Sporting ambitions and aspirations may be among the first casualties in the selection process, especially if the young person has other abilities which would help access academic/professional career pathways. As Chapter 7 clearly demonstrates, academic and sporting careers do not have to be in conflict and may actually complement each other, but so long as there is a widespread perception that there are problems associated with balancing competing demands on time, then this becomes an issue which needs to be addressed.

PARTICIPATION PATTERNS

Some 40 per cent of boys played competitively once or twice a week, compared with 16 per cent of girls. As noted elsewhere, the activities that afford opportunities for competition reflect on traditional gender and religious differences and preferences. Soccer was the sport in which boys were most active competitively (46 per cent), followed by Gaelic football (12 per cent) and swimming (7 per cent). For girls, swimming was ranked first (20 per cent), followed by netball (13 per cent) and soccer (7 per cent). It is interesting to note that Rugby Union, regarded as a major team game in the grammar school sector, provides only 4 per cent of the boys with competitive opportunities. Participation in club rugby is unofficially proscribed for competitive school rugby players and this may help to account for the low return in this activity, although interestingly, 22 per cent of those naming rugby as their 'top sport' were club members and very few claimed to be playing mini-rugby.

With the exception of swimming, the sports receiving greatest commitment at school are the traditional team games reflecting both gender and cultural differences. Returns indicate that these must be preferred activities as over 80 per cent of respondents from all school types recorded their intention to continue participation after leaving school.

As noted in Chapter 2, gender differences are evident in terms of the percentage with positive intentions to continue sport participation: 68 per cent of males and 54 per cent of females were planning for future participation. Both males (48 per cent) and females (45 per cent) were aspiring towards participation at a competitive level but a greater percentage of females (33 per cent) than males (14 per cent) intended to be involved in more informal types of recreation. Facilitating the latter would not appear to be problematic, with individual activities like jogging and walking requiring few purpose-built facilities. In addition, the availability of leisure, recreation and community centres that provide for recreational badminton, squash, fitness training and swimming are also plentiful, but the present use of these facilities by young people is less encouraging (see Chapter 1). However, competitive opportunities in the shape of organised leagues and tournaments for young people in the 'betwixt and between' years (that is, young people who are no longer juniors but are not yet seniors) appear to be scarce, with only 34 per cent of the entire sample recording that they were involved in competitive sport and 46 per cent feeling they had the potential to compete at a competitive level. It would appear therefore that affirmative strategies need to be devised in order to secure and harness this interest, with post-school clubs being the natural outlet for aspiring young competitors. However, to suggest that a simple open-door strategy would suffice would be naïve.

The present recruitment policy for sports clubs in general has its historic roots in the pursuit of excellence. In theory, the best performers are actively recruited to specialist clubs directly from either schools or general clubs, being persuaded to join with the promise of higher-level competition and its commensurate rewards. Such individuals are seen to be 'ready made', in the sense that they have already acquired the technical and tactical abilities that allow them to compete for places alongside the already existing club membership. The host club has therefore little to provide for such individuals; they are simply absorbed into the internal competitive selection system of the club. Competitive sports clubs will always be in the market for such sporting talent but the survey would suggest that this trawl system may be more effective for some sports than others (see Table 4.1 below).

That selection process aside, what of the larger percentage (46 per cent) who felt they had the potential to compete at a competitive level but were often unable to fulfil that ambition? How can clubs facilitate their competitive needs and aspirations? Realistically, if all of these aspiring competitors, or indeed a small proportion of them, turned up on a training night at clubs in their locality, existing club structures simply would be unable to cope with the logistical demands which such numbers would pose. In addition, overnight clubs would have to provide a player development strategy to include:

- access to coaching for these young players
- access to suitable competition
- systems to monitor young player development

All of these issues have resource implications for the hosting club, and in turn have implications for sports governing bodies. Market demand appears to be buoyant but facilities to cater for this demand would require careful scrutiny before the floodgates could even be unlocked, never mind opened.

As Table 4.1 shows, for many popular sports (including swimming, netball and athletics), the number of young, active participants who belonged to a club of any description at the time of survey was very small. In contrast, for a number of activities, and most obviously Gaelic sports and golf, club membership was extremely high. It is noteworthy that of the three Gaelic sports included in the list, all have club membership rates above 75 per cent.

In addition, despite the fact that nearly 600 different clubs were mentioned during the course of the interviews, only 18 per cent of the young people interviewed were members of sport-only clubs and only 36 per cent of the entire sample were members of clubs of any sort (a list including youth clubs, church groups, etc.) where their chosen or 'top' sport was played. There is a clear mismatch between young people's willingness to engage in sport and their opportunities to take part in organised activities outside of the formal education system. It is this disparity which forms the backcloth for the subsequent discussion and, it could be argued, which must inform policy over coming years.

Table 4.1 'Top sports' and club membership

Top sport	Participants	Club members	%
Gaelic football	127	113	89
Irish dancing	40	33	83
Golf	35	28	80
Camogie	42	32	76
Aerobics	21	14	67
Gymnastics	27	14	52
Horse riding	73	36	49
Badminton	52	25	48
Soccer	529	252	48
Lawn tennis	31	11	35
Athletics	90	25	28
Basketball	42	11	26
Ice skating	20	5	25
Rugby Union	36	8	22
Netball	129	23	18
Swimming	256	40	16
Other racket sports	19	3	16
Rounders	23	3	13
Cycling	44	2	5
Others	229	127	55

ACCESS TO COACHING

In terms of the present survey, of those young people who attended clubs of any sort, only 29 per cent specifically mentioned that they were supervised by a coach. As to the type of instruction and help which they received in clubs, these are detailed in Tables 4.2 and 4.3 respectively.

Table 4.2 Type of instruction offered in clubs

Club instruction	% of club members
Practice games	84
Skills help	87
Tactics talk	64
Team management	59
Total	827

Table 4.3 Ways in which clubs are perceived to have helped

Help given	% of club members
Training	55
Improve technique	49
Encouragement	19
Organise meetings	19
Fitness	9
Meeting people/friends	9
Confidence	8
Total	827

The data suggest that coaching provision is limited, and beyond this, the expertise or qualifications of these coaches remains undetermined. Club members have to provide time and expertise to coach these young players, and often these members are themselves players, finding time for their own personal sporting aspirations within a busy social, professional or commercial life style. The question of 'expertise to coach' needs careful consideration also because traditionally clubs have tried to retain the older player to fulfil such a developmental role within the club's coaching structure. However, increasingly, governing bodies of sport have been encouraging their clubs to ensure that coaches are properly qualified for the role. Once again, the time and effort needed to qualify as a coach in the sport becomes a potential deterrent to the individual wanting to share his or her playing expertise with young players. The situation is further complicated if one includes the legal ramifications of a situation in which a young club member is injured in a training/competitive session in which the coach in charge is not fully qualified. Moreover, the ability to coach adults is not necessarily commensurate with the skills required to coach and develop young people.

ACCESS TO SUITABLE COMPETITION

It would be quite pointless if one or two clubs within a sport were to provide a competitive youth development infrastructure if the remaining clubs then failed to match this commitment and instead concentrated on senior competition. Youth competition needs quality and variety if it is to have the desired developmental and motivational effect on young players. It requires an informed incremental approach with accessible intrinsic and extrinsic rewards and goals for the participating individual. All clubs, or the majority, must begin to make such strategic investments designed to enhance participation levels throughout the sporting infrastructure if they are to retain the majority of perhaps initially less recognisably gifted but potentially valuable club members, and so to build a solid foundation for the future wellbeing of the sport.

SYSTEMS TO MONITOR YOUNG PLAYER DEVELOPMENT

Young players need to know that their playing performances are being monitored and recorded by individuals who select the teams and who represent the club at the highest level of competition. If young players realise that such mechanisms exist for their competitive advancement then this can act as an incentive for them to improve competitively. Again, this initiative needs to be resourced properly, with senior officials being released to observe the competitive performances of young players throughout the club. In tandem with a monitoring system, young players need to know that if they perform well they will be recognised and given the chance to play at the highest level within the club. This knowledge and associated feedback can catalyse a motivational response within the young player, but this system is predicated on ample opportunity for competition. As the survey shows, a great many young people never actually compete in their chosen activity and without the chance to play at a competitive level, the sporting experience of the young person is necessarily incomplete, and in turn the development of their interest in that sport may well be stifled even before birth.

EXAMPLES OF GOOD PRACTICE

Internationally, sports which have developed mini-versions of the adult competitive form are seen to have taken the lead in providing for the needs of the young developing sports participant. Almond (1989), when alluding to strategies of change in sport, stated that 'Too often people have to adjust to the inappropriate demands of the event rather than modify the event to enable a person to perform adequately.'

Such a statement embodies reflective good practice in providing open access to all young people who wish to avail themselves of the benefits of sports participation. It also highlights a strategy which fairly well guarantees success in bridging the gap between youth and adult sport. To date, a number of governing bodies have produced very well-developed mini-versions of their sport and indeed some even offer a coaching qualification that allows individuals to coach the restricted version of the major game. Innovations of this type lower the threshold for both coaching opportunities and participation and therefore improve access to sport generally. With this in mind it is surprising how few young people in the survey had experience of mini-sports. Indeed, of the entire sample, only 19 young people (0.8 per cent) appeared to have had experience of mini-sports. Given the energy which has been devoted to the development of these games by a great many people, this uptake must be a source of deep concern.

PEERS

It is widely accepted that considerable importance is attached to peer friendships across the adolescent years. Their influence on sport participation appears to be most focused between the ages of 13 and 16. Hendry *et al.* (1993) argue that peers generally provide security at a time of rapid personal and social growth. The social growth and development of the individual, in both same-sex and mixed-sex contexts, is facilitated in peer group contexts, and conformity in lifestyle, dress, interests and appearance becomes endemic to social life for adolescents. Gender differences have also been recognised, with females valuing individual friendships more highly than males. On the whole, though, Hendry *et al.* (1993) found that friends promoted involvement simply by being fellow participants.

The importance of friends being involved in sport is obvious in this study, with 21 per cent of the sample detailing that it was their friends who initiated their interest in sport and who helped maintain this interest. Also, 63 per cent also responded that 'making friends' through the context of sport was a major factor in making them more keen about participation. Not surprisingly the respondents recorded a close concordance of sports that they played with sports played by their friends. High rates of coincidence were found particularly in relation to some major team games. For example, soccer, as a 'top sport', was found to have 63 per cent of friends playing the game; likewise Gaelic football (46 per cent) and camogie (47 per cent). Minority sports such as basketball, gymnastics, tennis and cycling recorded much lower concordance rates. Nevertheless with very few exceptions young people had more friends associated with their own sport than any other sport. In addition 40 per cent of those who were club members recorded that it was a friend who introduced them to their sports club. Parents (31 per cent), siblings (10 per cent) and other relatives (6 per cent) were of less significance in this respect. Alongside this pattern of positive peer influence there is a need to consider the issue of gender-mixed sport. Qualitative observations confirm the conclusion across mixed sporting activities that if a sport can retain a gender mix among older participants, then this can act as an added incentive, for older adolescents in particular. An example of good practice in this regard is swimming, where clubs normally maintain a healthy gender balance. Indeed this particular sport has gone further in order to try to maintain involvement. Swimming-related activities such as water polo have been developed alongside competitive swimming clubs in order to continue to provide for a competitive vehicle for members who may no longer wish to devote the time to swim training but nevertheless would like to continue to swim competitively. Initiatives like this facilitate the retention of interested and talented individuals within the sport with the likely consequence of these participants perhaps eventually devoting their accumulated expertise to assist the development of the next generation.

WE ALL KNOW BETTER

The implementation of the National Curriculum for Physical Education (NCPE) has unashamedly and explicitly provided for a transition from a games-dominated physical education programme to a broad and balanced curriculum with a strong health focus. Green (1994) suggests that the refocusing of the subject away from traditional team games and towards health-based physical activity has still to be proved as a worthwhile change. He maintains that despite the increase in awareness of the value of participation, the actual practice of physical activity has not increased greatly. Harris (1995) reinforces this claim by stating that differences exist between knowledge, beliefs and practice. Armstrong and McManus (1994), in their investigation of activity patterns of 11–16 year olds in Great Britain, found evidence to support the latter claim, with low levels of habitual exercise in terms of both duration and intensity. The question remains as to why, despite a clear understanding of the benefits of participation, more children are not more active. Cale and Almond (1991) collated common factors affecting low levels of participation from the scarce studies based on British children. Technology, pressure of work, gender stereotypes, social factors, cost, peer group and parental influence, variations in maturation rates and the association of physical education and sport with school and lack of enjoyment, represent the complex array of reasons for low or no commitment to physical activity, and, as various other chapters testify, this array of reasons has been confirmed in the present study in various forms.

Green (1995) also suggests that the development of positive attitudes, that will be transferred into positive actions, is more difficult during the adolescent and young adult stage as the individual is more vulnerable at this time. Such findings are hardly surprising when one considers that the implementation of the National Curriculum has not significantly increased the amount of time devoted to the teaching of physical education in schools. Moreover, it is further argued that the identification of attainment targets in the subject has led some physical education teachers to ask pupils to observe and evaluate their peers in a non-active manner, thus reducing the already short time when pupils can actually be physically active within the subject. It is therefore important that movement, activity and enjoyment remain at the heart of the physical education curriculum, with pupils exploring physical questions in a challenging environment. Teachers of physical education need to argue for time and resources to teach the subject properly to their pupils and they need to remind their colleagues who make timetable provision for the subject of the contribution which it can make to the physical, social and emotional potential of the pupil.

As far as the longer view and active lifestyle is concerned, teachers can but continue to teach their pupils effectively why and how to use what they learn wisely, in the hope that they will continue to exercise in the post-school years.

SCHOOL-COMMUNITY LINKS: SERVICING THE SPORTS CLUBS

Hendry (1978) has shown that the gradual decline in levels of participation in physical activity, both inside and outside school boundaries, emerges in the latter years of compulsory schooling, and as Chapter 5 shows, this pattern has been replicated in the present data set. Already we have explored how attitudes to physical activity may become established prior to leaving school. The withdrawal of young people from club structures which reflect a heavy adult, organised, conformist influence (sports clubs, youth clubs, church clubs and youth groups) begins to take place in middle adolescence (Hendry et al., 1993), at a stage of development when these are considered to be conservative socialising mediums (Synder and Spreitzer, 1978). The transition to leisure activities that emphasise the informal then begins to take place, with rates of change tending to reflect gender differences. Girls are more likely to enter more adult-led, commercial leisure time pursuits earlier than boys, and boys are more likely to remain in organised sport and leisure.

Evidence from the SCNI survey suggests that, on the whole, previous research may have underplayed the extent of positive attitudes to sport and physical activity among both boys and girls. Gender differences do not appear to be significant, yet males appear to be provided with, and use, a great many more opportunities than females. In this study 75 per cent of respondents were spending at least one hour a week on their favourite sport outside of school and over half (53 per cent) devoted between 2 and 10 hours per week. However, only 24 per cent actually competed on a weekly basis, with 73 per cent of the time devoted to practice and 54 per cent to instruction. In all, 43 per cent said that they never competed in their top sport. Gender differences are in evidence once again with only 33 per cent of girls having received opportunities to be competitive in their 'top sport' compared with 51 per cent of boys. Given that 'getting better' was rated by 75 per cent of the sample as a factor making them more keen about sport it would appear that the shortage of competitive opportunities for those who are genuinely interested in competition needs to be considered, if sport is to maintain young people's interest. By way of example, many of the relatively popular activities (sports attempted most often) do not provide many playing opportunities outside the school setting, for instance basketball (27 per cent), badminton (26 per cent) and cycling (24 per cent).

This survey has shown that only 36 per cent of the entire sample were members of organised clubs and just over half of these were involved with clubs where the primary focus was sport. This small percentage also reflects a gender imbalance, with boys over twice as likely to be members of sports clubs than girls. However, despite the low membership rates the commitment to sports clubs does increase over the adolescent years with 16 per cent of those at Key Stage 2 being club members, 25 per cent of those at Key Stage 3, 39 per cent at Key Stage 4 and nearly half (46 per cent) in the sixth form.

The general participation profile, however, suggests that the work undertaken in schools which is designed to bridge the gap between school and club has some way to go. In addressing this issue some schools have demonstrated considerable initiative, for example inviting representatives of local sports clubs to talk to pupils who were about to leave school. Unfortunately such practices are rare and have not been systematically evaluated, but clearly there is a large untapped resource of sporting enthusiasm which awaits further initiatives of this kind.

OTHER SPORTING OUTLETS

The Sports Council for Wales (1992) found in a study of children's sports that 86 per cent participated in sport but outside the traditional networks of schools, sports clubs and youth organisations. The report indicated that the narrow base of sports clubs which are devoted mainly to traditional team games provide more of a constraint than an opportunity to young people and went further to state that where clubs do exist some are unable or even unwilling to create necessary junior sections. Evidence may exist from this survey to support a similar vein in Northern Ireland, with fewer than 1 per cent of the sample recording that they have experienced a mini-version of sport. This problem is then possibly further compounded by implications of the philosophy of the broad and balanced National Curriculum taking effect. Now more children are possibly willing to try a number of activities. This diversified interest may possibly be reducing complete commitment to just one sport, and could foster low levels of commitment to a variety of activities. Alternatively it may open the opportunity for appetising tasters of a range of activities.

This would seem to suggest that there may be a large pool of potential participants if clubs were to establish appropriate junior sections and competitive structures. However, if mass participation is the goal, in order to address both sport and health needs, the question needs to be asked, 'Are sports clubs the answer?' Roberts (1996) states that throughout Europe, club membership is in decline across all age groups but especially among young people who are acting on a preference for 'do-it-yourself ' styles of participation.

Lack of communication between clubs, public sports provision and physical education departments is partly responsible for young people failing to realise the potential and opportunity for participation at recreative and competitive levels beyond school boundaries. Murphy and Tomlinson (1989) advise that these interfaces need to be addressed so that respective roles can be rationalised. Links and partnerships are surely crucial if the needs of young people are to be met fully. With the wider spectrum of sports now on offer, the need for an integrated policy is now more than ever a priority. Schools cannot provide either all the expertise or facilities to satisfy fully both the pupils' interests and the needs of traditional sports clubs.

The establishment of school–community links has long since been identified, most recently by the government White Paper *Sport: Raising the Game*, as one important vehicle for facilitating continuity of participation in, and a lifelong commitment to, physical recreation. Murphy and Tomlinson (1989) suggest that to reduce the void substantially from school to community participation, planned preparation of pathways for entry into the community is a prerequisite. Roberts (1996) argues that the Youth Service Study, carried out by the Department of Education this year (1996), suggests that whether young people continue to play sport after leaving school may well be strongly related to whether they are already using community facilities. Northern Ireland would appear to be at an advantage in this case given the number of leisure centres per head of population (28,000 people per leisure centre (Mahoney, 1995)). On the surface therefore it would appear that opportunities are in abundance. However, it must be noted that the context of Northern Ireland means that every facet of life is constrained by the politics of division (Sugden and Bairner, 1993), and sport and leisure are no exception. Consequently, public policy has facilitated the establishment of sport and leisure facilities in clusters, in trouble 'hot spots'. Given that only 14 per cent of sixth form students in this study participated in activity in leisure centres, and 10 per cent in a youth club, the use of community facilities could be seen not as a problem of overuse but as a potential growth area. Hendry *et al.* (1993) found that involvement in sports clubs experienced a more gradual decline than other organised clubs that were not sport specific, and so they have the potential to bridge the gap between adolescence and young adulthood.

Bridging this gap and maintaining involvement and activity remains a key concern for sport. In the real world, the majority of young school leavers directly enter the labour market (on a low wage), or higher/further education (on a grant or parental support), or job training schemes (on a pittance), but whatever is the case, it is almost inevitable that they will face financial hardship. In these circumstances, expenses associated with sport and club membership will assume great significance and such factors are likely to act as a significant deterrent to participation. Only when a sound occupational status is achieved will a young adult acquire the economic means and freedom to choose their own type and frequency of lifestyle pursuits, and by that time the bond with their favourite, chosen or 'top sport' may have been broken for ever. To avoid that fracture there is a need to address basic, structural factors, such as expense, if we are ever to see these positive attitudes to sport among young people translate into healthy profiles of sporting activity among adults. This remains the challenge for sport.

REFERENCES

Almond, L. (1989). *The Place of Physical Education in Schools*. Guildford: Biddles.

Armstrong, N. and McManus, A. (1994). Children's fitness and physical activity – A challenge for physical education. *The British Journal of Physical Education, 25(2)*, 20–26.

Cale, L. and Almond, L. (1991). Children's activity levels: A review of studies conducted on British children. *Physical Education Review, 15(1)*, 111–119.

Cale, L. and Harris, J. (1993). Exercise recommendations for children and young people. *Physical Education Review, 16(2)*, 89–98.

Clough, J., Thorpe, R. and Traill, R. (1995). A cross cultural comparison of girls' participation in sport. In G. McFee, W. Murphy and G. Whannel (eds), *Leisure: Cultures, Genders and Lifestyles*. Eastbourne: Leisure Studies Association.

Coleman, J. (1979). *The School Years*. London: Methuen.

Department of National Heritage (1995). *Sport: Raising the Game*. London: HMSO.

Evans, J. (1989). Swinging from the crossbar, equality and opportunity in the physical education curriculum. *British Journal of Physical Education, Summer*, 84–87.

Green, K. (1994). Meeting the challenge: Health related exercise and the encouragement of lifelong participation. *The Bulletin of Physical Education (BAALPE), 30(3)*, 27–34.

Green, K. (1995). Physical education, partnership and the challenge of lifelong participation: A shared goal for the 21st century. *British Journal of Physical Education, 26(2), Summer*, 26–30.

Hargreaves, J. (1995). Gender, morality and the national physical education curriculum. In L. Lawrence, E. Murdock and S. Parker (eds), *Professional and Development Issues in Leisure, Sport and Education*. London: Leisure Studies Association (Publication No. 56).

Harris, J. (1995). Physical education: A picture of health? *British Journal of Physical Education, 26(4), Winter*, 32.

Hendry, L.B. (1976). Early school leavers, sport and leisure. *Scottish Education Studies, 8(1)*, 48–57.

Hendry, L.B. (1978). *School, Sport and Leisure*. London: Lepus.

Hendry, L.B., Shucksmith, J., Love, J.G. and Glendinning, A. (1993). *Young People's Leisure Lifestyles*. London: Routledge.

Kirk, D. (1992). *Defining Physical Education*. London: Falmer Press.

Lenskyi, H. (1991). *Women, Sport and Physical Activity*. Canada: Minister of Supply and Services.

Lloyd, J. and Fox, J. (1992). Achievement goals and motivation to exercise, adolescent girls: A preliminary intervention study. *The British Journal of Physical Education Research Supplement, 11*, 12–16.

Mahoney, C. (1995). Sport and young people in Northern Ireland: An appraisal. *British Journal of Physical Education, 26(1)*, 35–38.

Mason, V. (1995). *Young People and Sport in England, 1994: A National Survey*. London: Sports Council (GB).

Murphy, W. and Tomlinson, A. (1989). *Leisure, Labour and Lifestyles: International Comparisons, Volume. 5: Children Schooling and Education for Leisure*. Eastbourne: Leisure Studies Association.

Roberts, K. (1983). *Youth and Leisure*. London: Allen & Unwin.

Roberts, K. (1996). Young people, schools, sport and government policies. *Sport, Education and Society, 1(1), March*, 47–58.

Sallis, J.F. and Patrick, K. (1994). Physical activity guidelines for adolescents: Consensus statement. *British Journal of Physical Education Research, Supplement 15*, 2–7.

Schultz, R.W., Smoll, F.L., Carre, F.A. and Mosher, R.E. (1985). Inventories and norms for children's attitudes towards physical activity. *Research Quarterly for Exercise and Sport*, 56(3), 256–265.

Singer, R. (ed.) (1976). *Physical Education: Foundations*. New York: Holt, Rinehart and Winston.

Sports Council (Wales) (1993). *Children's Sports Participation, 1991/2*. Cardiff: Sports Council (Wales).

Sugden, J. and Bairner, A. (1993). *Sport, Sectarianism and Society in a Divided Ireland*. Leicester: Leicester University Press.

Synder, E. and Spreitzer, E. (1978). Socialisation comparisons of adolescent female athletes and musicians. *Research Quarterly for Exercise and Sport, 49(3)*, 342–350.

Talbot, M. (1994). The role of physical education in a national strategy for young people and sport. *The British Journal of Physical Education, 25(1)*, 2–29.

5   Age and sport participation

Craig Mahoney

INTRODUCTION

Contemporary research with young people of school age has consistently found that children become less active as they grow older (Armstrong and McManus, 1994), and quite naturally this decline in sporting participation has been of concern to parents, teachers, health professionals and government alike. By way of example, in 1995 the UK Prime Minister, John Major, refocused attention on school sport by making participation in team games in particular a major focal point of school physical education. This was followed in 1996 by a further initiative to develop school sport, launched in the wake of Britain's poor performance in the 1996 Atlanta Olympic Games.

Despite this concern, the SCNI survey represents one of a small number of studies which have considered how age may influence mode, frequency and number of sports undertaken. The survey yielded data on where and how these age-related changes begin, and what effect, if any, they may have on long-term activity patterns. This chapter seeks to use the data to identify key factors which alter as young people grow older and their lifestyles and behaviours change. The need to track sport and exercise-related behaviours from childhood to adulthood is now widely acknowledged, and it is hoped this survey will begin to address this need by providing baseline data on sport participation rates of young people, and hence the likelihood of their healthy involvement in sport through to adulthood.

A range of opinions exist regarding how sporting behaviours develop and how they should be nurtured in young people of school age. The recently completed survey of such behaviours in young people in England (Mason, 1995) describes few differences across age ranges but did identify that, by age 15–16, 'Sport for All' had become sport for some. This alarming trend has been noted in previous surveys completed elsewhere, including Northern Ireland. For example, Sutherland (1992) found that post-primary-aged students in their mid-teens were dropping out of sport, with girls much more prone to drop-out than boys. The English survey also found that girls devoted less time to sport than boys: between the ages of 6 and 9 years, on average girls played 10 different sports per year, while boys played 12 sports, these numbers increasing to 13 and 14 respectively between the ages of 9 and 11 years, before then declining (Mason, 1995).

In the SCNI survey, detailed information acquired from 2,400 interviewees has produced a massive data set from which only a small amount can be effectively presented in a short chapter such as this. It is intended to address age differences by focusing on changes in behaviour principally between primary and post-primary school, and then to develop this further by considering changes according to the key stage (KS) within the school curriculum. Primary school pupils were grouped as Key Stage 2 (KS2, normally aged 8 to 11 years), and post-primary students were divided into Key Stage 3 (KS3, normally aged 11 to 14 years), Key Stage 4 (KS4, normally aged 14 to 16 years) and sixth form students (6F, normally aged 16 to 18 years). The chapter will compare differences in relation to: main participant sports played; age of commencement in sport; the reasons for starting to play sport; the highest level played (and perceived potential); where young people participated in sport; what type of instruction they had received; age of drop-out from sports and why they dropped out; what time of the year young people were involved in sport; and how often per week they were participating. Finally where young people play their sport will be considered, all the while focusing attention primarily on age differences.

PARTICIPATION RATES

The actual number of sports which young people participate in each year provides baseline information on personal levels of physical activity. Owing to the significance of tracking behaviours it also yields a database of likely long-term possibilities for those promoting sport or those involved in sports' governing bodies. Figure 5.1 shows the percentages of primary and post-primary students attempting different numbers of sports. It indicates that the most common number of sports attempted by primary school children is three, for both boys and girls. This figure is substantially lower than the average of 10 sports for girls and 12 for boys as cited in the English survey, a finding which may reflect on many factors, including different survey techniques, the more

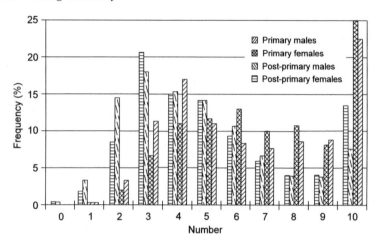

Figure 5.1 Sports attempted per year

traditional primary curriculum in Northern Ireland, or a restriction of
opportunities for involvement in sports away from school.

By post-primary school, these results have altered dramatically,
with 35 per cent of young people attempting 10 or more sports
regularly each year. Across the sample, it was encouraging that 99
per cent recorded that they were active in sport, and most often this
was throughout the year. Over 60 per cent of males and females were
involved for the entire year, with a further 11 per cent involved for the
winter only and 29 per cent during the summer.

When young people were questioned about the nature of their
participation in sports, over 90 sporting activities were listed. Table
5.1 shows the five most-often-cited sports for primary and post-
primary students. Given that the Digest of Sports Statistics (Sports
Council, 1991) and the General Household Survey (PPRU, 1994) list
walking, swimming and cue sports (for example, pool and snooker) as
the main participant sports in the UK, it may be surprising to find
that soccer emerged as the most prevalent sport among boys. However, other surveys of young people across the UK have found soccer
to be massively popular. For example, Riddoch (1990) similarly found
that it was considered the most popular participant sport by over 60
per cent of young people between the ages of 11 and 16 years. It is
perhaps surprising to note that Gaelic sports do not feature more
highly, being only ranked fourth in the top five participant sports
for males, but not featuring at all for females, and that other high-
profile sports (for example, rugby) do not feature at all. No major

Table 5.1 Top five participation sports – primary and post-primary

Ranking	Boys		Girls	
	Primary	*Post-primary*	*Primary*	*Post-primary*
1	Soccer	Soccer	Swimming	Swimming
2	Swimming	Swimming	Rounders	Netball
3	Cycling	Basketball	Cycling	Badminton
4	Gaelic football	Gaelic football	Netball	Hockey
5	Basketball	Badminton	Soccer	Athletics

differences appear to exist across the primary to post-primary divide, except that rounders, a traditional primary school sport, is represented for primary girls only but fails to appear in the post-primary listing.

TAKING UP SPORT

Involvement in physical activity is normally considered to be a fundamental part of everyday life, presumably driven by a primary human motive to be physically active rather than inactive (Robertson and Halverson, 1984). Given the right sort of encouragement it should be possible to channel these natural energies towards organised sport from an early age, and the survey did attempt to consider this issue by looking at the age of involvement and the primary agents involved in recruitment. First, young people were asked at what age they started playing sport. The retrospective nature of this question produced some interesting results (Table 5.2).

Table 5.2 suggests little variation between genders across the two broad age groupings, but does show what appears to be an unusual recollection of when the young person started playing sport. Given that sport participation profiles of primary and post-primary students

Table 5.2 Age at which young people reported starting sport

Age (years)	Boys		Girls	
	Primary %	*Post-primary* %	*Primary* %	*Post-primary* %
4–	11.4	6.0	10.0	4.8
5–7	51.9	20.0	47.5	15.3
8–9	30.3	21.5	32.5	18.0
10–11	6.3	28.8	10.1	29.3
12+	0.1	23.7	0	32.5

Craig Mahoney

are unlikely to have witnessed such a dramatic change in the space of a few years, instead it would appear that current age has a considerable effect on recall of when sport involvement commenced. This is evidenced by the difference of over 5 per cent between those who stated that they started sport at 4 years or younger among those currently in primary school, as opposed to those stating they started at that age when they had reached post-primary education. This trend is repeated across the age groupings, most dramatically in KS4 and 6F, and rather than reflecting a changing trend in terms of the age at which sport is being taken up by young people it is more likely the result of recency and primacy effects in recall.

When seeking information as to why young people have attempted various sporting activities, the primary/post-primary divide appears to be less significant. Scanning the top five reasons for starting sport (Table 5.3), it is apparent that parents have a considerable bearing on young people's involvement, with fathers more commonly associated with boys' sporting activities, and mothers with girls. Consistently girls rate school, friends and mothers as the main reasons for taking up sport across all age groups, with school playing an increasingly dominant role in secondary education. For boys in secondary education, peer influence features more prominently alongside school.

With friends and school acting in concert as the major reasons for attempting sports, it is likely that voluntary sport, away from

Table 5.3 Reasons for taking up sport

Ranking	KS2	%	KS3	%	KS4	%	6F	%
Boys:								
1	Friends	25.6	School	29.4	School	30.1	Friends	25.8
2	Father	17.5	Friends	21.2	Friends	22.0	School	25.6
3	School	15.1	Father	10.2	Father	12.1	Father	13.2
4	Siblings	8.5	Something to do	7.8	Something to do	5.4	Keep fit	5.1
5	Something to do	7.7	Siblings	5.7	Siblings	4.3	Something to do	4.9
Girls:								
1	School	26.9	School	45.8	School	46.9	School	44.1
2	Friends	19.0	Friends	15.9	Friends	16.1	Friends	14.0
3	Mother	15.6	Mother	7.9	Mother	6.8	Mother	6.9
4	Father	9.8	Something to do	7.6	Interest	5.5	Interest	5.2
5	Siblings	8.8	Father	4.6	Something to do	5.1	Father	5.1

school, reflects strongly on peer influence. Many studies have shown fun to be a major factor in promoting participation (Schmidt and Stein, 1991; Brustad, 1993), and friends equate with fun for most adolescents. The other major influence, the school, is likely to be influential in an entirely different way. The physical education curriculum, with its emphasis on a broad and balanced range of activities, should provide opportunities for continued and increasing exposure to a greater range of sports, especially as young people progress through the system. This probably provides the primary explanation for the increasing number of sports experienced by young people in post-primary education, in comparison with primary children.

SPORT IN SCHOOLS

The introduction of the Common Curriculum (in 1991 in Northern Ireland) brought about a standardisation in the provision of physical education within schools. The framework this provided for the delivery of physical education means that young people should be exposed to a wide range of sporting opportunities. In reality, given the restrictions of time, money and expertise, it was always likely that those attending primary school would benefit least. This imbalance should be reflected in data on the provision and balance of sports provided, although when the lists of the five most frequently available school sports are compared by age, the similarities are more remarkable than the differences (Table 5.4).

Soccer dominates the scene for boys at each of the key stages. Other major participant activities such as swimming are not so widely represented. This is especially surprising given that swimming is named as a discrete area of the physical education curriculum and is therefore mandatory from KS2 onwards. As expected, netball is the most commonly provided school sport for girls, with statistics suggesting that at any one time over 900 girls will be playing competitive netball at school. Unfortunately these participants are not tracking through to adulthood, since figures available from the sport's governing body would indicate that only 1,300 women are involved in competitive netball in club-based leagues in Northern Ireland.

The other surprising omissions are the Gaelic sports. While Gaelic football is the third most common sport provided for boys, and appears to maintain its participant base from KS2 to 6F, it still ranks only third in terms of commonality, with fewer than 10 per cent in each age band acknowledging availability.

Table 5.4 Five most commonly available school sports

Ranking	KS2	%	KS3	%	KS4	%	6F	%
Boys:								
1	Soccer	73.1	Soccer	77.6	Soccer	81.7	Soccer	72.3
2	Swimming	49.4	Basketball	65.0	Basketball	66.1	Basketball	56.6
3	Gaelic football	22.5	Gaelic football	46.1	Gaelic football	48.7	Gaelic football	49.4
4	Athletics	20.4	Swimming	40.8	Athletics	35.3	Badminton	43.4
5	Rounders	18.0	Athletics	38.5	Swimming	34.8	Swimming	39.8
Girls:								
1	Swimming	54.4	Netball	81.1	Netball	80.0	Netball	79.1
2	Netball	37.7	Swimming	46.4	Field hockey	54.0	Badminton	61.5
3	Soccer	25.1	Field hockey	45.6	Badminton	46.4	Field hockey	58.2
4	Athletics	22.7	Athletics	40.5	Swimming	45.1	Aerobics	48.4
5	Field hockey	21.2	Gymnastics	33.1	Athletics	37.4	Swimming	45.1

WHERE SPORT IS PLAYED

Given that young people spend much of their time at school it is likely that many early experiences in sport and exposure to new sports will occur there. Interestingly, when asked where they were most involved in their selected 'top sport' the dominant response, among both primary and post-primary students, was not in schools but in clubs outside school (Table 5.5).

It seems that school may be providing early exposure to a sport but the development of interest and involvement then occurs away from school. It is also noteworthy that an even higher percentage of those attending primary school than secondary school play their chosen 'top

Table 5.5 Where young people play their 'top sport'

Site	Boys		Girls	
	Primary %	Post-Primary %	Primary %	Post-Primary %
School	14.8	29.0	24.3	39.8
Club/outside school	63.0	47.0	59.3	41.5
Both	22.3	24.0	16.4	18.7

sport' away from school. At this early age it would be hoped that the school environment would be able to foster budding sporting interests and talent, but it would appear that the initiative is placed instead on children and their families to make arrangements for practice, instruction and competition.

To elaborate further on this issue, young people were asked to specify the place in which they most often played sport (Table 5.6). Informal arrangements (breaks at school, home, street, parks, etc.), as well as 'playing outdoors' (mountains, countryside, sea, etc.), characterise most primary school students' sport involvement outside school hours, with clubs and more formal facilities being more often used by post-primary students. Overall, however, use of leisure centres and swimming pools does not appear to increase substantially with age, a finding which is perhaps counter-intuitive. It is also noteworthy that when asked to identify where sport was played in this more general fashion, across all ages, school is credited with playing a far more important role in the provision of sporting opportunities than was indicated in relation to a more specific question about 'top sport'. This is in addition to informal settings (breaks at school, home, street, parks, etc.) and outdoors.

Table 5.6 Where 'top sport' is played

Location	Boys		Girls	
	Primary %	Post-Primary %	Primary %	Post-Primary %
Informal/various	20.2	13.1	15.3	9.3
School (in school hours)	12.6	20.9	19.4	29.0
School (out school hours)	2.2	2.9	3.2	4.5
School (both)	1.3	4.2	1.0	4.0
Sports club	11.4	16.8	10.5	12.9
Gym/leisure centre	1.1	1.8	2.0	2.6
Leisure centre (with club)	0.9	1.6	1.2	2.0
Leisure centre (other)	10.5	9.9	14.7	11.4
Swimming pool	9.8	6.6	11.3	7.1
Outdoors	29.9	22.1	21.4	17.1

INSTRUCTION

The type of instruction given to young people in sport is known to be influential in nurturing a long-term interest in sport (Smith and Smoll, 1990). Coaching experiences which are rewarding tend to support further participation while those which are negative often turn young

Table 5.7 Major sources of instruction in 'top sport'

	Boys		Girls	
Instruction	*Primary* %	*Post-primary* %	*Primary* %	*Post-primary* %
None	45.6	29.6	39.8	19.6
In school	19.3	35.8	25.4	49.2
Coach out of school	16.8	19.2	21.4	22.5
Parent	15.4	7.7	11.7	4.4
In and out of school	2.9	7.8	2.1	4.2

people away from sport (Brustad, 1993). In Table 5.7 the principal sources of instruction are shown for the elected 'top sport'. There are marked age differences here, with few opportunities for instruction before post-primary education, and beyond that, few opportunities outside school. Overall relatively few young people maintained that they received instruction from coaches away from school.

The source of this instruction likewise comes from a limited range of people. The young people were asked to indicate who had ever given them instruction in their 'top sport'. The four predominant groups of instructors are listed in Table 5.8. Mothers (for girls when younger) and fathers (for boys through to 6F) do appear to play a role but PE teachers and qualified coaches were cited more frequently. With age there was greater reliance on individuals other than the immediate family, with coaches' influence continuing to increase with age. PE teachers were regarded as important sources of instruction in KS2 and KS3 but less so in 6F.

Table 5.8 Source of instruction

	Boys				Girls			
Source of instruction	*KS2* %	*KS3* %	*KS4* %	*6F* %	*KS2* %	*KS3* %	*KS4* %	*6F* %
Mother	3.3	2.5	4.6	1.3	15.6	8.6	5.6	2.2
Father	31.1	33.0	30.0	22.1	19.9	11.0	8.4	5.6
PE teacher	9.4	56.3	59.4	37.7	9.3	46.9	46.7	33.3
Qual. coach	32.1	47.8	55.8	59.7	43.0	39.6	47.2	52.2

DROPPING OUT

The phenomena of burnout, staleness or overtraining have been considered in relation to élite sport, to the point where many of the underlying factors are well understood and problems can be foreseen,

Table 5.9 Age of drop-out from attempted sports

Age	Boys		Girls	
	Primary %	Post-primary %	Primary %	Post-primary %
4 and under	0.1	0	0	0
5–7 years	1.6	0.2	3.0	0.5
8–9 years	2.4	0.6	4.9	1.2
10–11 years	1.4	3.5	2.5	5.6
12 and older	0	11.0	0	20.5
Not applicable	94.5	84.6	89.6	72.2

if not avoided. Young people, however, enter and leave sports at an alarmingly high rate (Roberts, 1984; Gould, 1987). In part this may be due to their initially high participation rates across a broad range of sports. Given that a significant minority of young people in post-primary education may participate in over 10 sports per year, it is highly unlikely that they can sustain this breadth of commitment for any length of time, or with genuine quality of participation. Nonetheless, as Table 5.9 indicates, the rate of complete drop-out across the sample was surprisingly low, with only 17 per cent having discontinued a sport entirely. As would be predicted from previous research this drop-out occurs predominantly in post-primary education after the age of 12 years. In a further question designed to find out why young people had discontinued a sport, across each age range 'lack of interest' was cited as the most important reason, by around one-third. Other factors, such as 'friends stopped', 'too time consuming', 'to start other sports' and 'injury', did not appear to be significantly age dependent, although 'school commitments' were mentioned by 10 per cent of post-primary students but only 6 per cent of primary girls and no primary boys, and 'not played at school' was a significant factor for 17 per cent of post-primary students but only 8 per cent of those attending primary school.

By definition, top-level or élite sport is not a common experience for most young people. The pinnacle of excellence in any sport will only be available to a few, regardless of age. When considering the sample as a whole, the percentage who classified themselves as élite was understandably low. However, the number of young people who classified themselves as performing at a competitive level in sport increased, in both genders, from just below 10 per cent to around 18 per cent and 25 per cent respectively for girls and boys between primary and post-primary schools. Whether these figures are acceptable, or whether indeed competition at an early age is to be

Table 5.10 Highest level of attempted sports by key stage

Level of attainment	Boys				Girls			
	KS2 %	KS3 %	KS4 %	6F %	KS2 %	KS3 %	KS4 %	6F %
Basic	91.9	92.4	76.9	82.6	71.6	81.1	69.0	76.3
Competitive	8.1	7.6	22.5	17.0	27.2	18.0	29.3	21.3
Élite	0	0	0.6	0.4	1.2	0.9	1.6	2.4

Table 5.11 Highest level of 'top sport' by key stage

Level of attainment	Boys				Girls			
	KS2 %	KS3 %	KS4 %	6F %	KS2 %	KS3 %	KS4 %	6F %
Basic	65.8	77.5	47.8	62.9	26.7	61.2	28.6	62.9
Competitive	34.2	21.9	48.7	35.0	69.1	32.7	64.9	35.0
Élite	0	0.7	3.1	1.5	4.1	5.6	6.5	1.5

encouraged, must remain a matter for debate, but certainly the opportunities afforded for competition below the age of 12 years do appear limited. Table 5.10 provides information regarding the highest level of sport played by young people, encompassing all attempted sports, while Table 5.11 focuses on their 'top sport'. Élite-level representation increases with age in both genders, although both tables indicate that boys enjoy greater opportunities for competition as they grow older,

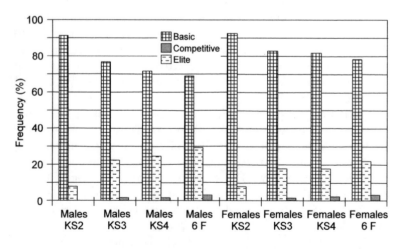

Figure 5.2 Highest level of attempted sport

whereas for girls, the percentage of those playing competitively remains relatively constant over time.

When asked what standard they believed they had the ability to achieve, while only 7 per cent in primary school felt they could perform at a competitive level in their 'top sport', among post-primary students this figure had risen to 14 per cent. Also, in terms of those who felt they had the potential to become élite performers, 1.9 per cent of boys and 1.4 per cent of girls attending primary school felt this was true, yet among post-primary school students (KS3) these figures had risen on transfer to 6.4 per cent and 3.5 per cent respectively. Therefore, aspirations among those in primary school were severely limited and this raises interesting questions as to why this was the case. Was the absence of competition, and hence the shortage of performance benchmarks, the most significant factor, or were primary students less interested in aspiring towards excellence in sport? These are interesting questions which may warrant further investigation.

Analysis of those sports identified by the young people as their chosen 'top sports' by age reveals some interesting differences (Table 5.12). For boys, soccer is the most popular sport across the key stages, although by 6F it is chosen by only around one-quarter of the sample, in comparison with 58 per cent at KS2. Other sports,

Table 5.12 Five most popular 'top sports' by key stage

Ranking	KS2	%	KS3	%	KS4	%	6th Form	%
Boys:								
1	Soccer	57.7	Soccer	44.0	Soccer	35.5	Soccer	24.7
2	Swimming	9.7	Gaelic football	12.3	Gaelic football	17.1	Gaelic football	11.7
3	Gaelic football	8.4	Swimming	6.3	Rugby Union	6.9	Rugby Union	10.4
4	Athletics	2.4	Basketball	5.0	Golf	4.6	Golf	6.5
5	Basketball	1.5	Golf	4.1	Swimming	3.7	Badminton	6.5
Girls:								
1	Swimming	31.8	Netball	20.2	Netball	14.0	Camogie	11.1
2	Athletics	8.9	Swimming	16.6	Swimming	12.6	Aerobics	10.0
3	Netball	7.0	Soccer	10.4	Field hockey	7.0	Swimming	8.9
4	Horse riding	6.6	Horse riding	8.3	Badminton	6.1	Badminton	8.9
5	Field hockey	5.6	Field hockey	7.1	Soccer	5.6	Netball	6.7

including Gaelic football, Rugby Union, athletics, golf and badminton, all attract support, and this tends to be more consistent over the years. For girls, swimming is chosen by almost one-third of primary-aged girls, but this sport declines in popularity through to 6F (9 per cent), a trend of declining popularity also noted among the boys. Netball appears most popular among girls in KS3, but again, by 6F only 7 per cent nominate this as their 'top sport', in comparison with 10 per cent who then chose aerobics and 11 per cent camogie.

When asked who or what had been the main influence behind them starting their top sport, those attending primary school were more likely to mention their same-sex parent whereas secondary students felt they had been more influenced by either peers or the school (Table 5.13). Consistently, boys said they were more influenced by friends or their father, while girls in primary school felt they were more influenced by their mother and, in post-primary schools, by which sports were on offer at school. Given the retrospective nature of this question, it may be that the reason at the time they became involved in their favoured sport does not reflect accurately in replies at the time of interview, but instead replies give insight into their contemporary perception of significant influences, and hence perhaps their future attitudes towards what governs sport motivation and commitment.

Table 5.13 Single most significant influence on starting 'top sport'

| | Boys | | Girls | |
Key stage	Main influence	%	Main influence	%
KS2	Father	31.6	Mother	27.8
KS3	Friends	25.8	School	49.4
KS4	Father	25.8	School	37.9
6F	Friends	31.2	School	34.4

PRACTICE COMPETITION AND INSTRUCTION

The following tables summarise information on participation in the young person's 'top sport'. The data reveal details of practice, competition and instruction, broken down by key stage and by gender (Tables 5.14–5.16). The tables indicate starkly contrasting profiles for girls and for boys but also significant changes in activity patterns over time.

For both genders, up until KS4 post-primary schools offered significant opportunities for practice and instructions in the young person's chosen sport, with approximately half of the sample of boys and

Table 5.14 Where 'top sport' practised, by key stage

	Boys				Girls			
Where practised	KS2 %	KS3 %	KS4 %	6F %	KS2 %	KS3 %	KS4 %	6F %
School (in hours)	41.1	55.0	59.0	28.6	24.2	43.9	37.9	25.6
School (after hours)	16.8	25.5	30.9	33.8	10.9	16.3	13.1	18.9
At home	40.6	51.6	44.7	28.6	25.8	35.6	23.4	24.4
Youth club	14.0	17.3	16.6	7.8	7.6	16.0	14.0	13.3
Sports club	21.8	37.4	54.0	59.8	9.5	12.8	24.8	33.3
Swimming pool	8.4	7.9	3.7	6.5	32.5	16.0	13.5	12.2
Leisure centre	12.5	14.2	11.5	9.1	11.9	4.9	11.2	17.8
The outdoors	11.7	12.6	12.4	16.9	8.9	6.1	8.9	11.1
Park/street	37.8	31.8	28.1	22.1	12.9	15.3	14.5	11.1

Table 5.15 Where 'top sport' instructed, by key stage

	Boys				Girls			
Where practised	KS2 %	KS3 %	KS4 %	6F %	KS2 %	KS3 %	KS4 %	6F %
School (in hours)	25.5	51.6	52.5	20.8	16.6	46.9	38.8	27.8
School (after hours)	10.7	17.3	25.8	26.0	8.9	12.6	11.7	13.3
At home	19.9	21.4	14.7	9.1	6.6	6.7	5.1	2.2
Youth club	8.4	9.1	10.1	9.1	6.6	9.8	12.1	8.9
Sports club	21.9	32.4	47.5	53.0	10.0	15.0	24.3	35.6
Swimming pool	7.4	7.0	2.3	5.2	31.5	15.0	11.6	10.0
Leisure centre	6.4	3.5	4.1	2.6	8.6	3.4	5.6	8.9
The outdoors	5.4	5.3	7.8	9.1	3.0	2.8	6.1	5.6
Park/street	11.7	9.1	8.3	6.5	4.0	3.4	3.3	5.6

Table 5.16 Where 'top sport' competed, by key stage

	Boys				Girls			
Where practised	KS2 %	KS3 %	KS4 %	6F %	KS2 %	KS3 %	KS4 %	6F %
School (in hours)	23.2	29.9	38.7	19.5	11.3	30.7	25.2	17.8
School (after hours)	12.2	13.8	24.9	29.9	6.6	11.0	8.9	18.9
At home	3.8	3.8	2.3	2.6	1.0	0.6	1.9	0
Youth club	10.7	11.9	13.4	13.0	4.6	8.9	11.7	10.0
Sports club	23.5	48.8	64.5	70.2	10.6	8.2	24.7	35.5
Swimming pool	1.8	4.4	1.0	3.9	8.3	2.8	5.1	5.5
Leisure centre	5.4	6.6	6.0	1.3	7.3	2.8	6.5	11.1
The outdoors	3.8	2.5	6.0	9.1	1.3	3.4	5.1	3.3
Park/street	6.9	5.3	9.7	10.4	1.3	3.4	0.9	6.7

40 per cent of the girls maintaining that they had experience of practice and instruction. In contrast, fewer than one-third of the sample had enjoyed actual competition in their favoured activity. Primary children, whether boys or girls, appear to have had very few opportunities for competition and practice, and instruction, perhaps predictably, tended to be informal. As time goes by, while schools continue to offer assistance, the maintenance of interest in sport appears to hinge crucially on the availability of sports clubs, with an almost linear increase in the involvement of clubs in relation to practice, competition and instruction from KS2 to 6F for both genders.

By 6F, over two-thirds of boys with a nominated 'top sport' cited a sports club as a place where they were involved in their sport. For girls, the picture is somewhat less rosy; only one-third of female 6F students who had a 'top sport' were receiving practice, instruction or competition from clubs, and this is despite the prevalence of sports such as camogie, badminton and netball in the list of most popular sports for young women of that age (see Table 5.15).

CONCLUSION

The results of the SCNI survey support the notion that while overall levels of participation in sport do appear to decline somewhat with age, the nature of this decline is not nearly so dramatic as many would expect. There appears to be a strong groundswell of support for continued involvement among a great many young men and women through to the age of 18 years, with no marked decline of interest in mid-adolescence as has often been noted elsewhere, or at least among this sample who are still in full-time education. As an aside, it may be interesting to compare the involvement of young people still attending school beyond the age of 16 years with those who have left school.

Instead of attitudes and motives playing a key role in the continuance of participation in sport, the data seem to suggest that structural rather than personal factors may play a more significant role in the decline of involvement. Put simply, it becomes more difficult to maintain an interest, first, when opportunities at school become more restricted and, second, when sports clubs are not readily available to take up the mantle of responsibility. Young people move from a position of having facilities and opportunities made readily available, to themselves having actively to seek out facilities. This transition from 'object' to 'agent', covered in greater detail in Chapter 4, is clearly one which many fail to make.

Therefore, although the curricular time may be reduced, support from parents, relatives and friends may be less forthcoming, and pressures of time and other interests may be debilitating, nevertheless the enthusiasm to participate appears to be little affected. Great play may continue to be made of the sociological, psychological and physiological changes associated with maturation, and how these interact with gender to determine participation in sport and physical activity. However, this survey provides no evidence to refute the hypothesis that young people continue to want to be involved in sport, and analyses and interpretations based on the interplay between gender and age should not be allowed to divert attention, or resources, from the undeniable fact that the gap between young people's commitment to sport and their opportunities to fulfil that commitment leaves a great deal to be desired.

REFERENCES

Armstrong, N. and McManus, A. (1994). Children's fitness and physical activity–A challenge for physical education. *The British Journal of Physical Education, Spring*, 20–26.

Brustad, R.D. (1993). Youth in sport: Psychological considerations. In R.N. Singer, M. Murphey and L.K. Tennant (eds), *Handbook of Research on Sport Psychology*. New York: Macmillan.

Gould, D. (1987). Understanding attrition in children's sport. In D. Gould and M.R. Weiss (eds), *Advances in Paediatric Sciences, Volume 2*. Champaign, IL: Human Kinetics.

Mason, V. (1995). *Young People and Sport in England, 1994: A National Survey*. London: Sports Council.

PPRU (1994). *The General Household Survey*. Belfast: HMSO.

Riddoch, C. (1990). *The Northern Ireland Fitness Survey–1989*. Belfast: The Queen's University of Belfast.

Roberts, G.C. (1984). Achievement motivation in children's sport. *Advances in Motivation and Achievement, 3*, 251–281.

Robertson, M.A. and Halverson, L. (1984). *Developing Children–Their Changing Movement–A Guide for Teachers*. Philadelphia: Lea & Febiger.

Schmidt, G.W. and Stein, G.L. (1991). Sport commitment: A model integrating enjoyment, dropout and burnout. *Journal of Sport and Exercise Psychology, 8*, 254–265.

Smith, R. and Smoll, F.L. (1990). Self-esteem and children's reactions to youth sport coaching behaviors: A field study of self-enhancement processes. *Developmental Psychology, 26*, 6, 987–993.

Sports Council (1991). *A Digest of Sports Statistics for the UK*. London: Sports Council.

Sutherland, A. (1992). Physical Education and Games in Post-Primary Schools in 1991. Belfast: Sports Council Northern Ireland.

6 Sport and community background

Anthony M. Gallagher

INTRODUCTION

It is an often-stated cliché that Protestants and Catholics in Northern Ireland are divided by many things, including the sports that they play. It is possible to hear, just as often, the claim that sport provides a great unifying force in an otherwise divided society. Research evidence accumulated over a number of years would suggest that both claims are only partially true (Sugden and Bairner, 1993). To consider these and other related issues, the general patterns emerging from existing research will be explored briefly in this introductory section, while the chapter itself will provide an account of the additional insights to be gained from the SCNI survey.

Not surprisingly, the idea that Protestants and Catholics play different sports has always been linked to the fact that, in practice if not in law, separate school systems operate in Northern Ireland for the two religious communities. One of the first major studies to explore some of the consequences of separate schooling was that of Darby *et al.* (1977). Among the issues explored in the study was an examination of the type of sports that Protestant and Catholic schools offered to their pupils. Darby *et al.* (1977) found that the wide variety of sports available in schools fell into three categories. Gaelic sports, including football, hurling and camogie, were not played in any Protestant school. Rugby, cricket and hockey were popular in Protestant schools and were markedly less popular in Catholic schools, although all of them except cricket were played to some extent. The third category comprised a range of sports that were available generally across all the schools. This category included association football (soccer), tennis, netball and basketball.

The next significant contribution came from two studies which explored the curriculum of schools, based on the timetables followed by pupils. Sutherland and Gallagher (1987) found that pupils in Catholic schools spent more time on languages (mainly accounted for by the teaching of Irish) and religious education in comparison with pupils in Protestant schools. Pupils in Protestant schools, on the other hand, spent much more time on physical education than pupils in Catholic schools. This pattern was confirmed by Cormack *et al.* (1992) in their secondary analysis of a larger-scale survey of the curriculum in schools carried out by the Department of Education for Northern Ireland (DENI). However, Cormack et al., (1992) found also that this pattern of greater time being devoted to physical education in Protestant schools was more consistent, and existed to a greater extent, among pupils in grammar schools.

Sutherland (1992) provided further detail in a survey of the sports actually provided by post-primary schools just before physical education became part of the mandatory Common Curriculum. Her study provided a basis for assessing whether any change had occurred since the pioneering study of Darby *et al.* (1977). Sutherland found that, for boys up to age 16 years, differences existed between Protestant and Catholic schools in the sports offered. As in previous research, Gaelic games were commonly offered in Catholic schools but were not offered in Protestant schools. By contrast, cricket, rugby and, to a lesser extent, hockey were frequently offered in Protestant schools but in very few Catholic schools. Boys in Protestant grammar schools were offered the widest range of sports. In an echo of the earlier curriculum research, Sutherland (1992) attributed this to the greater time allocation to physical education in Protestant schools. A similar pattern emerged for girls in that camogie was offered in over half of the Catholic secondary schools and a quarter of the Catholic grammar schools but in none of the Protestant schools in the survey. Hockey was offered in almost all the Protestant schools, in about half the Catholic grammar schools, but barely a quarter of the Catholic secondary schools.

For sixth form pupils a wide range of sports was available to boys and girls in Protestant grammar schools and to boys in many Catholic grammar schools. For girls in Catholic grammar schools, and boys in Catholic secondary schools, a narrower range of options were available, while for the remainder in secondary schools the range was narrower still. In part this appeared to be explained by the enrolment of the sixth form, which was found to be small in many Protestant secondary schools. The pattern of options available for extra-curricular activity mirrored the differences highlighted above, with an emphasis, in Catholic schools, on team games. There was more use of weekends for extra-curricular sport in grammar than in secondary schools, and in Protestant rather than Catholic schools.

The final piece of evidence to be presented here is derived from a research project with a somewhat different focus. Sugden and Harvie (1995) examined the role played by sport in community relations in Northern Ireland. They were less directly interested in schools than in the views and policies of the governing bodies for sports, although clearly the context provided by physical education in schools was important. Among the conclusions offered by Sugden and Harvie (1995) was the suggestion that sports' preferences and patterns of participation are governed by cultural tradition and community affilia-tion, particularly for the major team games. They suggested also that differential sports affiliation is rooted in the system of separate Pro-testant and Catholic schools, because this provides a divided games curriculum. Further weight was given to this claim by their conclusion that sports which were not grounded in the school curriculum appeared to offer more opportunities for cross-community interaction.

They found that the use of key national symbols, including flags and anthems, allied with disputes over the representation of Northern Ireland at regional, national and international levels, can become overlain with political significance and can exacerbate tensions. Furthermore, Sugden and Harvie (1995) did not find consistent prac-tice across different sports in these areas. An important finding was their suggestion that

> Governing bodies generally believe that a considerable amount of cross-community interaction takes place in the name of sport. Under closer questioning this proves not to be the case. In fact, there is relatively little inter-community interaction fostered through sport in Northern Ireland.
>
> (p.92).

They go on to suggest that most governing bodies do not see commu-nity relations as relevant to their sports and prefer to keep away from this work because of the issues which may be provoked. By contrast the one sport which has embraced community relations, soccer, is believed to have benefited by widening its recruitment base and bring-ing in extra resources. Despite eschewing any formal commitment to community relations' aims, the sport which they felt offered one of the best examples of cross-community sport in Northern Ireland was boxing. This was attributed to its ethos and traditions, its open-door approach to recruitment and the way it is internally controlled.

THE PRESENT SURVEY

Chapters 1 and 11 provide details of the sampling frame, achieved sample and research instruments used in the SCNI survey. For the purposes of this chapter, interest focuses on similarities and differences in the research findings between young people in Protestant and Catholic schools. On the basis of previous research, as outlined above, it may be expected that a discrete range of sports will be predominantly pursued by pupils in either school type, and an additional range of sports will be common to both school types. Perhaps more interesting, however, is the evidence revealed by the survey on the broader context of sports activity by young people in what has been described as a divided society, Northern Ireland.

Regardless of the particular types of sports played, the survey allows us to examine a range of other issues including where and when young people play sports, who, if anyone, provides support and training, and the attitudes and motivations they have towards sport. These could be described as the culture of sports activity in Northern Ireland. Not only does this survey provide the first detailed opportunity to examine these issues but it also offers an alternative perspective on religious differences in social behaviour. The evidence from the survey examined below considers young people in primary and post-primary schools separately.

YOUNG PEOPLE IN PRIMARY SCHOOLS

Table 6.1 provides an overview of the pattern of responses by primary school students. When asked which sports they had tried, the only two sports mentioned by more than half of the sample were swimming (85 per cent) and soccer (59 per cent). Thereafter those attending Catholic schools were slightly more likely than those in Protestant schools to mention sports such as athletics, cycling and rounders, while students in Protestant schools more frequently mentioned field hockey. All of these sports, however, were tried by pupils in both school types. This contrasted with Gaelic football which was mentioned by 139 (31 per cent) pupils in Catholic schools but only one pupil in a Protestant school. When the question is posed in a slightly different way, that is asking pupils to identify their 'top sport', the pattern changes a little in that about a third mentioned soccer (35 per cent) and about a fifth mentioned swimming (16 per cent). Of the remaining sports, 7 per cent of pupils in Catholic schools, and half that proportion in Protestant schools, mentioned athletics, while 10 per cent of pupils in

Table 6.1 Sports available in school, attempted sports and 'top sports' for primary age students by religious affiliation of school

	Sports available in school		Sports attempted		Top sports	
	Prot.	Cath.	Prot.	Cath.	Prot.	Cath.
Association football	57.4	45.0	59.0	57.1	35.1	33.8
Athletics	16.5	27.0	14.0	27.8	3.6	7.2
Badminton	12.8	1.9	18.9	5.2	2.1	0.0
Basketball	6.6	8.1	16.6	16.0	0.0	2.3
Cricket	4.1	0.5	11.0	3.8	0.3	0.0
Field hockey	28.3	3.6	26.0	6.1	3.0	0.6
Gaelic football	0.0	31.1	0.2	31.4	0.0	10.1
Gymnastics	6.6	8.1	13.6	7.2	3.6	1.4
Hurling	0.0	6.5	0.0	10.2	0.0	1.2
Irish dancing	1.1	1.4	3.9	18.3	0.9	4.3
Netball	25.9	20.3	14.8	13.5	3.3	3.2
Rounders	17.6	20.3	19.9	25.3	1.2	2.3
Swimming	50.7	53.1	85.2	83.7	21.9	15.9
Field hockey mini	7.7	1.4	8.7	1.1	1.5	0.6

Catholic schools and no-one in Protestant schools mentioned Gaelic football.

The patterns identified above are largely consistent with those which would be expected from the existing literature, but beyond this, one of the most striking features of the survey data is the degree of similarity that exists between primary age pupils, regardless of the type of school attended. Most of them took up their sports between the ages of 5 and 7 years, about a fifth said they took their sports up because of friends or school, and an equally small proportion from each school type aspired to competitive levels of sports activity. About a quarter said that their father was the most important influence in them taking up their top sport and a slightly higher proportion described their father as the most important reason for maintaining their top sport. About two-fifths of the sample said they had received no instruction in their sports, or coaching in their sports. For those who did receive instruction and coaching a little over a fifth mentioned receiving this in school, a little under a fifth received coaching outside school and just over a tenth received coaching from a parent. The main point of interest, however, is that these patterns are almost identical for pupils from Protestant and Catholic schools.

For general sports, in fact, the only area in which differences appear between pupils in Protestant and Catholic schools lies in where they take part in their sports. Pupils in Catholic schools are slightly more likely than pupils in Protestant schools to be involved with sports clubs (12 per cent vs. 10 per cent) or outdoors (29 per cent vs. 23 per cent), while pupils in Protestant schools are slightly more likely to participate in their sports in leisure centres (14 per cent vs. 11 per cent). As the figures cited above emphasise, however, even these differences are small.

Slight differences can be found also when considering their 'top sport'. Pupils in Catholic schools were slightly more likely to practise and to compete in their 'top sport' during school hours, and were more likely to compete in a sports club. This appears to be explained by the greater likelihood of the 'top sport' of pupils in Catholic schools (often Gaelic games) being a compulsory part of physical education or games lessons. Pupils in Catholic schools were more likely than those in Protestant schools to describe a number of factors as 'very important' in maintaining their interest in their top sport; interestingly, a twin pattern exists such that these pupils were more likely to rate as 'very important' competitive aspects (winning, feeling good about performing well) and social aspects (being with friends, meeting people). However, even these differences tend to be in degree rather than in direction. The main emergent theme of similarity between pupils in Protestant and Catholic primary schools is reinforced further by the finding that over four-fifths of both groups said they found it easy to find time to engage in their 'top sport', and over two-thirds intended to keep up their 'top sport' after they had left primary school.

YOUNG PEOPLE IN POST-PRIMARY SCHOOLS

The pattern of responses of the young people from post-primary schools can be seen in Table 6.2. This table identifies the sports which were most commonly available in their schools, and also the proportion who said they had tried these sports and the proportion who described these as their top sports. For the present purposes, the most interesting feature is, once again, the relatively high degree of overlap found in sports' participation. The exceptions are the Gaelic sports, which are almost exclusively found in Catholic schools, and a few other sports, such as cricket, field hockey and Rugby Union, which are largely found in Protestant schools.

In terms of their responses to questions on sports in general, there is some indication that school-based activity is more important for

Table 6.2 Sports available in school, attempted sports and 'top sports' for post-primary age students by religious affiliation of school

| | Sports available in school | | Sports attempted | | Top sports | |
	Prot.	Cath.	Prot.	Cath.	Prot.	Cath.
Aerobics	13.9	10.9	12.2	11.6	2.4	1.1
Association football	50.9	38.9	61.5	56.3	25.1	20.8
Athletics	52.4	35.8	28.8	29.7	2.5	5.3
Badminton	50.1	22.1	49.1	30.5	5.4	2.6
Basketball	48.6	44.8	38.2	34.8	3.0	2.5
Camogie	0.0	15.9	0.0	14.5	0.0	5.2
Cricket	36.0	0.5	24.3	4.1	2.5	0.0
Field hockey	66.3	20.4	51.6	16.1	9.8	0.6
Gaelic football	0.0	41.7	1.5	37.7	0.0	12.7
Gymnastics	29.8	23.7	16.1	19.0	1.4	0.4
Hurling	0.0	22.0	0.5	16.9	0.0	1.8
Lawn tennis	23.8	13.3	30.5	22.4	1.4	2.6
Netball	35.0	46.5	31.8	42.4	8.4	7.9
Rounders	3.5	8.2	15.9	12.3	0.5	1.3
Rugby Union	25.3	0.5	20.8	2.3	8.2	0.0
Swimming	44.4	38.3	76.2	76.7	5.4	10.4

young people in Protestant schools. Thus, 42 per cent of these young people said that school was the most important reason for taking up sports, while this was so for only 33 per cent of young people in Catholic schools. Further, 40 per cent of young people in Protestant schools said their involvement with sports was school based as opposed to 38 per cent who said it was based outside school. This contrasts with the pattern for young people from Catholic schools where 49 per cent said their involvement with sports was outside school, as compared with only 30 per cent who said it was school based. In keeping with these data, a higher proportion of young people from Protestant schools said they took part in their sports in school, either as curricular or extra-curricular activity. A higher proportion of young people in Catholic schools, on the other hand, said they participated in their sports in sports clubs.

This pattern of results is replicated when considering responses regarding 'top sports'. Here we find that whereas 42 per cent of young people from Protestant schools started their top sport in school, this was so for only 26 per cent of those from Catholic schools. In fact, among the latter group almost as many said they started because of their friends as said it was because of school. This can be seen also by the fact that the largest proportion of those from Protestant schools say that their PE teacher was the most important person in maintaining their interest in their top sport, while for those in Catholic schools the most important person was their father.

The highest proportion of both groups said that they practised their top sport during school hours, or at home, but whereas school was mentioned more often by those from Protestant schools, a slightly higher proportion of those from Catholic schools mention home. In addition, those from Protestant schools were more likely to practise their top sport as extra-curricular work in school, while those from Catholic schools were more likely to practise in a club. This is seen also in relation to patterns of competing; those from Protestant schools were more likely to compete during school hours or as extra-curricular activity, while those in Catholic schools were as likely to compete in school hours as in a club. Indeed, the former said that their most important instructor was their PE teacher, while the latter said the most important instructor was their club coach.

The consistency of this pattern of results is belied only by the young people's responses to a question on the status of their 'top sport' in school; while 35 per cent of those from Protestant schools said that their top sport was compulsory at school, this was so for 43 per cent of those from Catholic schools. However, part of the explanation of the importance of school for sports in Protestant schools may be linked to the finding that 36 per cent of pupils in these schools said that their 'top sport' is available, in school, to those who are interested. By contrast, the comparable figure for pupils in Catholic schools is only 20 per cent. As a final note, one interesting consequence of the greater importance of school-based activity generally for pupils in Protestant schools is the finding that while half these young people said they would maintain their 'top sport' after leaving school, this was true for just over 60 per cent of those from Catholic schools.

DISCUSSION

Previous research on participation in sports in Northern Ireland has highlighted differences between the experience of pupils in Protestant and Catholic schools, while at the same time reminding us of the fairly high degree of commonality in the sports followed. This pattern of similarity and difference has been found in a number of studies over quite a long period of time. At this level, data from the present survey serve to confirm this general pattern. There are some sports, particularly Gaelic games, that are almost exclusively found in Catholic schools, there are a range of sports that are largely, although not usually exclusively, found in Protestant schools, and there are a wide range of sports that are found, to some extent, in all schools.

The present survey suggests that this pattern holds true for pupils in both primary and post-primary schools, although perhaps more so for the latter because of the greater concentration of activity in two sports, soccer and swimming, among the primary school pupils. Furthermore, we can see elements of this pattern when we look at the sports that are available to pupils in schools, the range of sports which they have tried at some point, or the sports which they identify as their chosen or 'top sports'.

The present survey allows us to move beyond the specific sports played in order to examine aspects of what might be considered to be the broader culture or context of participation in sports. When we do this we find an even higher degree of overlap among the experience of pupils in primary schools. For pupils in this sector there appears to be relatively little difference in where they play sports, who they play with, and who provides them with help and instruction. Similarities here certainly overshadow any differences.

However, the pattern begins to become more differentiated when we look at the responses from young people in post-primary schools. Despite the high level of commonality in the sports these young people follow, there does appear to be a marked difference in the context of sports participation. In particular, the SCNI survey suggests that school-based sports participation is more important for young people in Protestant schools, whereas participation outside school, especially in sports clubs, is more important for young people in Catholic schools. This is not to downplay the importance of school-based activity for Catholic schools but rather to highlight what may be the beginning of an institutional separation in the way these young people pursue sports. In this regard it is perhaps noteworthy that of the sports which form the most popular 'top sports' for our oldest sample, the ones with arguably the strongest post-school infrastructure are also the ones that display the higher degree of difference in participation between young people from Protestant and Catholic schools.

If our survey evidence adds to our existing picture of the nature and extent of sporting activity in Northern Ireland, how does this fit into the wider social concern of the promotion of better community relations? This will be addressed in the last section of this chapter.

SPORT AND COMMUNITY RELATIONS

To some people better community relations can only be achieved if we remain blind to ethnic or other labels that are felt to encourage difference. To others the promotion of community relations is best achieved by concentrating on those things which we have in common. Both views try to achieve harmony by downplaying or ignoring difference. It is questionable whether, in practice, difference can be subsumed in this way. Regardless, there are good grounds for believing that this represents an inappropriate approach. The main reason is that a failure to recognise difference can lead some people to fear that the distinctive aspects of their culture and heritage are being removed, and that they, and their community, are being assimilated into some artificially created melting pot. Such perceptions fuel a sense of unease and insecurity, and in the long run act as a constraint on the achievement of reconciliation. To some extent such an assimilationist approach may have informed the government's policy towards community relations in the past, but this is no longer the case (Gallagher, 1995). In saying all this, of course, it is recognised that establishing the principles of diversity and pluralism as the lodestars of community relations policy is not without difficulty or controversy. This is particularly evident in debates in the USA (see, for example, Schlesinger, 1991; Berude, 1994) and Great Britain (Gill, Mayor and Blair 1992).

In recent years government policy on community relations has been organised around three broad objectives. The first of these is to promote more opportunities for Protestants and Catholics to meet together; the second objective is to encourage greater tolerance of cultural pluralism; and the third objective is to promote equality of opportunity. To paraphrase the intentions behind this policy, we can say that community relations in Northern Ireland are about recognising and celebrating commonalities *and* differences. Furthermore, this sits within an overall framework of equity and fairness. How might this approach be enacted in a policy for sports?

Clearly each of these elements of government policy, as outlined above, has some resonance for sports policy. Equity is achieved through the fair distribution of resources and support for the different sports that operate in Northern Ireland. A fair distribution in this context will recognise that some sports are played largely within one or other of the main communities and so their comparative levels of participation will be gauged taking this into account. Community relations in sports emphatically do not mean the discouragement of 'ethnic' sports in favour of those activities engaged across all communities. It is necessary, in other words, to recognise the divergent cultural influences that have helped to shape the world of sport in Northern Ireland, glimpses of the development of which we can see in the survey evidence discussed above.

The legitimation of difference may, however, carry with it a responsibility to encourage further opportunities for contact between Protestants and Catholics through sport. The simplest and most obvious way to achieve this is through the sporting activities commonly practised by young people from both communities, and here soccer becomes an obvious candidate. In addition, however, it would be of value for the various sports authorities to consider ways in which they can contribute to bridge building. This could be achieved by broadening the range of experience of trainees in the main teacher training colleges to include sports activities they themselves may not have tried in their own schools. If the colleges are unable to provide this wider experience within their own resources, then students could spend some time in the other college to gain this experience, building on contact work which is already carried out by the two teacher training colleges in Belfast. Alternatively, or perhaps in addition, the authorities of particular sports bodies conceivably could consider ways in which to package a version of their sport so that teachers who have no experience of that activity would be able to pick up the basic rules and hence organise games for their pupils; the relative lack of participation in mini-sport or alternative versions of various sports was a very noticeable feature of the survey. Such organised packages of materials have worked successfully in other areas of the curriculum, so there seems every reason to believe that the same approach could be used for sports.

The key lies in the effort people are willing to make. A plural society is one which consciously sets out to include all the diverse groups that make up its population and encourages the diversity of cultural forms arising from those communities. Sport is an important cultural activity not only because of the large number of participants but also because of the even larger number of spectators. The SCNI Survey confirms a picture such that schools in Northern Ireland provide part of the basis for community-based sporting activity, alongside other sports that are shared across all communities. If we are to build a successful plural society in Northern Ireland then we should welcome, encourage and support this diversity, while building bridges and making connections where these are appropriate. This is the challenge for Northern Irish society. Sports bodies of every type can and should contribute to the achievement of this challenge. Our young people deserve no less.

REFERENCES

Berude, M.R. (1994). *American School Reform: Progressive, Equity and Excellence Movements, 1883–1993*. New York: Praeger.

Cormack, R.J., Gallagher, A.M. and Osborne, R.D. (1992). *Secondary Analysis of the DENI Curriculum Survey. Annex F, Annual Report of the Standing Advisory Commission on Human Rights. House of Commons Paper 54*. London: HMSO.

Darby, J., Dunn, S., Murray, D., Farren, S., Batts, D. and Harris, J. (1977). *Education and Community in Northern Ireland: Schools Apart?* Coleraine: Centre for the Study of Conflict.

Gallagher, A.M. (1995). The approach of government: Community relations and equity. In S. Dunn (ed.) *Facets of the Conflict in Northern Ireland*. London: Macmillan.

Gill, D., Mayor, B. and Blair, M. (eds) (1992). *Racism and Education: Structures and Strategies*. London: Open University/Sage.

Schlesinger Jr, A.M. (1991). *The Disuniting of America: Reflections on a Multicultural Society*. New York: Whittle.

Sugden, J. and Bairner, A. (1993). *Sport, Sectarianism and Society in a Divided Ireland*. Leicester: Leicester University Press.

Sugden, J. and Harvie, S. (1995). *Sport and Community Relations in Northern Ireland*. Coleraine: Centre for the Study of Conflict.

Sutherland, A.E. (1992). *Physical Education and Games in Post-Primary Schools in 1991*. Belfast: Sports Council for Northern Ireland.

Sutherland, A.E. and Gallagher, A.M. (1987). *Pupils in the Border Band*. Belfast: Northern Ireland Council for Educational Research.

7   Time for sport? Activity diaries of young people

Karen Trew

INTRODUCTION

This chapter is based on four-day diary records which were completed by almost half of the post-primary school students who participated in the SCNI survey. The diaries recorded the students' main activities out of school hours during term time and complemented the questionnaire by providing the following:

- An independent basis for establishing the time devoted to sport by young people with differing levels of commitment to competitive sport.
- A record of the relative importance of sport in the daily lives of young people based on the time devoted to sport compared with the time spent on both leisure and work activities outside school hours.
- An insight into differences and similarities in the leisure pursuits of males and females of different ages outside school hours.

The time devoted to specific leisure activities by young people has been of interest to researchers concerned with adolescent lifestyles (for example, Meeks and Mauldin, 1990; Fine, Mortimer and Roberts, 1993) and the impact of social background on development (for example, Whyte, 1995), as well as those who study young people's involvement in sport and physical recreation (for example, Reeder *et al.*, 1991).

The use of a diary to record time use has been seen as a prime example of the 'micro behavioural' approach to survey research. Reviews of this methodology (for example, Robinson, 1988; Harvey, 1990) highlight the range of large national and international studies which have employed time budgets to investigate the use of time and the relationship between the use of discretionary time and attitudes towards the chosen activities. As Robinson concludes:

time-diary data ... have shown that there seems to be a clear relation between general attitudes toward activities and time spent on
those activities as reported independently in time diaries.

(Robinson, 1988, p,142)

The time budget studies usually involve participants recording the
sequence, duration and context (for example, location) of all their
activities for at least 24 hours. Analyses of time budget data are
usually based on classification systems which enable researchers to
employ fine-grained categories for areas of specific interest (for example, travel) to the research team. A number of methodological studies,
cited by Robinson, provide evidence of the reliability and validity of
this form of time-diary survey and analysis. Furthermore, Meeks and
Mauldin (1990) note that children on average give as much information in time diaries as adults.

As Harvey (1990) argues, time diaries are essentially neutral since
they permit the recording of the flow of events. However, the categorisation and coding of these reports is usually determined by the focus
and the scope of the investigation. In this chapter the method of
analysis and reporting of the quantitative data, which were derived
from the diary records, has been focused mainly, but not exclusively,
on sport.

THE SAMPLE

Diaries and questionnaires were made available for 602 students.
Table 7.1 summarises some of the key characteristics of these students.

As Table 7.1 indicates, the sample included equal numbers of males
and females and grammar and secondary school students. Grammar
schools were therefore slightly overrepresented in the subsample, as
were Catholic schools. Of the diary writers 58 per cent were attending
Catholic schools whereas only a third were attending Protestant or

Table 7.1 Sample characteristics

Gender:	50% males, 50% females
Age:	Age range 11–19; mean age =14.00
Type of school:	47% grammar, 47% secondary, 6% comprehensive
Religion of school:	32% Protestant, 58% Catholic, 11% integrated
Key stages:	52% Key Stage 3, 34% Key Stage 4, 14% sixth form
Education Board:	21% Belfast, 18% North Eastern, 17% South Eastern, 27% Western, 18% Southern
Sport involvement:	8% no sport, 44% basic, 44% competitive, 4% Élite

controlled schools and 11 per cent were attending integrated schools. The students were from all areas of Northern Ireland, as represented by the five Education and Library Boards (these boards control education in five regions in Northern Ireland, under the aegis of the Department of Education for Northern Ireland). Half of the students were at Key Stage 3 (post-primary classes 1–3), a third at Key Stage 4 (post-primary classes 4–5) and 14 per cent were in the sixth form.

The categorisation of the students' levels of sport involvement was based on their identified top sport: 8 per cent (21 males and 29 females) had no top sport, 44 per cent reported that they were involved in their sport at a basic level, 44 per cent were involved at competitive club level and 4 per cent (13 males and 11 females) were involved in their top sport at an élite level. These 24 young people were involved in 14 sports, with three sports attracting three players (soccer, Gaelic football, netball) and four sports attracting two players (athletics, camogie, judo, Irish dancing). Each of the remainder of the sample who reported that they played at an élite level followed a different sport (namely, boxing, hurling, gymnastics, field hockey, lawn tennis and contemporary dancing).

THE DIARY

The survey interviewers asked pupils to complete a diary for four days, including Saturday and Sunday and two weekdays, before they came to the interviews. At this stage the young people should have had no idea that we were interested in sports participation. There were 2,386 days of diary records but the sampled days were not balanced across the week. Table 7.2 shows that there were very few diaries completed on Wednesdays and, as requested, Saturdays and Sundays were included in most of the students' diaries.

Table 7.2 also shows the distribution of diaries across the school year. No diaries were completed during the summer holidays (July and August) or during the Christmas and Easter breaks. The majority (76 per cent) of diaries were completed between October and March but a fifth of the diaries were completed in the summer term from April to June.

Diarists were asked to indicate whether the weather was mainly sunny, mixed sun and rain or mainly raining. The weather was recorded on 2,194 diary records and 31 per cent of these days were described as 'mainly sunny', 51 per cent as 'mixed' and only 18 per cent as 'mainly raining'.

Table 7.2 Distribution of diary records by day of the week and month

Day of the week	Number of diaries	%	Month	Number of diaries	%
Monday	278	12	January	232	10
Tuesday	207	9	February	315	13
Wednesday	68	3	March	412	17
Thursday	303	13	April	162	7
Friday	387	16	May	312	13
Saturday	574	24	June	41	2
Sunday	569	24	September	48	2
			October	216	9
			November	344	15
			December	266	11

The diary was semi-structured, with students given the following instructions:

> We are asking you to fill in this diary for two school days and two days when you are not at school. You have been chosen as one of many pupils who will be asked to fill in these diaries so that we can have a clear idea about how young people are spending their time outside school hours and in break. We are not interested in the details of the activities but just the main sort of things you find worthwhile. You will not be asked to put your name on the diary but we will be asking you some questions about some of your activities so we can get a clear picture of what is important to young people like you.

There was one page for each day. On each diary day, the students were asked to note the times when they got up, had their main meals and went to bed. In recording their behaviour, they were asked to note the times when they started and ended each activity, where they were and who they were with. The school days were divided into before school, break time and after school. The weekend days were divided by meal times (see Appendix 7.1).

The diaries were checked after the interviews with the students and any problems noted. Figure 7.1 is an example of a four-day diary completed by a boy from a Catholic secondary school and Figure 7.2 the four-day diary of a girl from a Protestant secondary school.

The bracketed behaviours in the example diary record (for example, 'I went for my lunch') were not coded. Most of these activities can be classified as maintenance activities and were not of primary

Activity	Time	Where	Who with
THURSDAY MARCH 3rd	Get up time 7.30		
Dinner time (I went for my lunch)			
Then I played a game of football	13.05–13.30	School	Friends
After school I did my homework	16.00–17.00	Home	Alone
(I got my dinner)			
I went out to play football	17.25–18.35	Home	Friends
I watched TV	19.00–20.00	Home	Family
(I went for a bath)			
Did some more homework	8.50–10.00	Home	Alone
Bedtime 10.20 Weather: some sun/some rain			
FRIDAY MARCH 4th	Get up time 7.45		
Dinner time (I had my lunch)			
I played football	13.10–13.30	School	Friends
After school (I got my dinner)			
I watch TV	17.00–17.30	Home	Family
I did my homework	17.30–18.30	Home	Alone
I got my bike and went for a cycle	19.00–19.45	Home	Friends
I did more homework	19.45–20.45	Home	Family
I watched TV	20.50–12.00	Home	Family
Bedtime 12.00 Weather: mainly raining			
SATURDAY MARCH 5th	Get up time 12.30 p.m.		
(I went and got my breakfast)			
(I went for a wash)			
I went for a ride on my bike	13.20–14.00	Home	Friends
I went out for a game of football	14.00–14.25	Home	Family
I watch the TV	14.25–15.00	Home	Family
After lunch (I went out with my friends)			
I watch TV	16.50–17.15	Home	Alone
I went out for a game of football	17.15–18.00	Home	Friends
After tea			
I played the computer	18.00–19.25	Home	Family
I went to Mass	19.25–20.30	Home	Alone
I watch TV	20.30–23.00	Home	Family
Bedtime 23.00 Weather: Some sun/some rain			
SUNDAY MARCH 6th	Get up time 9.30 a.m.		
(I got up and had my breakfast–I went for a wash–I left for football practice)			
I togged out and we had our practice	10.50–12.30	Town	Friends
I left for home			
After lunch (I went for a rest)			
I watched TV	15.00–16.30	Home	Family
I played football	16.30–17.15	Home	Friends
I watched TV	17.15–18.00	Home	Family
After tea			
I watched TV	18.30–20.00	Home	Family
I played the computer	20.00–20.30	Home	Alone
I went for a walk	20.30–21.30	Home	Friend
I watched TV	21.30–22.45	Home	Family
Bedtime 22.50			

Figure 7.1 Example diary (boy, Catholic secondary school)

Activity	Time	Where	Who with
FRIDAY MARCH 11th	Get up time 7.45		
Dinner time (Walked around school, talked with friends)			
After school (Walked home, had a snack)			
Did homework	16.05–17.00	At Home	Alone
After tea			
Washed dishes	18.30–19.00	At Home	Brother
Tidied bedroom	19.00–19.20	At Home	Alone
Watched TV	19.25–22.00	At Home	Family
(Got ready and went to bed)			
Bedtime 10.30 Weather: some sun/some rain			
SATURDAY: MARCH 12th	Get up time 10.00		
(Got washed and dressed, Ate breakfast, washed hair, went into town)			
Dinner time			
Looked around shops	13.30–14.20	In town	Friend
Played tapes	14.45–15.15	At Home	Friend
Played game gear	15.20–16.00	At Home	Friend
Watched TV	16.00–17.05	At Home	Friend
After tea			
Watched TV	17.45–18.30	At Home	Family
Played badminton	19.00–19.30	Youth club	Friends
Played table tennis	19.35–20.00	Youth club	Friends
Played on Bouncy castle	20.05–21.15	Youth club	Friends
(Home/Bed)			
Bedtime 11.00 Weather: mainly raining			
SUNDAY MARCH 13th	Get up time 9.45		
(Got washed and dressed, ate breakfast)			
Went to church	10.30–13.00	Church	Friends/family
Watched TV	13.30–14.10	At Home	Family
After lunch			
Washed dishes	14.35–14.50	At Home	Alone
Did homework	14.55–15.30	At Home	Alone
Read book	15.30–16.00	At Home	Alone
Watched TV	16.05–17.20	At Home	Alone
After tea			
Tidy bedroom	18.00–18.20	At Home	Alone
Listened to radio	18.20–19.30	At Home	Sister
Watched TV	19.35–21.00	At Home	Family
(talked on phone, had supper and went to bed)			
Bedtime 22.00 Weather: Some sun/some rain			
MONDAY MARCH 14th	Get up time 7.30 a.m		
Dinner time (Walked around in playground, talked to friends)			
After school (Walked home)			
Did homework	15.45–16.30	At Home	Alone
Watched TV	16.30–17.30	At Home	Brother
After tea			
Wash dishes	18.30–19.00	At Home	Alone
Hoover bedroom	19.00–19.15	At Home	Alone
I went for a walk	19.20–20.30	At Home	Family
Watched TV			
Bedtime 21.00			

Figure 7.2 Example diary (girl, Protestant secondary school)

interest in this study. Other reported activities were not classified if the diary entry was vague and non-specific (for example, 'went out', 'chatted to friends') or referred to a very trivial event (for example, 'went for message to shop for mother', 'walking around playground').

The main activities were coded using the 116 sports categories which had been used for the main survey (see Chapter 1), plus an additional 25 categories for the main types of non-sport activities (see Appendix 7.2). In practice, 66 sports were coded. Appendix 7.2 lists the 51 sports which were not identified in any diaries. Most of these are esoteric sports (for example, aikido, croquet), adult sports which require specialist equipment (for example, sub aqua, parachuting, hang gliding) or mini-sports. There was no obvious explanation as to why none of the diarists reported involvement with rowing, Scottish dancing or volleyball.

There was a maximum of 10 coded activities per day or 40 per four-day diary. In practice, an average of 16 activities and the associated time, place and accompanying people codes were recorded in the 602 four-day diaries. The method of coding can be illustrated using the boy's diary shown in Figure 7.1. The first activity 1, on the first day, was football, which started at 13.05 and ended at 13.30. He carried out the activity at school with friends. The boy recorded five coded activities on the first day including another session of football from 17.25 to 18.35. This means that football has a frequency of 2 for that day and he spent a total of 1 hour 35 minutes playing football. Homework also had a frequency of 2 and he spent 2 hours 10 minutes on this activity. The next day he only played football for 20 minutes but he went out on his bike, watched television and did homework. On Saturday, he played football and watched television and rode on his bike but he also played on his computer and went to Mass.

This coding scheme enabled us to present the frequency of reporting each activity across the four diary days, the mean time per student devoted to the activities during the four days, and the percentage of respondents who carried out the activities at any time during their four diary days. It also enabled us to establish where specific activities occurred and who was involved with the diarists when they carried out their activities. In this chapter, these measures have been used to compare groups differing in gender and sports involvement. Individual activity times are then used to establish whether groups of students can be identified who have adopted different patterns of activities or lifestyles.

RESULTS

Overall frequency of activities

A total of 9,494 activities were recorded by the 602 students in their diaries. The most frequently mentioned activity, as shown in Table 7.3, was watching television, which accounted for 32 per cent of all the recorded activities. Most diarists reported at least one period of television viewing on each of their diary days.

Television viewing could feature twice in one evening if the diarist went away from the television to do homework or go out. Homework was also a frequently mentioned diary activity and was referred to more than once in the majority of diaries. Football was widely reported as a break-time and lunch-break activity as well as an activity for after school. Most diarists reported 'playing football' without specifying the nature of their activity; hence they could have been referring to a variety of ball games including soccer, Gaelic football, rugby or merely kicking a ball in the street. Given the respondents' lack of specificity, perhaps in turn reflecting the general nature of this play, it was decided to include a generic term 'football' to capture these various activities involving feet and a ball.

Table 7.3 The 20 most frequent activities (sport and non-sport)

Activity	Count	% of responses
Watch TV/video	3,024	32
Homework/revision	1,377	15
Football	801	8
Home computing	576	6
Listen to music	431	5
Church	409	4
Work incl. farm	318	3
Walking/running	245	3
Reading/writing	213	2
Help housework	205	2
Shopping	171	2
Youth clubs	134	1
Non-organised games	127	1
Party/outing/trip	113	1
Swimming	110	1
Play/sing music	98	1
Disco dancing	80	1
Voluntary work	77	1
Cycling	74	1
Extra curricular	71	1

Table 7.4: Top 20 activities (sport)

Activity	Count	% of responses
Football	801	8.4
Swimming	110	1.2
Disco dancing	80	0.8
Keep fit	50	0.5
Riding	47	0.5
Billiards/snooker	32	0.3
Netball	32	0.3
Jogging	27	0.3
Badminton	26	0.3
Lawn tennis	26	0.3
Golf	24	0.3
Squash rackets	21	0.2
Athletics	18	0.2
Pool	18	0.2
Irish dancing	18	0.2
Rounders	17	0.2
Hurling	14	0.1
Darts	14	0.1

Some of the frequently reported activities involve physical effort but they are not included among the list of recognised sports. These include walking/running and cycling which are categorised as general activities rather than sports. Table 7.4, which shows the top 20 sport activities, reveals that there were only three sporting activities which accounted for more than 0.5 per cent of the reported activities. These were football, swimming and disco dancing. Although disco dancing is classified as a sporting activity, it was not always clear whether the young person was simply attending a disco or actually involved in competitive disco dancing, but almost certainly the former rather than the latter. This 'sporting' category may therefore be somewhat artificial, irrespective of the physical energy expended in this activity!

As the vast majority of categories were not widely used it was appropriate to combine some of the specific activities into more global categories for further analysis. Five of the six most frequently reported activities ('Watching television', 'Homework', 'Church', 'Computing', and listening to 'Music') were retained, together with three other general activity categories which subsumed all other specific activities. These general categories were 'Sport' (football, together with the other 65 sporting activities included in the diaries), 'Work' (voluntary work, paid work and housework) and 'Non-sport' (all other non-sport activities ranging from reading to youth club).

Number of diarists engaging in activities

In addition to reducing the original 142 activity categories to eight, the data were further compressed by combining the activities reported in the four daily diaries for each student to produce a mean activity count for each diarist. This procedure enabled us to determine the percentage of the sample who had reported carrying out each of the activities in any of the four days, as shown in Table 7.5.

Table 7.5: Percentage of diarists mentioning activities at least once

Activity	Males %	Females %	All %
Television	91	90	90
Homework	76	87	81
Sport	85	67	76
Other activities	65	83	74
Church	51	63	57
Work	35	52	43
Music	32	46	39
Computing	47	24	35

Nine out of 10 of the diarists mentioned that they watched television at some time during the four days of their diary records. Those who did not mention television viewing may not have watched television but it seems more probable that they did not record their television viewing. For example, one male diarist, who did not mention television viewing, confined his entries to 'swimming', 'jogging' 'go to the tuckshop' or 'nothing'. His diary entries were clearly incomplete and they serve to highlight some of the potential shortcomings of the data. Nevertheless while the absolute level of responding may not be an accurate reflection of the extent of television viewing in the sample, the relative frequencies of reporting the eight activities would seem to reflect the relative engagement of young people in these types of activities.

Reported television viewing was equally popular with males and females, whereas more boys (85 per cent) than girls (67 per cent) reported some involvement in sport. Given the possibility that activities may have been underreported in the completion of the diary records it is surprising that as many as three-quarters of all diarists report some involvement in sporting activities outside school hours. Similarly, a suprisingly high percentage of boys (47 per cent) but not girls (24 per cent) reported using the computer at least once in their diary records. In contrast, more girls than boys reported activities which were categorised as 'Non-sporting activities', 'Homework', 'Church attendance', 'Music' or 'Work related'.

Overall, over three-quarters of the young people reported that they watched television, engaged in a sporting activity and worked on homework at least once in their four-day diary. Over half of all the students reported carrying out non-sport activities and attending church and over half of the females, but just over a third of the males reported some work-related activity in their diaries. Musical activities were less widely reported but they were mentioned by four out of ten of the diarists.

Time spent on activities

The average time spent on each of the activities is based on the sum of the total times spent on the activity across the four diary days divided by the total sample number. The average activity time is therefore strongly influenced by the number of students who report that activity. For example, if 100 students spent six hours each on an activity over the four diary days, the average or mean time for the sample (600/602) would be one hour. Another way to establish the relative time spent on an activity is to examine the median for a category. This measure of central tendency is the value above which and below which half of the cases fall. Table 7.6 reports the mean, median, standard deviation and minimum and maximum times spent on each of the eight categories of behaviour over the four days and Figure 7.3 displays the distribution of the time spent on sport.

Viewing television was the most frequently reported activity and was also the activity to which most time was devoted across the four diary days. On average, the diarists recorded almost six hours of

Table 7.6 Total hours spent on activities–summary statistics

Activity	Mean	Standard deviation	Median	Minimum	Maximum
Television	5.52	4.10	4.95	0	25.2
Sport	3.74	3.98	3.00	0	28.2
Other	3.07	3.32	2.08	0	22.3
Homework	2.85	3.02	2.00	0	19.7
Work	2.41	4.43	0.00	0	23.0
Computing	1.02	1.99	0.00	0	14.2
Church	0.74	0.91	0.75	0	8.5
Music	0.94	1.88	0.00	0	24.0

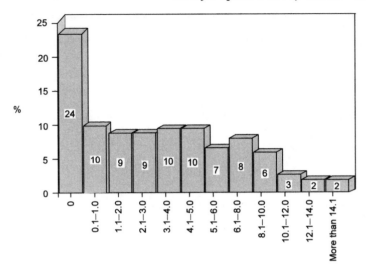

Figure 7.3 Percentage of total diary time devoted to sport

television viewing across four days. The most dedicated viewer recorded 25 hours of television viewing or over six hours per day.

The average time devoted to sport was 3.7 hours across the four days. Figure 7.3 shows that this is derived from a wide spread of involvement in sport ranging from 24 per cent of the sample who did not spend any time during their diary days on sport, to the 13 per cent of the sample who spent eight or more hours engaged in some sporting activity during the four diary days.

The mean times for each of the eight major activity categories reported by boys and girls according to their reported level of sports attainment are shown in Table 7.7. Boys reported a mean of 21.0 hours of activities, while girls reported 19.7 hours. Both genders spent similar mean times watching television and on work-related activities but girls devoted significantly more time than boys to 'Homework' (3.4 vs. 2.4 hours), 'Church' activities (0.8 vs. 0.6 hours) 'Music-related' activities (1.1 vs. 0.8 hours) and other 'Non-sports' pastimes (3.6 vs. 2.5 hours). Males reported significantly more time than females on 'Computing' (1.6 vs. 0.4 hours) and sport (4.9 vs. 2.6 hours).

As expected the time spent on sport was also closely related to the level of sports involvement. The 13 élite sportsmen reported that they spent double the time (6.7 hours) involved in sport than the males who had no top sport (3.3 hours). Similarly, the 11 girls who participated in sport at an élite level devoted 3.8 hours to sport compared with the

Table 7.7 Mean activity time by gender and level of sports involvement

	Sport	Work	TV	Home-work	Comput-ing	Church	Music	Other	Total
Males:									
no sport	3.3	2.2	6.2	3.3	1.9	1.0	0.8	3.1	21.7
basic	3.9	3.4	5.5	1.8	1.8	0.6	0.6	2.5	20.0
competitive	5.7	2.0	5.9	2.5	1.6	0.6	0.9	2.4	21.5
élite	6.7	0.8	5.1	3.0	0.6	0.4	0.3	3.2	20.0
All males	4.9	2.4	5.8	2.4	1.6	0.6	0.8	2.5	21.0
Females:									
no sport	1.7	4.9	5.9	4.3	0.2	0.5	1.5	2.8	21.8
basic	2.0	2.3	5.8	3.2	0.4	1.0	1.2	3.7	19.7
competitive	3.5	2.1	4.5	3.3	0.4	0.7	1.0	3.5	18.9
élite	3.8	2.2	4.5	4.3	0.5	0.7	0.9	6.0	22.9
All females	2.6	2.4	5.3	3.4	0.4	1.0	1.1	3.6	19.7
All	3.7	2.4	5.5	2.9	1.0	0.7	0.9	3.1	20.3

1.7 hours reported by the 21 girls with no top sport. It is notable, however, that the élite females devoted less time on average to sport than the males who had attained only a basic level in their top sport.

One explanation for the variation in mean time spent in sporting activities by boys and girls at the same level of attainment could be that a greater proportion of girls than boys did not participate in sports during the diary period. This is a partial explanation, as Table 7.8 indicates. Although all of those who played sport at an élite level reported some sports activities, more females than males at other levels of sporting attainment did not report sporting activities in their diaries. Table 7.8 also illustrates the association between reported level of sports attainment and time spent engaged in sporting activities which is reflected in the mean times devoted to sport (Table 7.7) as well as the percentage participation rates.

Not only was level of sports involvement related to the time spent on sport but there was also a significant relationship between level of

Table 7.8: Percentage reporting sporting activity by gender and level of sports involvement

	No top sport %	Basic level %	Competitive %	Élite %
Males	79	76	90	100
Females	57	61	75	100

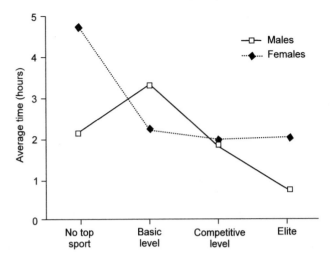

Figure 7.4 Mean time spent on work-related activities by gender and level of sports involvement

sports involvement and time spent on homework. From Table 7.7 it is apparent that time spent on sport is not taken at the expense of home-work time but that those who have attained an élite level in their sports and those with no 'top sport' spend more time on homework than those involved with sport at either a basic or competitive level.

The level of sports involvement was not related statistically to the time spent on music, computing or other non-sporting activities but there was a relationship between the level of sports involvement, gender and time spent on work-related activities. Figure 7.4 and Table 7.7 show that boys with a basic level of involvement in sport devote more time to work-related activities than males with both more and less involvement in sport. In contrast, girls at all levels of involve-ment with a 'top sport' showed a similar commitment to work-related activities. However, those with no top sport spent on average over twice as long as their peers on work-related tasks.

Table 7.9 presents a more fine-grained analysis of the relationships between level of involvement in sport and differing types of work. It tabulates the time spent on voluntary work, helping with housework and paid work, which includes work on the family farm as well as work outside the home.

The level of involvement in sport was not related to the time spent on voluntary work, housework or paid work. It was notable, however, that no boys or girls involved in sport at an élite level spent time on

Table 7.9 Mean times spent on work-related activities by gender and level of sports involvement

| | Voluntary work | | | Housework | | | Paid work | | |
	Male	Female	All	Male	Female	All	Male	Female	All
No top sport	0.14	1.63	0.78	0.46	0.20	0.35	1.55	3.03	2.19
Basic level	0.13	0.13	0.45	0.30	0.46	0.40	2.97	1.25	1.88
Competitive level	0.12	0.57	0.30	0.16	0.64	0.35	1.70	0.92	1.39
Élite	0.00	0.00	0.00	0.10	0.50	0.28	0.65	1.66	1.11

voluntary work during the diary period. In contrast, girls with no top sport spent an average of 1.6 hours on voluntary work during the diary period, as compared with the 0.14 hours of voluntary work reported by boys with no top sport.

In general, girls spent more time than boys on housework as well as voluntary work but boys spent longer than girls on paid work. Overall, the time spent on paid work decreased as the involvement in sport increased but this relationship was not statistically significant.

In summary, evidence from the time-based data derived from the diaries indicates that sport has an important role in the out-of-school activities of the majority of young people but as other research studies (for example, Meeks and Mauldin, 1990; Fine, Mortimer and Roberts, 1993) have demonstrated, it is more important for males than females. It would seem that time spent on sporting activities replaces voluntary work rather than homework, television or other non-sports pastimes.

Sporting activities: location and participants

In order to establish where the young people took part in sport, all activities on each of the four diary days which had been categorised as sport were found and the location of each of these sporting activities was identified. These locations were then aggregated for all students as shown in Table 7.10.

As Table 7.10 shows, a quarter of the sporting activities reported in the diaries took place at school. The diarists were not only engaged in sport in their own schools but also in schools they visited as team members. However, the vast majority of school-based sports involved boys playing football either before class or at break time. Almost a fifth of the sporting activities were home based. These included playing outside the home but also activities such as those of the female grammar school student who noted in her diary 'weight trained' and 'worked out' at home.

Table 7.10 Reported locations of sporting activities

Location	Count	%
School	398	23.8
Home	306	18.3
Youth/leisure centre	152	9.1
Park/field	138	8.2
Sports club	116	6.9
Street	114	6.8
Entertainment centre	98	5.9
Football pitch/tennis court	94	5.6
Swimming pool	41	2.4
Outdoors	37	2.2
Friend's house	24	1.4
Laser Quest	17	1.0
Others	35	2.1
Not specified	104	6.2
Total	1,674	99.9

Only 7 per cent of sporting activities were carried out in a sports club. Finer-grained analysis indicates that 19 of the sports activities associated with a club involved playing pool, snooker or billiards, 14 referred to horse riding, 12 football, 10 athletics, 8 golf and 4 squash. The other sporting activities located in a club (for example, lawn tennis, basketball, cycling, keep fit) occurred less frequently. Three-quarters of the sporting activities located on a football pitch or tennis court were football, with only two references to tennis.

Table 7.11 summarises the diarists' reported companions when they were involved in sporting activity. As with Table 7.10, frequencies refer to activities, not students. Over two-thirds of the sporting activities involved fellow pupils or friends and a further 7 per cent of the activities involved siblings. This means that at least three-quarters of the sporting activities were perceived as involving peers only, but it is clear from the diary entries that some of these activities must have included adults (for example, matches against other schools). A coach or teacher was specifically mentioned for only eight of the 1,532 activities categorised as sport-oriented.

A coach was involved with diarists who were playing netball (2), badminton (1), football (1), athletics (1) and 'Other sports' (3). In contrast with the eight sporting activities in which the diarist was with a coach or teacher, there were 23 occasions when diarists reported being with a music teacher and 19 when the diarists were engaged in other non-sporting activities with a coach or teacher.

Table 7.11 Reported companions for sporting activities

Companion	Count	%
No-one	155	10.1
Sister/brother	107	7.0
Father/mother	21	1.4
Whole family	66	4.3
Other relation	12	0.8
Fellow pupils/friends	1,042	68.0
Coach/teacher	8	0.5
Unknown	121	7.9
Total responses	1,532	100.0

ACTIVITY PATTERNS

Although the diary records provide a rich source of information on the activities of young people, the account is limited by its reliance on aggregated information and univariate statistical analysis. Further analysis was therefore carried out in order to establish the relationships among the activities for individual diarists. This analysis aimed to develop a typology of leisure activities which would enable us to examine the characteristics of young people who had adopted differing patterns of activities and specifically to establish if there were identifying characteristics of those who had chosen to devote a high proportion of their out-of-school time to sport.

Cluster analysis

As part of their study of the daily life of the unemployed, Kilpatrick and Trew (1985) showed that activity times derived from diary records could be used to identify groups of diarists with similar patterns of time use. They used the technique known as cluster analysis to sort their sample into groups of relatively homogeneous cases or clusters. Cluster analysis is a statistical procedure that identifies homogeneous groups or clusters of cases based on their similarity of values in relation to a specified set of variables. It was used in the present study to identify groups of students with similar lifestyles in order to assess if clear patterns of leisure activities could be found for young people and if these lifestyles were related to either biographical characteristics (for example, gender, age, school involvement in sport) or psychological effect (for example, global self-worth). Following the procedure adopted by Kilpatrick and Trew (1985), the variables used

Table 7.12 Characteristics of clusters by mean time on categories of behaviour

	Cluster 1 Non-sports	Cluster 2 Sports	Cluster 3 Passive	Cluster 4 Work	Sig.[†]
No. in group	147	110	266	79	
Sport	2.66	**10.00**	2.11	2.53	***
Work	1.25	0.51	0.95	**12.15**	***
Television	**10.83**	4.80	3.15	4.61	***
Homework	**3.70**	2.37	2.50	3.09	***
Computing	1.35	1.36	0.83	0.58	**
Church	0.71	0.58	0.81	0.76	NS
Music	0.97	0.55	**1.20**	0.50	**
Other	**3.73**	1.77	3.59	1.90	***

[†] The significance values relate to F-tests
***$p < 0.001$ **$p < 0.01$
NS = Not significant

for the cluster analysis in this study were the aggregate time each diarist reported for the eight categories of behaviour.[1]

The cluster analysis provided four main clusters. The characteristics of these clusters are defined by the mean times for each of the activities and the variables which show the greatest contrast between the different groups. The mean times for seven of the eight behaviour categories varied significantly between the four clusters (see Table 7.12), church attendance being the only category which did not vary across the groups of young people. Students from the four groups spent an average of 30 to 40 minutes in church during their diary period.

Cluster 1, made up of 147 students, is characterised by long hours in front of the television but the members of this group also spent more time than those in other groups on homework and other non-sport activities. This cluster has been labelled the 'Non-sports' cluster. Cluster 2, which includes 110 students, is typified by the time the members spent on sport activities; hence it has been named the 'Sports' cluster. Cluster 3 is the largest and the least clearly defined cluster. It includes 266 members who are characterised by the length of time they spent listening to music. Generally, members of this cluster spent the least time on sport, and television. The cluster was therefore called the 'Passive' cluster. Finally, cluster 4 is notable for the time spent on work which was an average of 12.15 hours compared with the 30 minutes spent by those in the 'Sports' cluster or around one hour by those in the 'Non-sports' (1.15 hours) and 'Passive' (0.95 hours) clusters. Cluster 4 is called the 'Work' cluster.

Background characteristics

The gender, age, school religion and level of sports involvement of members of the four clusters were as shown in Table 7.13.

Four out of five of those in the 'Sport' cluster were male while the 'Work' and 'Non-sports' clusters included almost equal numbers of males and females and the 'Passive' cluster was predominantly female. The 'Sport' cluster was also distinguished by including a higher proportion of members from Catholic schools than other clusters; only a quarter of the cluster were attending Protestant schools as compared with almost a third of the total sample.

In the sample as a whole, approximately half of the students were at Key Stage 3 with approximately a third at Key Stage 4 and 14 per cent in the sixth form. This distribution was reflected broadly in the age profile of the 'Non-sports', 'Sport' and 'Passive' clusters, but the majority of the members of the 'Work' cluster were at least at Key Stage 4 or in the sixth form.

Table 7.13 shows that a majority of those in the 'Sports' cluster reported that they were involved in their 'top sport' at either competitive or élite levels with less than a quarter of the members of this cluster reporting that they played sport at a basic level. In contrast,

Table 7.13 Biographical characteristics of students in the four clusters

	Group 1 Non-sports %	Group 2 Sports %	Group 3 Passive %	Group 4 Work %	Sig.[†]
Gender:					
% females	5	19	62	50	
% males	95	81	38	50	***
Age:					
% key stage 3	48	56	59	27	
% key stage 4	34	37	31	42	
% sixth form	18	6	10	32	***
School religion:					
% Protestant	31	25	34	37	
% Catholic	60	68	52	58	
% integrated	9	7	15	5	*
Sport level:					
% no sport	10	4	7	14	
% basic	46	24	48	54	
% competitive	42	65	41	30	
% élite	2	8	4	1	***

[†] Significance relates to chi-square values: *** $p < 0.001$, * $p < 0.05$

those involved in sport at a basic level comprised at least 46 per cent of the members of other clusters. It should be noted, however, that although seven of the boys who were involved in sport at an élite level were included in the 'Sport' cluster, only two of the 11 girls were in this group. Six girls and five boys who reported that they were involved in their top sport at an élite level were included in the 'Passive' cluster.

Activity patterns and psychological affect

The relationship between activity patterns and psychological health was examined in order to establish if there was an association between active involvement in sport or other activities and mental health, as suggested by numerous authors (Hendry, 1983; Willis and Campbell, 1993). Self-worth was used as an indicator of psychological health in the present study. Self-worth, defined as 'adolescent's perception of themselves as being satisfied with the way they are and the way they behave' was measured using a scale devised by Harter (1986; see Chapter 3 for further details). The scores on the self-worth scale ranged from 5 to 20 with the average student reporting a moderately positive score of 14.1.

An analysis of variance was carried out to assess whether the students' typical activity patterns, as represented by the four clusters, were reflected in their feelings of self-worth. As males tend to report higher scores than females on measures of self-esteem and self-worth (Granleese, Turner and Trew, 1989), the analysis took account of gender as well as cluster membership. As Table 7.14 shows, boys did have significantly higher self-worth scores than girls. Furthermore, both boys and girls who were members of the 'Sport' cluster had significantly higher self-worth scores than their peers.

Table 7.14 Self-worth scores by cluster membership and gender

	Group 1 Non-sports	Group 2 Sports	Group 3 Passive	Group 4 Work	All
Males	14.9	15.6	14.1	13.5	14.7
Females	13.1	14.6	13.7	13.3	13.6
All	14.0	15.4	13.8	13.4	**14.1**

DISCUSSION

This chapter has employed the diary records completed by 602 adolescents to examine a number of questions associated with these young people's choice of out-of-school activities. Methodologically there are many issues concerned with how the diary data are reported. The reliability and veracity of diary records were not measured directly for this investigation but comparisons between the diary records and the questionnaires, some of which are included in this chapter, provided a means of establishing consistency in patterns of response. For example, because the diaries only sampled activities over four days, it is possible that one or more of the diarists who played their 'top sport' at an élite level may not have been involved in sport during the assigned period. However, as expected, on average the level of sports involvement was closely associated with time spent on sport.

The analysis of the diaries revealed some fascinating insights into the leisure interests of young people in the 1990s, as well as specific information on sporting activities. As in other studies (for example, Fitzgerald *et al.*, 1995) television viewing was found to be central to young people's lives but sport was also important for the majority of young people. It is notable that 85 per cent of males and over two-thirds (67 per cent) of females mentioned involvement in some type of sporting activity during their four-day diary. However, this also means that almost a quarter (24 per cent) of the sample did not record any involvement in sport in their diaries.

Boys spent almost five hours on average during the four diary days engaged in sport whereas girls spent 3.7 hours. Overall, sport was a more important characteristic of boy's out-of-school activities than of girls, and only one in five of those categorised as having a sporting lifestyle was female. Previous research on time use by young people (Hendry, 1983; Mauldin and Meeks, 1990) has demonstrated that differences in the time males and females allocate to leisure activities, household work and personal care accord with traditional male–female roles, and this survey confirms that these traditions still permeate lifestyles in the 1990s.

Because of the emphasis in the present study on sport, detailed analysis of non-sporting activities was not carried out and a diverse range of pastimes was subsumed under a general 'other non-sports' category. However, it was interesting to note that girls who played their top-sport at an élite level spent almost twice as long as those without a top sport on these 'other activities'. More refined analysis is required to determine the relationship between specific sport and non-sport pursuits but, in general, the diary records provided an opportunity to establish whether time spent on sports activities displaced other leisure pursuits or work activities. There was no evidence that time spent on sport was replacing time spent on home-work, but sporting activities did seem to be replacing some work activities – for girls at least. Alternatively it is possible that the work commitments of these girls did not allow them any time for sports involvement.

The overwhelming choice of football as a 'top sport' by males in the survey was mirrored in the diary record by the relative frequency of their references to playing football. Overall it was the third most frequently reported single activity after television viewing and home-work. Football was also more frequently referenced than all other sports together. Although the term football can cover a wide range of activities from the solitary child kicking a ball around a field to a formal match under a variety of sporting codes (including rugby, Gaelic football, soccer) its predominance over other sports is still noteworthy given its appeal to males of all ages and a growing number of females.

The small number of references to the presence of a coach or teacher in relation to sporting activities was one of the more unex-pected findings to emerge from the analysis. A coach or teacher was referenced for only eight of the 1,532 sports-related activities. This may have been a gross underestimate as the presence of teachers was not always recorded during team games but, alternatively, the limited availability of coaching may be reflected in this finding.

The chapter concluded with details of the cluster analysis which produced four patterns of activity associated with a range of back-ground variables and a measure of self-worth. The characteristics of these clusters were as follows:

- *The non-sports cluster* ($n = 147$): Long hours in front of the televi-sion and a relatively long time spent on homework and other non-sports activities; approximately equal numbers of males and females; almost half the group at Key Stage 3; 56 per cent of the group with no top sport or involved in their top sport at a basic level; on average, self-worth low for females but high for males.
- *The sports cluster* ($n = 110$): Long hours devoted to sport; four out of five of the group are males; only 6 per cent are in the sixth form; 68 per cent attend Catholic schools; 65 per cent are involved in sport at a competitive level and 8 per cent at an élite level; the highest mean self-worth scores for both males and females.
- *The passive cluster* ($n = 266$): On average members did not devote their time to any one activity; they also spent the shortest time

engaged in sport or watching television; 62 per cent were female; 54 per cent either had no top sport or played their top sport at a basic level; females had an above average self-worth score but the score of males was below average.

- *The work cluster* ($n = 79$): On average this group spent over 12 hours of their four diary-days engaged in work-related activities; half the group were female; almost a third were in the sixth form; over half played their top sport at a basic level; 14 per cent of the group had no top sport; self-worth scores of both males and females were low.

These clusters provide a useful way of characterising the activities of the young people in this sample. However, it is important to stress that the grouping of respondents was dependent on the level of aggregation of the activities employed in the analysis. For example, it would have been possible, on statistical grounds, to have included time spent on football as a separate category from time spent on other sports. However, because football is a predominantly male activity inevitably this would have produced a strong gender-related distinction which may have hidden any underlying commonalities in the activity patterns of boys and girls. Football was therefore included in the sports category for this analysis. Furthermore, sample size did not justify separate cluster analyses for the two genders in this study although this approach was used most successfully by Hendry *et al.* (1993) in defining young people's lifestyles.

In conclusion, this chapter has provided a snapshot of the activities of adolescents growing up in Northern Ireland in the 1990s. Not surprisingly, it reveals that, as in other western countries, television plays an important part in almost all young people's lives. At the same time it also clearly demonstrates that sport is an integral part of the out-of-school lives for the majority of young people, and that sport does not have to interfere with other life domains but may actually enhance them. Watching television can be a solitary activity involving little or no organisation. Taking part in sport requires more effort, yet these young people were taking part but most often outside of any organisation and structure which could perhaps have facilitated or encouraged their sporting development. In future, it is to be hoped that this enthusiasm is duly recognised and hence channelled, so as to avoid their physical activity regressing to little more than shifting furniture when searching for the remote control.

APPENDIX 7.1 ACTIVITY CATEGORIES

Activities reported in at least 20 diary records

Activity	Frequency	Activity	Frequency
Watch TV/video	3,024	Cycling	74
Homework/revision	1,377	Extra-curricular	71
Assoc. football	801	Cinema/ theatre	70
Home computing	576	Basketball	67
Listen music	431	Keep fit	50
Church	409	Riding	47
Work, incl. farm	318	Watch sports	32
Walking/running	245	Netball	32
Reading/writing	213	Billiards & snooker	32
Help housework	205	Arts and crafts	29
Shopping	171	Bingo/amusements	29
Youth clubs	134	Jogging	27
Non-organised games	127	Learning activity	26
Party/outing/trip	113	Lawn tennis	26
Swimming	110	Badminton	26
Play/sing music	98	Golf	24
Disco dancing	80	Squash rackets	21
Voluntary work	77		

Activities reported in fewer than 20 diary records

Activity	Frequency	Activity	Frequency
Athletics	18	Mountaineering	2
Pool	18	Windsurfing	2
Irish dancing	18	Laser Quest etc.	2
Rounders	17	Archery	1
Hurling	14	Ballooning	1
Darts	14	Baseball	1
Field hockey	12	Bobsleigh	1
Rugby Union	12	Camping	1
Angling	10	Canoeing	1
Cricket	10	Fencing	1
Ten-pin bowling	10	Five's	1
Medical	10	Judo	1
Non-school drama etc.	10	Flying ms	1
Gaelic football	9	Karting ms	1
Table tennis	9	Orienteering	1
Weightlifting	9	Petanque	1
Aerobics	9	Rugby League	1
Ice skating	8	Sailing	1
Karate	8	Roller skating	1
Camogie	7	Trampolining	1

50   *Karen Trew*

Activity	Frequency	Activity	Frequency
Motor cycling ms	7	Triathlon	1
Jujitsu	7	Water-skiing	1
Boxing	5	Bodybuilding	1
Surfing	5	Chinese martial arts	1
Adult venues	5	Ballet dancing	1
Handball	3	Contemporary dancing	1
Gymnastics	3	Rugby Union mini	1
Shooting	3		
Bowls	2		

ms = motor sport

Sport activities not recorded in any diary

Bicycle polo	Caving	Croquet	Ballroom dancing
Folk dancing	Gliding	Hang gliding	Ice hockey
Roller hockey	Lacrosse	Modern pentathlon	Model aircraft fly.
Hovering ms	Power boating ms	Parachuting	Parascending
Quoiting	Racketball	Rambling	Rowing
Land & sand yachting	Shinty	Skateboarding	Skiing
Softball	Sub aqua	Life saving	Water polo
Tennis & rackets	Tobogganing	Tug of war	Volleyball
Wildfowling	Wrestling	Yoga	Powerlifting
Rock climbing	Aikido	Scottish dancing	Tae kwondo
Badminton mini	Basketball mini	Camogie mini	Cricket mini
Gaelic football mini	Field hockey mini	Lacrosse mini	Lawn tennis mini
Netball mini	Rugby League mini	Assoc. football mini	

ms = motor sport

APPENDIX 7.2 NON-SPORT ACTIVITY CATEGORIES

Watch TV/video	Homework/revision
Home computing	Listen music
Youth clubs	Walking/running
Reading/writing	Arts and crafts
Play/sing music	Non-organised games
Extra-curricular school activities	Shopping
Church	Cinema/theatre
Medical (visit doctor etc.)	Work (including farming)
Housework	Voluntary work
Bingo/amusements	Watch live sporting event
Party/outing/trip	Learning activity
Non-school drama	Adult venues
Laser Quest etc.	

NOTES

1 The method used to carry out the cluster analysis was Quickcluster on the Statistical Package for Social Sciences. This technique is a non-hierarchical approach to clustering. See Goss (1995) for a discussion of the advantages and disadvantages of this approach.

REFERENCES

Fine, G.A., Mortimer, J.T. and Roberts, D.F. (1993). Leisure, work and the mass media. In S.S. Feldman and G.R. Elliott (eds), *At the Threshold: The Developing Adolescent*, Harvard, MA: Harvard University Press.

Fitzgerald, M., Joseph, A.P., Hayes, M. and O'Regan, M. (1995). Leisure activities of adolescent schoolchildren. *Journal of Adolescence, 18*, 349–358.

Goss, M. (1995). Stress and coping in carers of patients with Alzheimer's disease. Unpublished Doctoral Thesis, The Queen's University of Belfast.

Granleese, J.,Turner, I. and Trew, K. (1989). Teachers' and boys' and girls' perceptions of competence in the primary school: The importance of physical competence. *British Journal of Educational Psychology, 59*, 31–37.

Harter, S. (1986). *Self-Perception Profile for Adolescents*. University of Denver, Colorado.

Harvey, A.S. (1990). Time use studies for leisure analysis. *Social Indicators Research, 23*, 309–336.

Hendry, L. B. (1983). *Growing Up and Going Out: Adolescents and Leisure*. Aberdeen: Aberdeen University Press.

Hendry, L.B., Shucksmith, J., Love, J.G. and Glendenning, A. (1993). *Young People's Leisure and Lifestyles*. London: Routledge.

Kilpatrick, R. and Trew, K. (1985). Life styles and psychological well-being among unemployed men in Northern Ireland. *Journal of Occupational Psychology, 58*, 207–216.

Mauldin, T. and Meeks, C. B. (1990). Sex differences in children's time use. *Sex Roles, 22 (9/10)*, 537–554.

Meeks, C.B and Mauldin, T. (1990). Children's time in structured and unstructured leisure activities. *Lifestyles: Family and Economic Issues, 11, (3)*, 257–281.

Reeder, A.I., Stanton, W.R., Langley, J.D. and Chalmers, D.J. (1991). Adolescents' sporting and leisure time: Physical activities during their 15th year. *Canadian Journal of Sport Science, 16, (4)*, 308–315.

Robinson, J.P. (1988). Time-diary evidence about the social psychology of everyday life. In J.E. McGrath (ed.), *The Social Psychology of Time: New Perspectives*. Newbury Park: Sage.

Whyte, J. (1995). *Changing Times: Challenges to Identity? 12 year-olds in Belfast 1981 and 1992*. Aldershot: Avebury.

Wills, J. and Campbell, D. (1993). *Exercise Psychology*. Champaign, IL: Human Kinetics.

8 Focus group interviews with élite young athletes, coaches and parents

Janthia Duncan

INTRODUCTION

Over recent years, in both the commercial and academic arenas, the value of focus group research has become increasingly recognised. Focus groups involve bringing together a small number of people, normally between five and 10, in order for the group to discuss a particular topic, be that a washing powder, a political party, a social problem or, in this case, young people and sport. The aim of a good focus group is to provide a forum for open discussion, giving participants the freedom to work through an agenda which genuinely reflects their own priorities and concerns, rather than those brought along by the researcher. In this way, the methodology and the resulting data are ethnographic, hopefully reflecting on the perspectives brought to the research by the participants themselves.

While the other chapters in this text draw primarily on more structured data obtained from the face-to-face interviews with young people, this chapter stands apart as it reports on a separate branch of the project, namely focus groups which were held with young élite performers, with coaches of young élite athletes, and finally with parents of children of different ages, from different educational backgrounds and with varying levels of involvement in sport.

The four focus groups with young élite performers and coaches were carried out at the Dale Farm Olympic Youth Camp held at Greenmount College, Antrim, in August 1993. The Dale Farm Olympic Youth Camp is a week-long residential course held each year for young athletes from a wide range of (primarily) Olympic sports. The camp enables these élite performers to benefit from coaching given by invited experts, many of whom come to Ulster specifically for the event. The performers who were interviewed were all on the Ulster team for their chosen sport, or were expected to achieve provincial standard in the near future. Some had already achieved even greater distinction: for example, three had represented Ireland in their chosen sport, one was a former British Champion, and one had already participated in the Commonwealth Games.

The members of these two groups of élite performers were chosen to include a balance of representation in terms of age, gender, sport and type of sport (individual/team, contact/non-contact), religion and family background. Except for one individual (aged 25), all participants were within the age range of 12 to 18 years. Group 1 consisted of five boys and three girls, representing swimming, hockey, wrestling and judo, with the ages of group members ranging from 12 to 25 years. Individual contributors were all articulate though, as would be expected, the younger members were initially more hesitant. This was also true of the second group, made up of five boys and one girl, representing fencing, swimming and cycling and aged between 12 and 16 years.

The first of the coaches' group was made up of two women and four men, representing the sports of hockey, athletics, swimming, judo and boxing. All were articulate and appeared well informed. This was also true of the second coaches group which consisted of four male coaches representing boxing, judo, hockey and athletics.

Four months later, four groups of parents were also interviewed, with group sizes of nine, eight, seven and six respectively. These were parents of children with mixed sporting abilities, including roughly equal numbers of mothers and fathers. The first group comprised parents with one or more child aged 7–18, but children who were not necessarily involved in sport. In the second group, all group members were parents of children aged 7–18 years who were actively involved in sport, that is they were on a school team or a member of a sports club (in or out of school). Group 3 comprised parents whose children were aged 7–11 years; but were not necessarily involved in sport, and those in Group 4 had one or more children aged 11–18 years, either at grammar school or secondary school, again with varying involvements in sport. These interviews were arranged during evenings at three different locations. The most relaxed group was the first, which took place in the ante room of a public house, characterised by low lighting and the background hum of a bar. In contrast, the three other groups were in well-lit rooms with a more formal atmosphere. Where interviewees knew other group members they settled down more quickly (for example, the first two groups). There were occasions when the desire to be seen as a model parent or as an iconoclast may have influenced behaviour and attitudes conveyed, but parents normally relaxed as the focus group progressed.

ISSUES

The focus group interviews with performers and coaches were designed to address the following issues:

1 what élite performers get out of sport
2 parents and sport
3 the school and sport
4 coaching and élite performers
5 how young people can be attracted to sport

In the case of parents, the following themes were also introduced:

1 parents' perception of the value of sport
2 the place of sport within the family:
   (a) various attractions competing for young people's time
   (b) parents' views about their role
3 the role of sports facilities outside the school:
   (a) sports clubs
   (b) coaching

In keeping with focus group research, these agendas were not slavishly followed; instead issues were allowed to emerge during discussion and digressions were pursued. The time allotted for each focus group was one hour but in practice this varied depending on the commitment or enthusiasm of contributors. All interviews were tape recorded.

During discussions, the researcher had to play a more active role in generating responses from the élite young performers. Coaches required little prompting, and in the case of parents' groups, the researcher occasionally had to steer the conversation back to the key issues in order to avoid overrunning. However, parents were generally extremely articulate and opinionated and required little prompting. The following themes are those which emerged during the course of discussion and it is these which have been used to structure the report.

YOUNG ÉLITE PERFORMERS

What élite performers get out of sport

There was general consensus among these élite athletes that sport:

- *Is enjoyable, particularly in relation to competition*
  These young athletes were very clear that winning was important and satisfying, claiming that achieving something for your country gave you a 'good' feeling. At the same time, the desire to win

inevitably meant that they had to be prepared to lose. As one cyclist put it, 'losing means someone else is fitter', although one swimmer claimed he had never yet lost a competition. Two fencers said they derived enjoyment from pitting their wits against an opponent and both liked to win but recognised that it was more difficult to win the higher the level of competition. A 17-year-old female hockey player claimed that winning gave you 'a great feeling of pride'; it was about 'doing something for yourself', but was not a means of gaining respect from parents, or the friendship of peers. Winning for older members was likewise often referenced in terms of 'a great feeling of honour and pride'. Their more personal elaborations suggested that these opinions were deeply felt. The personal nature of this experience was reinforced by a 12-year-old swimmer who said that she did not tell her friends about her achievements because her friends would not be interested: 'If I tell them about winning they just think it's bragging'; 'Jealous, probably' interjected one of the boys.

However, the subject of winning also prompted a more negative response. A 16-year-old male hockey player contended that sometimes a sport could become too competitive and this spoilt the fun, 'There's nothing wrong with competition but sometimes people are OTT [over the top]'.

- *Is fun*
  The younger élite performers placed greatest emphasis on the fun side of sport, whereas the older ones were more inclined to mention having a good social life. For example, the swimmers and the fencers described how, when they went away for competitions (without their parents), they worked hard all day but then went out on the town, normally with other competitors, perhaps to have a meal and then see a film. One young cyclist who had yet to participate in international competition described the aftermath of racing as 'fun' but when asked to describe it said, 'No comment!', which could be interpreted in a host of ways! The word 'fun' was occasionally qualified; the fencers pointed out that the English team tended to look down on the Ulster team although the Welsh and Scots were seen as friendly. A female fencer remarked that if asked about bombs she just said that there was one in her back garden every day...and people seemed to believe her!

- *Leads to a good social life*
  However good the experience of winning, the most compelling feature of sport for most of these élite performers was undoubtedly the opportunity to go on trips, normally without parents. There

was consensus about the pleasure of competing outside Ulster where they met other performers. Élite performers often found that it was only other élite performers who understood their interest in sport. One 17-year-old hockey player said that, through her hockey, she now had 'friends all over Northern Ireland'.

- *Keeps you fit*
  When the researcher probed further to assess the significance of the uniform response on fitness, by asking about the value of fitness, a few of the youngest athletes expressed contempt for anyone who could not grasp its value but offered no explanations beyond this. This reaction seemed to reveal that they had not thought the issue through as clearly as their initial automatic response suggested. The older members of the group were more convincing. There was consensus about the value of fitness, for example, with swimmers rising at 5.00 a.m. daily to go to training sessions. At the same time the athletes listed the advantages of fitness with a kind of automatic thoroughness which suggested programming: 'It's good for your body'; 'By not exercising you can do it damage'; 'You've only one chance so look after your body'.

- *Provides family enjoyment*
  Virtually all élite performers were supported and followed by their parents, though some of the older athletes pursued their chosen sport alone. Sport was seen to provide a focus for family activity; sometimes this meant that the parents, together with younger brothers and sisters, travelled to events to offer support; sometimes the entire life of the family revolved around the performer's sports needs.
  Other thoughts offered by some, but not all, élite performers were that sport:

- *Gives you a discipline*
  One 14-year-old boy said, 'It becomes a habit'. He explained how the routine of training and performing for judo created a regular pattern for his life. For him, as for many élite performers, sport was a discipline around which the rest of his life was structured.

- *Is an outlet for letting off steam*
  This was the response of a 25-year-old wrestler. Although other members of the group did not disagree, they did not seem to regard letting off steam as a priority.

- *Sets you apart from your friends*
  Some élite performers felt that it was not easy to get on with people who did not share the same interests; others considered that you lost touch with friends at home. In contrast, one contributor said that the higher you went, the more you were drawn into a sport's

social environment but you never actually lost your friends at home – you just saw less of them because sport intervened.

- *Provides extrinsic rewards*
  An added attraction, for example in swimming, was the distribution of 'freebies' – free hats and tee-shirts. The mild envy expressed by other group members indicated that not all sports had this kind of sponsorship. Two young swimmers considered these extrinsic rewards to be particularly important. It was almost as if tangible, fashionable items were visible proof of a return on their considerable personal investment; these rewards made them feel as if they had been shrewd in their choice of leisure pursuit.

The role of parents

Élite performers were unanimous that parents were instrumental in their success. For example, they offered moral support, they provided transport, and they funded travel, equipment and kit. One girl (whose mother was a single parent) remarked that her mother travelled round Ireland to see her play; another that her parents had committed their lives to taking her and her sisters to swimming. Except for one female fencer, élite performers could find no fault with their parents. This fencer said that her parents sometimes nagged by asking too many questions when she returned from a trip (especially when she had lost!). They were also inclined to push her into keeping up her training, especially during the summer when she felt like a break. However, she expressed no real annoyance and was very straightforward about how much she appreciated her parents' support. She even said that she felt their enquiries were justified bearing in mind how much money she cost them. One swimmer's advice on how to deal with parents nagging about training was 'Just say you don't want to go'! The confident way in which this remark was made suggested that the young swimmer had had some experience of dealing with nagging parents and that family relationships were not always completely harmonious.

Almost all had parents or grandparents who were high-achieving sportsmen or women in their youth. The parents of some involved themselves in the administration or fund raising side of their children's sport.

School and sport

Younger contributors considered that school provision for sport was adequate, even if their particular sport was not catered for. Older group members emphasised that schools had limitations, especially for élite performers. There was general agreement that teachers had 'a hard time of it' and could not do much more than they were already doing. While these young athletes would have welcomed the opportunity to pursue their sports to a high level at school, they did not normally appear to consider that schools were responsible for specialist provision.

In terms of each sport's response to the role of schools and clubs, there were marked differences. Judo players pointed out that contact sports such as theirs were rarely part of the curriculum, though a number of schools did have a judo club and these, they felt, would benefit from more involvement by outside expert coaches.

Swimmers generally had a very positive attitude to sport at school, especially in the case of two young swimmers (aged 12 and 13 years) who said that the swimming pool could be used at lunchtime, and the coaches (PE and non-PE staff) and facilities were good. Some felt schools should be more competitive and include more swimming in the timetable, while others saw that having it in the timetable did not at present guarantee pupils regular swimming. All were completely satisfied with their clubs.

Wrestlers felt that more could be done in schools, for example more fitness training and greater involvement of outside coaches. They claimed that at a club level there was insufficient challenge; hence élite performers had to train abroad.

Hockey players suggested that schools could supplement their limited resources by bringing in outside help from local clubs, and generally felt that school provision left something to be desired. For example, they pointed out that international hockey was played on astro-turf but that Northern Ireland schools only had gravel pitches.

The cyclists competed through a club but they had no complaints about sport in school, except that there was not enough of it.

Fencing was available at school but only as an extra-curricular activity. One fencer described how fencing had been frowned on by the principal at her school and how pupils had had to organise the club themselves. One boy said that money was not normally given to fencing at his school because the head was a rugby fanatic, nor would the school sponsor him as an individual. Similarly, since it represented a minority sport, fencing results were not usually announced during assembly.

Coaching

With only one exception, each had received specialist coaching, and all were in agreement as to its importance: 'You could never know everything about a sport'; 'Coaching helped you to progress at your level'; 'The coach gave you incentive and spurred you on'; 'Coaching gave you "a kick up the backside to push you on"'; 'Without it you'd be rubbish'; 'Coaches teach you all you know'.

In terms of what coaches did to help, the list included: 'worked on your technique'; 'helped you lose bad habits'; 'cheered you on, psyched you up, helped your confidence'; 'taught you how to avoid injury'; 'showed you how to mend faulty gear'; 'told you how to handle competitions'; and 'told you what unfamiliar situations would be like'.

How young people can be attracted to sport

'Come and try it sessions' were suggested and it was recommended that sports should be shown to be fun. They said more advertising was needed in the papers. On the other hand, they considered that sport was not for everyone. Some people preferred using their minds rather than their bodies, the emphasis depending on upbringing. Dedication was required and a sense of realism; it was not all fun. Additionally, time, money and parental support were needed – very few athletes could hope to get on in sport without parental support.

COACHES

What élite performers derive from sport

Coaches listed the following attractions of sport for young élite performers:

- *The opportunity for fun*
  In the first place coaches argued that sport had to be enjoyable at primary school; the sports' profile of a particular area depended heavily on there being a local interest in sport and ultimately this interest had to be nurtured in the schools. Although most coaches accepted that sport had to be enjoyable, some rated fun higher than others. For example, the boxing coach regarded sport as a discipline; although it was possible for young athletes to approach training through games and as a result have fun, time in the gym was at a premium and he had top athletes who needed him. He therefore had to establish early on whether a young athlete was really interested. He did not want to invest in those young people who may quit.

Coaches were very much aware of major distractions from sport, including the opposite sex, discos, examinations and weekend jobs. A hockey coach (also a PE teacher) mentioned that when coaching the national hockey team she discussed with players what they could offer and worked with this.

There was an interesting digression as to whether or not a young athlete could return to a sport if he or she dropped out of it. It was felt in judo and boxing that in early adolescence it could actually be an advantage because if the young person continued to train for another sport in the interim then they may acquire the necessary weight and strength. Likewise in hockey it was considered feasible provided the athlete already had spatial awareness. However, in swimming the coach said that if people left the sport they rarely returned to perform at the same high level.

- *A chance to build self-confidence*
Parents often pushed their children to take on a sport, so that they could toughen up or learn to defend themselves. By improving their skills it was felt that self-confidence then grew.
- *A chance to focus energies and keep out of trouble*
This was felt to be especially true in areas with poor amenities. For example, in the case of boxing, parents often pointed youngsters in that direction in the absence of any other local activities.
- *The money and glory of professional sport*
Although some coaches highlighted extrinsic rewards to motivate young athletes, at the same time they all agreed that money had spoiled sport. It was argued that, in the past, performers were thrilled and honoured just to wear the national vest. Nowadays amateur performers had to buy their own kit and pay their own expenses. It was felt that national teams should have their kit presented to them.
- *Winning*
This was seen to encourage young performers to stay in a sport. However, since winning was so important it was felt that some sports were chosen simply because they were easier to succeed in. For example, the judo coach argued that it was easier to become Yorkshire Judo Champion than to have a football trial for Leeds United.
- *Background*
Coaches also commented that social class played a role in determining the choice of sport; some sports were regarded as working class, others as middle class, and this could affect chances of success.

The role of parents

Coaches acknowledged that parents provided moral, financial and practical support for young performers. However, parents could be a nuisance and even a serious problem if they interfered with their child's coaching. Coaches went on to describe different tactics for dealing with parents. For example, the boxing coach referred them to the treasurer of the club so that they could help with fund raising but he forbade them entering his gym during coaching. The athletics coach would occasionally give them a clipboard and pen and ask them to observe certain actions very closely and make notes. In reality, this information was usually carefully collected and from a coaching perspective was invaluable because the coach could not watch everything at once. The hockey coach said that diplomacy was essential; parents could wreck a child's chances by shouting the wrong instructions yet their moral support was invaluable. The judo coach was very strict (intolerant?) with parents when he was an amateur but now as a professional coach he had to listen more patiently to them.

The school and sport

Coaches generally portrayed a degree of frustration with schools. Several coaches had worked on initiatives to promote their sport in schools with virtually no response from staff. The athletics coach had tried to organise athletics days in schools yet in a mail shot of around 50 he received no more than four responses.

Schools were seen to have a strong bias towards the PE teacher's sport, and traditionally hockey for girls and rugby for boys. Thus, hockey for boys was not a priority in many schools.

Contact sports like judo and boxing were not part of the PE curriculum and were seen to be supported primarily at club level. The attitude of schools was felt to be unhelpful, but at the same time judo had been introduced to quite a number of schools as an extra-curricular activity. These tended to be grammar schools where money, it was claimed, was less of a problem.

Primary schools which did not have a specialist PE teacher were blamed for the often poor level of physical co-ordination found in 12-year-olds. The introduction of the Common Curriculum was seen to offer some hope, as primary schools were now to have specialist PE teaching available. Primary schools also tended to use full-size pitches and equipment which were not always appropriate for small children.

The swimming coach remarked that the inclusion of swimming in the Common Curriculum may actually put pupils off swimming altogether, and he also felt that the link between schools and clubs was very weak. Clubs were currently oversubscribed and many had had to introduce waiting lists to cope with demand. A filter system was needed which would enable the clubs to drop less keen youngsters. It was felt that schools could help by setting up swimming clubs with an affiliation to the national governing body for swimming and by offering coaching at a more advanced level.

Coaching and élite performers

Coaches considered that these young athletes derived a range of benefits from coaching as follows:

- *Self-discipline for life*
  The swimming coach mentioned that a study of swimmers showed that the highest performers were amongst the intellectually brightest and that the discipline which had been learned in swimming transferred itself to other aspects of life. The hockey coach pointed out that coaches helped players to cope with pressure by promoting time management. Generally it was argued that young athletes achieved a discipline by using their bodies correctly and by eating properly. This could also be fun.
- *Self-respect and respect for others*
  Coaching was seen to teach young athletes respect for themselves and for others. For some young people coaching was their first experience of one-to-one teaching where someone was actually talking to them. This, it was argued, generated self-respect and respect for others. Coaches claimed that they did not just teach skills, they also made better people. Furthermore, coaching could be life saving. The boxing coach said that in his experience the young people who worked hard at a sport like boxing turned out well, the others ended up dead or in prison. Although coaches expressed strong views about the moral value of sport they clearly aimed not to impose their own value systems on young athletes.
- *Friendship and fun*
  Coaches appeared to be well aware of the need to make sport enjoyable for teenagers, otherwise they would lose interest. The boxing coach operated in a club situation and at a higher level than school. Having experienced many situations where parents sent their children to boxing to get them out of the way he was

emphatic that he was neither a childminder nor a welfare worker. On the other hand, he said that if a young athlete was not getting much attention at home he would tend to focus on the coach. The coach had to be straight and set a good example so as to build up trust; then the young athlete would confide in the coach. Several other coaches said that students often talked to the coach about problems rather than approaching their parents. Most coaches clearly derived great pleasure from working with young people and tried hard to make repetitive training fun.

One coach misinterpreted the question but in a revealing way. Instead of explaining what students got out of coaching she talked about her own experience. She said that she enjoyed being involved in a cross-community sport. She also said that young athletes called her their second mum and claimed they were her friends, though they knew where the dividing line between friend and coach lay. She remarked that a Russian coach at the Dale Farm Olympic Youth Camp was extremely strict and tough. She claimed that far more could be achieved with young athletes through mutual respect. The rest of the group did not suggest in any verbal or physical way that her attitudes were unusual or out of line.

- *The opportunity to travel*
Especially when competing in international events, this was seen as a valuable form of education, particularly for those brought up in Northern Ireland.

Several other benefits of coaching were also mentioned, including the opportunity to:

- participate in competition
- obtain help in the search for financial support
- observe good models of professionalism

How young people can be attracted to sport

This was a topic which generated considerable interest, and coaches were particularly vocal on this subject. For example, there was consensus that leisure centres should be open on Sundays.

It was suggested that the Sports Council could further promote individual sports. For example, amateur boxing was seen to have a bad name in schools because of its association with professional boxing, and this reputation was seen to be unfair. More generally it was argued that the Sports Council could adopt a higher profile and ensure that the achievements of amateur sportspeople were well publicised. In addition, government should be pressurised into seeing that coaches visit schools and start work with athletes when they are young.

The athletics coaches in particular described the need for improved facilities, including an indoor running track and shot circle (claiming that if putting was done outdoors in winter, two buckets of boiling water were needed to thaw out the 16 lb shot!).

PARENTS

Parental attitudes to sport

Parents generally recognised the value of sport although normally this varied according to the degree of personal involvement in sport which the parent had experienced, either currently or when younger. Parents' previous or current involvement included currently playing a sport competitively, playing on school or county teams when younger, taking up a sport in later life, being currently involved in some kind of physical activity. In addition, there were parents who either found that it was not possible to be involved personally in competitive sport because of family commitments, or had keen armchair interests in sport, particularly in their former sport, or personally were not interested in sport, but still encouraged their children because they could see how valuable it was for their development.

Unsolicited, parents were quick to list the advantages of sport for their children. Only one parent argued that he would prefer his children to focus on academic work. Parents said that sport 'got children involved in teamwork'; 'stimulated children mentally'; 'gave them some "childhood" '; 'helped them let go, and get rid of aggression, after the pressures of school and homework'; 'helped them to mix and to get on with their friends'; 'helped them have a good time'; 'provided exercise which is good for health'; 'got children outdoors'; 'could be useful for young people when applying for a job'; 'helped them build up confidence'; 'helped children learn to compete'; 'was valuable for physical development (i.e. unimportant how good the children were at the sport)'; 'was an excellent discipline'; 'encouraged children to adopt good habits and helped keep them from drinking and smoking'; 'encouraged children to organise their time so as to fit in homework, sport and other activities'; 'was good for university applications and careers prospects'; 'kept children busy during the summer vacation (though at a cost in terms of time and money to parents)'; 'taught them how to get on with other children'; 'was a form of relaxation after school'; 'was a means of achieving balance'; 'was a means of helping children to develop good time management skills'; 'could be interdenominational, e.g. inter-school matches at primary level run through the Education for Mutual Understanding (EMU) programme'.

It was generally felt that if a shorter working week became the norm, people would want more sport and leisure facilities in their free time and therefore a sports education was important for children.

Less positive views included the association in Northern Ireland of sport with religious groups (e.g. Gaelic games) or class (e.g. rugby), mild resentment at the idea that some academically weak students could gain college places on the strength of sports performance, and a dislike of Sunday sport since it was offensive to religious people.

Attractions competing for young people's time

Sport undoubtedly played an important role in children's time outside school hours, though constant sources of competition were seen to include watching television and videos, playing computer games, listening to music and carrying out homework. Other interests were occasionally represented, including drama, playing musical instruments, reading, Cubs and Brownies, Scouts and Guides, Boys and Girls Brigade, extra-curricular studies and numerous hobbies.

Their children played a wide range of sports (rugby, rowing, table tennis, badminton, canoeing, swimming, water polo, soccer, cricket, athletics, running, horse riding, netball, handball, hockey, running, basketball, snooker, motor cross, cycling, triathlon, gymnastics, golf, netball, Gaelic football, hurling, rowing, shooting, fishing and Duke of Edinburgh's Award). Some sports had been initiated by the school (rugby, hockey, netball, basketball, athletics, table tennis, swimming and badminton), with a significant number of others initiated through the family (fishing), sports clubs (running, swimming, badminton), or leisure centres (badminton).

The role of television and computer games was much discussed. They were seen by some as a distraction, leading many parents to restrict their use. One parent had banned computer games but permitted his daughter to use a computer for educational purposes. Another mother said that her two boys had visited a neighbour's house to play computer games after school because they did not have a machine at home, but this was stopped when one of her sons became aggressive following these visits. Others saw them as a means of occupying children so giving parents some peace. One woman said she preferred the children to be in the house with the television or computer games rather than being out in the town where worse problems existed, including drugs. Another woman said that her son finished his homework more promptly when he wanted to watch television and yet others saw television as a positive means of stimulating interest in sport. One woman observed that during Wimbledon attendance at her children's tennis club increased dramatically.

In a less positive vein, television was seen as a stimulus for dangerous copycat acrobatics. One woman said that after watching 'Gladiators' with her children she found her 3-year-old attempting to tie a rope round the bannisters to see if she too could swing; another mother described how her baby son jumped off the top of the bannisters shouting 'He-man' and spent seven weeks in traction. One woman pointed out the problem which arose when children had their own computer or portable television; parents could not control how they used their time. It was also agreed that family life was disrupted and that children stopped reading books and people ceased to have conversations.

Although television helped to stimulate children's interest in sport, often the wrong messages were conveyed. For example, equipment, sports clothing and footwear were now fashion accessories and children did not want to take part in a sport unless they were wearing the right clothing and using the equipment advertised on television. This meant that parents could not necessarily afford to support their children in sport. One father also remarked that his youngest two children tended to become very enthusiastic about a recently publicised sport for a few months but then the interest would die.

A parent who was also a PE teacher said that many children wanted to be as brilliant as the top class sportsperson they saw on television. If they were not good at the sport within a month, rather than work at it, they changed to something else according to what caught the imagination.

This point raised the importance of dedication in sport. One father felt that dedication was a prerequisite for success in sport; if you kept changing sports you would not improve. One woman explained that her middle son used to skip from one sport to another while at school. He finally took up rowing when he went to university and dedicated his time to it, becoming open champion in the British Eights. He then decided there was no point dedicating every minute of his free time to a sport in which he could go no higher so he gave up rowing and tried different sports again, most recently rugby. Her explanation for his intense interest in rowing was that neither of his brothers – both rugby enthusiasts – had pursued it.

One man remarked that others were saying that 'if you're dedicated to sport you should be of Olympic standard', when he felt that sport should be regarded primarily as a pastime. Another participant suggested that the problem of children losing interest in sport might be counteracted by having coaches to drive them on. This idea prompted one man to point out how important it is for children to be good at a sport, otherwise they become demoralised. Another suggestion was that this was where coaching would come in, but for the less able children rather than the high achievers.

One woman said that at her child's school a different sport was tackled every year, thus adding some variety. Another woman praised the Duke of Edinburgh's Award scheme which covered a range of sports and then complained that it should be more generally available; her son wanted to take part in the scheme but it was not available locally. Another man said that the attraction of the Duke of Edinburgh's Award scheme was that it 'only lasts a week: young people don't do it for long and so they think it's great'. He could imagine that, after a few months, his children would have to be pushed to attend. On the strength of this, one man said that maybe this boredom factor could be counteracted by having different sports in school every week.

Parents' views about their role

It was generally agreed that children's involvement in sport depended on their parents taking an interest in what their children were doing, and providing encouragement, alongside practical support in terms of finance, transport, equipment and general assistance. It was also agreed that parents did not themselves have to be sporty but they did have to be interested. While it was argued that children had to be allowed to make up their own minds, one mother said that occasionally a little pushing was needed and described how from time to time her sons would decide to give gymnastics a miss. She would insist that they go and they always thoroughly enjoyed it.

Parents were also essential as a taxi service. The interviewees expressed no annoyance at having to give up their time in this way. In fact, one mother said it was a good way of meeting other parents. One man argued that the real reason for having to provide children with transport was the current security situation. Other parents were quick to say that Northern Ireland was no more unsafe than anywhere else in the UK and that the main reason for providing transport was either lack of public transport or a desire to enable children to have more time for homework and hobbies.

Some parents found that their child's preferred sport was too expensive; one working woman had prevented her daughter from becoming involved in Irish dancing because of the cost of the dresses and the time commitment required of parents. However, in the meantime her daughter had become interested in another expensive sport, horse riding, but had got herself a job to pay for it!

Parents could also influence children's choice of sport: for example, one father who was keen on racket sports said that his children had also opted for these sports.

Parents were particularly aware of the cost of sports equipment and clothing and their fashion accessory status. They felt there was a need to find ways of making sport cheaper and thus more widely available, and it was argued that sporting celebrities could do more to promote sport and play down the importance of accessories.

It was argued that it was often difficult to get other parents involved in community sporting activities for children. One woman described attempts to set up a youth club in her local parish; parents began by running the club on a weekly rota but it did not last long. It was felt that 'People have this belief that they don't have time'. Thus parents were often unwilling to give up their free time.

One single parent said that she felt that parents were responsible for their children's outside interests outside school hours. She explained how she had been worried about how to help her boys learn to play football before they became too old to learn easily and how she had asked her brother for help.

The role of the school in promoting sport

It appeared that many parents were unaware of the place of sport in the new school curriculum, one man observing that it put increased pressure on children to achieve academically: 'Everyone is going for all these "A" levels and "O" levels and forgetting about sport'. It was even felt that sporting achievements did not count any more. One woman, a school vice-principal, recognised that some parents had a limited awareness of the role and scope of school sport. Parents did not seem to realise that sport was now part of the curriculum and had to be squeezed into an already full timetable. She also remarked that parents should not be so quick to write notes excusing children from school sport since they would not consider doing this for academic subjects. In this way children lost out because they failed to discover the value of sport, in her view an essential alternative to academic work.

One parent, however, pointed out that within the new curriculum there was simply not enough time available for sport. She referred to a school in Belfast where 'almost any kind of physical movement was called sport', so that the amount of time spent on sport looked good on paper but did not impinge too much on the timetable. This wrongly lowered its importance in the eyes of children.

One father said that sport had been pushed to the bottom of the heap, with some sports only available after school: 'you don't do maths after school'. In some schools children were finding that by the time they had changed and showered there were only 30 minutes left for PE; in one school children were asked to arrive in their PE clothes.

Although some schools succeeded in providing a range of sports, parents in one group felt that little or nothing was on offer at primary schools. They felt the problem existed because general primary school teachers were not trained in sport and this problem should be rectified. In contrast, members of another group felt that primary school provision was good in terms of both facilities and qualified teachers. In other groups, parents had mixed views. Some felt that primary school provision suffered from the lack of specialist sports teachers, others pointed out that organised games were not available for children until they were 9 years old.

Parents focused particularly on how schools should interest children in sport, for example by teaching the basics when children are young enough to benefit, and by introducing children to a range of sports. The question of how to gain and sustain children's interest raised a number of issues. One mother said that a note was sent home by her child's primary school asking parents to encourage children to become involved in sports such as badminton. Since her child did not even know what badminton was, this presented difficulties. One man suggested that since children mature earlier these days, teaching the basics in sport should start sooner, for example age 9 to 11 years. In his view children were past basic learning in sport after age 11 years, and another suggested that children should be taught the basics as early as age 7 or 8 years. Another man agreed and said that if boys were shown more about how to play football it would encourage them and they would take more interest.

Even at primary school, parents considered that children associated certain sports with particular genders. One mother pointed out that at primary school there was more for girls (that is, netball and hockey) than for boys (that is football and only occasionally rugby). It was generally agreed that at break time boys played football (at the expense of their trousers) whereas girls played hopscotch, tag, skipping and clapping games.

Parents maintained that sport was catered for much better at secondary school, though there were still problems. One man said that teachers did not stay after school to take extra-curricular sport because of the need to spend time developing the new curriculum and possibly also because they had lost interest since teaching was no longer perceived as a job for life. He also pointed out that some older teachers who specialised in games such as rugby had been replaced by younger teachers who wanted to spend their non-classroom hours with the family. Indeed one woman described how a member of the Board of Governors of a school with a long-standing interest in rugby resigned because he was so disgusted at teachers' lack of commitment to sport. At some schools Saturday sport had been discontinued and this was seen as unfortunate. This meant that children were not getting up and out on a Saturday, that less academically able children were not having the opportunity to excel at sport, and that pride in playing for the school team was becoming a thing of the past.

The value of Parent–Teacher Associations (PTAs) was stressed; these associations were considered to be a valuable if underutilised resource for contributing to the cost of coaching.

A parent who also happened to be a PE teacher argued that schools could only cater for majority interests; they did not have the resources to help individuals in minority sports and so they let these pupils down. In the case of gymnastics, schools did not have the facilities, the expertise or the staff. Gymnastics at school was thus an introduction but to go further pupils then needed to join a club. In any case PE teachers did not normally feel they were knowledgeable enough to teach the like of double somersaults. If there were an accident there would inevitably be litigation.

In the case of minority sports such as golf, therefore, the school could not take credit for pupils' successes except that it allowed them to play golf during school hours. Asked why gymnastics equipment was not used in many schools, the PE teacher said that this was because many children could not vault properly or needed help and these days there was a policy of not humiliating children. The idea was that they should develop their skills in a school club. However, schools rarely had a gymnastics club so children had to join outside clubs. Furthermore, teachers' morale had been greatly undermined by claims made against them as a result of accidents; the more equipment that was out, the greater the risk of injuries.

Teachers' understanding of children's motivation and health problems and how these affected a child's attitude to and performance at sport was questioned. One man maintained that teachers needed a course in sport psychology. His children had been put off rugby because they were required to run round the field six times before they even started, with no explanation as to why this running was relevant. Another parent reinforced the need for greater understanding on the part of teachers; her son normally wore glasses but had to take them off for sport with the result that he could not even see the teacher properly (to his great embarrassment).

Within the group, parents felt that teachers needed a refresher course on how to deal with children psychologically, and specifically in relation to asthma. The recent death of a child on a sports field as a result of an asthma attack left parents of asthmatic children very concerned. One woman asked if asthmatics were not helped by sport and was told that swimming helped; one man commented that chlorine affected his asthmatic daughter; another woman said that her asthmatic son hated sport, not least because he often had to use his nebuliser which embarrassed him; one man reinforced the need for teachers' attitudes to be changed because otherwise asthmatic children were branded as invalids; one woman said that the teacher had phoned her and asked her to bring in her child's nebuliser because the inhaler was insufficient – something which happened if her child did too much exercise. She felt the school should have a clear policy about how to deal with asthma.

The role of sports facilities outside school

The main kinds of facilities used were leisure centres (offering archery, badminton), youth clubs (featuring a wide range of sports), Gaelic Athletic Association (GAA) clubs, Boys Brigade and specialist sports clubs (running, badminton, rugby, hockey), including those run by the local church (for example, badminton). Parents generally commented on the limited scope of facilities, especially outside towns and cities, and on the problem of obtaining information about specialist coaching and clubs.

Several parents maintained that leisure centres were underutilised and should be visited more frequently by primary schools. One woman said the schools should not be blamed since children could go to leisure centres after school if they wished. It was agreed that with large classes sports teaching had to be directed at the majority rather than the most able children.

Parents felt that facilities in country areas were not adequate. Some parents had children who attended clubs for triathlon, cycling or gymnastics. It was generally felt that facilities in the north-west of the province could be better, and that opportunities for young people to get onto national teams were much fewer than for their Belfast counterparts. One woman had great difficulty finding out where to take her sons for gymnastics in the first place. She reluctantly settled for a small gym with poor facilities but endowed with an excellent coach. One college did not have the requisite spring flooring for gymnastics so pupils had to go elsewhere to train for competitions. In Belfast, it was enviously claimed, they had Russian coaches.

Progress in the sport of tennis was seen to depend on the availability of indoor courts which cost money. Tennis was not a priority in the eyes of councils so private money was required. It was suggested that Northern Ireland had much to learn from tennis enthusiasts in the south who were accustomed to having no government support; for example, it was recounted that in Sligo a club with 1,000 members had raised £100,000 to build good facilities.

One general problem identified in relatively small communities was that a small number of people in each sport carried a heavy burden for that sport. People in rural areas generally believed it was easier in more densely populated areas to find people to share the load. Asked if there was a solution to this problem the response was that people must be educated. Another general problem was that of obtaining qualified instructors. With the risk of litigation the qualifications were much more difficult to obtain and required a considerable time investment. The result was increased difficulty in obtaining qualified instructors for enterprises such as the Duke of Edinburgh's Award scheme.

Being selected for national teams was considered to be much more difficult for children who lived outside Belfast. For example, parents from the Derry area argued it was more difficult to get onto the national hockey team because they were not so well known to the selectors. At selection trials, comments were often made such as 'She didn't do herself justice today'. By not having known 'form' it was argued that players from the Derry area had to be even better to gain selection.

One woman stressed the value of encouraging children to participate in sport and thereby discouraging them from drinking, smoking and generally lounging about. At the same time there was general dissatisfaction with public facilities and the lack of information about sports' opportunities for children. One man complained that cutbacks at leisure centres had resulted in restricted opening hours and limited access to facilities. He noted that many now have high-tech gyms but said they were there to bring in more money. He also said that council playing fields were of a poor standard with no changing rooms, no caretakers and problems with dog fouling and broken glass.

Youth clubs, GAA clubs, Boys Brigade and leisure centres provided the main sports facilities outside school. Youth clubs were considered to be an extremely cost-effective way of exploring new sports, especially outdoor pursuits, while GAA clubs and the Boys Brigade offered a wide range of competitive sports. Leisure centres were regarded as excellent places for sport after school with the advantages of qualified instructors and on-site first aid. When one woman heard that trampolining was available at some centres she said that leisure centres should advertise their attractions because had she known about the trampolining she would have taken her children.

The role of coaching

Not all parents had experience of coaching and did not necessarily recognise it as an activity distinct from the teaching of basic skills. Indeed there seemed to be general confusion about the difference between the two but the value of systematic teaching of basic skills was recognised. One mother said that her boys had had swimming lessons and if they had not had coaching they would never have learned to swim. Another woman said that her girls had the opportunity to attend specialist teaching on jumping hurdles (run by a Northern Ireland coach) at the local leisure centre. They protested about this because they were the smallest. However, with some misgivings, she insisted on taking them and they thoroughly enjoyed it because, she claimed, someone had taken a real interest in them and shown them how to jump hurdles properly. She was delighted to be able to say, 'Mummies always know best'!

One woman's children received weekly tennis lessons and also attended a summer tennis clinic (two weeks) and one at Easter (four days); another woman remarked that her child was enjoying individual ski lessons at the artificial ski slope and was benefiting considerably from individual attention. One man said he would like his children to have access to specialist peripatetic sports lessons at school.

At the same time some less positive experiences of the system were reported. For example, two women once took their children to swimming classes but since they never seemed to get anywhere, and also the whole activity was very inconvenient and time consuming for the parents, they gave it up. At first the parents thought it was the fault of their children but at a later stage the children were taught to swim by someone else and had no problems. One man took his son to judo classes as a result of his son seeing it on television. However, although the coach was good the boy was put off by the discipline, 'It wasn't boisterous enough for him'.

Occasionally some concern was expressed about the implications of training children in competitive sports. One woman referred to her brother who trained swimmers including his own son. Both rose at 5.00 a.m. and in her view the son was unpleasantly competitive. He was in fact two years younger than the people he competed against and still won medals. A man who initially raised the subject of Sunday sport complained about athletics coaching on Sundays, claiming that it should be on Saturdays, but one woman pointed out this would clash with sports matches. She also noted that no one forced coaches to work on Sundays but they did it out of choice. The mother of a triathlon champion commented that had her son not cycled on Sundays he would have missed vital races watched by selectors.

Coaching and associated support was considered essential for success in a sport. One example cited as good practice was tennis, where the Ulster Branch sent out coaches to local areas to coach players and encourage aspiring coaches. In contrast, the mother of an Irish Junior Triathlon Champion from Derry could now see that he had received very little in the north-west before moving to England.

How young people can be attracted to sport

Various suggestions were made, including making it more fun, having extrinsic rewards, and making parents support children's sporting events. One mother commented, 'If the parents don't care the children don't'. It was also argued that parents should focus more on the importance of physical fitness than on winning and that winning should not be a prequisite for parental support. In addition, sporting personalities (such as The Gladiators) should be introduced to school children, as had happened at one primary school where the visit made a considerable impact. 'Try it and see' events should also be run for school children on a regional basis, and leisure centres should be encouraged to focus on sport for the family.

Youth clubs which focus on sport were considered useful vehicles for attracting children to sport. However, some parents had experienced problems setting them up. One woman described how she and some friends attempted to set up a youth club but they found that they ended up providing a minding and taxi service for other people's children and hence became disenchanted.

DISCUSSION

In the first place, the value of sport was recognised by all. As parents pointed out, children appeared to spend the majority of their leisure time involved with sport, although a range of other activities continued to compete significantly for their time. However, it was felt, particularly by those from rural areas, that children were not always getting the right type of tuition or receiving suitable introductions to a range of sports at the appropriate stages of their young lives.

Élite athletes' justifications for participating in sport were persuasive, and at the same time it should not be forgotten that those interviewed seemed to be extremely content and satisfied with their lives and had very positive relationships with their parents. Indeed, their sports activities attracted a good deal of family attention, also involving other brothers or sisters, to the extent that sport became the centre of family life. At the same time, they enjoyed an exhilarating yet loosely supervised social life, much of it away from home at a time when other parents may have been carefully monitoring curfews and anxiously wondering what their children were really doing when they went out.

These young athletes enjoyed attention from parents and coaches alike, yet when they went away for competitions they had the opportunity to enjoy personal freedom, to explore, meet new people and develop self-confidence. Thus they experienced independence without sacrificing parental approval and attention. Indeed, parents were respected for the effort they put into supporting their chosen sport. For their part, parents felt needed and proud of their children. Hence the pay-off for both parties was extremely positive. Undoubtedly there were tensions, yet there appeared to be an unwritten contract which ensured that the interests of both parties remained in balance. While the élite performers were succeeding and as long as parents provided the necessary resources and support, the contract remained intact.

Explanations about what attracted the young élite performers to sport can be summed up as the pleasure of winning, a good social life and fitness, but not always in that order. Younger athletes were also attracted by extrinsic rewards; they tended to place a higher value on the fun side of sport while older athletes emphasised fitness and a good social life. It would also appear that athletes were aware that they were paying a price for achieving excellence. They made every effort to present themselves as completely normal and uncomplicated, yet there was evidence that they experienced peer jealousy, difficulties in maintaining close friendships with non-élite performers and some suggestions that they were motivated by the desire for parental or peer approval, rather than personal achievement.

Coaches accepted the above list of motivators but added self-confidence and improved level of skills. They also highlighted how important a child's first impressions of sport could be, emphasising that sport should be enjoyable at primary school.

The role played by the media in the presentation of sport was also identified. This worked in two ways. On the one hand children could develop awareness and enthusiasm for sports through seeing these sports on television; on the other hand they may come to expect success quickly and were consequently disappointed and demotivated when they failed. Additionally, many children appeared to perceive sport as an activity with an image comprising fashion accessories as well as the performance itself. Parents then find themselves under pressure to purchase expensive equipment which for the reasons just outlined may soon be discarded when interest in the sport is lost.

Élite performers were unambiguous about their dependence on their parents who provided them with moral support, transport and finance. These necessities were likewise recognised by both parents and coaches, though coaches were firm about the need to prevent parents from interfering with coaching. Parents' occasional attempts to push reluctant athletes were interpreted as 'nagging', though generally recognised as the unfortunate downside of parental support. Parents also acknowledged that children needed skills and the means of acquiring them, as well as individual attention and inspiration from other sources (for example, media personalities).

As regards the role played by schools, it was generally recognised that schools provided a useful starting point or introduction to sport. At the same time it was felt that many schools concentrated too heavily on a small number of sports, usually the PE teacher's own specialism, and there was perceived favouritism towards team sports over individual sports and a general avoidance of contact sports and especially those regarded as minority sports. In addition, both parents and coaches felt that schools did not normally seem to respond to external coaching programmes, nor was there sufficient space available in the timetable for sport, and specialist sports teaching in primary schools was seen as limited in some areas.

Parents seemed uninformed about the role of sport in the new Common Curriculum and at secondary level there was evidence that some teachers (both of PE and of other subjects) had lost interest in extra-curricular sport, whether because of the Common Curriculum, additional calls on their time or because of generally low morale and discontentment.

As regards sports facilities outside the school, it was maintained that facilities, particularly outside urban areas, could be improved and that more schools should be provided with purpose-built facilities. Accurate information on the availability of existing facilities was seen as patchy, for example there seemed to be misconceptions about what was currently available in certain localities. Bearing in mind the need for facilities, it seems surprising that leisure centres were viewed as offering restricted services, and parents in particular felt that primary schools would benefit from greater access to leisure centres. Many parents indicated that they were hungry for more information and constantly searching for activities suitable for their children.

Turning to coaching, the élite athletes were unambiguous about the benefits they derived from coaching. However, parents and coaches both identified communication problems. On the one hand, parents seem to have had difficulty obtaining information about the availability of coaching; on the other, offers of specialist coaching which were sent out to schools often received little response. Several parents thought peripatetic coaches should visit schools and indeed volunteered that they would be willing to help raise money through their PTAs to help finance such schemes. Parents also seemed to confuse basic skills teaching with more specialised coaching. This seemed to be indicative of a wider lack of parental awareness about the structure of sports education and access routes to sporting opportunities.

Hence, these focus groups have revealed yet again the groundswell of support and enthusiasm for sport among young athletes, parents and coaches alike, and the findings from this qualitative research match results outlined in other chapters very closely indeed. The motivation is plain to see, the perceived value of competitive sport is acknowledged and the willingness to invest heavily in terms of time, money and effort is unmistakable. Against this backcloth, each group was able to identify a series of structural barriers to progress. Some have major resource implications, others involve the fine tuning of existing procedures or the opening of effective lines of communication. It is to be hoped that these voices are heard and are acted upon in order to ensure that enthusiasm for sporting involvement is able to translate into young people's increased involvement in sport and physical recreation.

9 Modelling participation motivation in sport

Garnet J. Busby

INTRODUCTION

Over recent years the benefits associated with habitual exercise and physical fitness have become better understood. However, the psychological mechanisms which underlie successful adherence to exercise regimes still remain obscure. Indeed it is only in the last 20 to 30 years that the systematic study of motivational processes in sport and, more recently, in exercise has received significant and sustained attention from sport and exercise psychologists. This chapter stands apart from other contributions to this book by taking as its starting point not the data set itself but the process of motivation. In this sense it is primarily driven by theory, or the need to set in place a theoretical substrate to our discussion of the data. Along the way the data are referenced, but always in the context of a process model of participation.

Typically in the research literature the term motivation has been used to refer to those personality factors, social variables, affective states (or moods) and/or cognitions that come into play when a person undertakes some form of physical activity. Hence participation motivation refers to the reasons which individuals adopt for initiating, continuing and then sustaining involvement in physical activity, as well as the reasons which individuals choose to discontinue involvement (Roberts, 1992).

According to Fishbein and Middlestadt (1987), the more one knows about the factors underlying a decision to perform a given behaviour, the greater the probability of influencing that decision. Looking back at the history of research, it would be fair to say that the majority of studies on participation and discontinuation motivation have been descriptive in nature. A review of these studies reveals several common themes. First, self-report studies have produced a fairly consistent set of motivational factors. These include competence (to learn skills and improve skills), health/fitness (to lose weight and to feel better), affiliation (to be with friends), enjoyment (to experience fun, challenge and excitement) and competition (to prove oneself). By way of example, Gill, Gross and Huddleston (1983) questioned 720 boys and 480 girls about their motives for participating in a number of sports. Factor analytic results indicated that 'success, team-atmosphere, friendship, fitness, energy release, skill development and fun' were basic dimensions of participation motivation. Similarly, Sapp and Haubenstricker (1978) studied the participation motivation of over 1,000 young sportspeople. They found that 'having fun' and 'improving skills' were the most popular reasons for participation. In yet another study, Gould, Feltz and Weiss (1985) found that fun, fitness, skill improvement, friendship and challenge were cited as the primary motives for participation by young swimmers. More recently, a study by Thuot (1995), which examined the reasons given by 100 college students for sports participation from childhood through to adulthood, found that the most frequent reason given for post-college involvement was enjoyment. In a study of participation motivation among Italian youth, Buonamano, Cei and Mussino (1995) also found that enjoyment (49 per cent) was the most popular reason for participation, followed by health/fitness (32 per cent), social reasons (9 per cent) and competitive motives (4 per cent).

A second common finding in these studies is that most individuals advance multiple motives for their involvement in sport and exercise (Gould and Horn, 1984; Ebbeck, Gibbons and Loken-Dahle 1995). A third is that gender (Gill, 1988) and culture (Weingarten *et al.*, 1984) have also been found to have a significant impact on the motives cited for participation. Finally, Weiss and Chaumeton (1992) found age differences in the reasons given for participation; for children and older adults, fun seems to provide the main motivation, whereas for young and middle-aged adults, health and fitness appears to be the motivating force. However, according to Willis and Campbell (1992) no matter what their initial motivation for sport and exercise participation, few people continue in a sport programme unless they find a form of exercise they enjoy.

The descriptive research on discontinuation motivation has paralleled that for participation motives. Orlick (1973), for example, interviewed 60 former Canadian sports participants ranging in age from 7 to 18 years and found that negative experiences were a major factor for discontinuing sports participation. 'Dislike for the coach', 'lack of playing time' and 'too high an emphasis on competition' were cited as the main reasons for dropping out. However, later research has failed to replicate these findings.

Gould *et al.* (1982) studied the reasons for dropping out given by 50 former swimmers, aged 10 to 18 years. The most frequently cited motives were 'other things to do', 'not enough fun', 'wanted to participate in another sport' and 'not as good as I wanted to be'. Overall, 84 per cent of the swimmers identified factors related to conflict of interest as an important or very important motive in their decision to discontinue swimming involvement.

In studies of healthy adults, the primary reason given for dropping out of a programme is 'lack of time'. In a representative study, participants said that the programme took too much time away from family and work (Gettman, Pollock and Ward, 1983). Medical problems, such as injury or illness, being unmotivated or lazy, and contextual factors such as expense, travelling distance and class times, were other reasons cited for dropping out.

In sum, the research findings on sport attrition have identified a number of reasons why individuals discontinue their involvement in sport and exercise. The most commonly identified motives for withdrawal were 'lack of time' and 'having other things to do', but it is unclear from this descriptive research whether these reasons are, at least in part, the result of dissatisfaction with the 'sport experience', or whether they are genuinely unavoidable.

Although there is much of interest in these descriptive studies, in order for understanding to advance, description and interpretation must go hand in hand. Hence, researchers need to focus on testing and modifying models and theories in relation to the accumulated data. Reflective of the infancy of exercise psychology, the current theoretical explanations of exercise motivation are best described as tentative. So far, few efforts have been made to develop theories unique to exercise, although some researchers have attempted to adapt existing psychological theories to explain and predict exercise behaviours. These theories and models include competence motivation theory (Harter, 1981), the psychological model for physical activity participation (Sonstroem, 1978), the health belief model (Rosenstock, 1974) and self-efficacy theory (Bandura, 1977), among others.

Perhaps one of the most popular and indeed productive theories for studying youth sport participation motives has been competence motivation theory (Harter, 1981; see Chapter 3). According to Harter, individuals are motivated to demonstrate competence in the social, cognitive and physical domains of achievement and do so by engaging in mastery attempts (Harter, 1978). The appeal of the model for sport and exercise psychologists is obvious, especially as the original scale already incorporated 'perceived competence in the physical domain' as a sub-scale. According to competence motivation theory, individuals high in perceptions of competence and internal control will exert more effort, persist at achievement tasks longer and experience more positive affect than individuals who are lower on these characteristics. One prediction of Harter's theory is that children who perceive themselves to be competent in sport in turn will be more likely to participate in sport. Roberts, Kleiber and Duda (1981) tested this prediction and found that sport participants were higher in perceived competence, as measured by Harter's physical competence scale, than were non-participants. However, the relationship was not strong. Indeed while competence motivation theory has been one of the most frequently cited theoretical frameworks in relation to participation motivation, the relationships which have been noted between perceived competence and participation generally have been weak (for example, Feltz and Petlichkoff, 1983; Feltz and Brown, 1984; Ulrich, 1987). As a result, it has been suggested that children may participate for many reasons other than just to demonstrate competence (Klint and Weiss, 1987). Perhaps perceived self-competence therefore represents one significant part of the jigsaw of participation motivation but possibly does not provide the whole solution.

The health belief model (HBM) represents an alternative approach. It has been one of the most enduring theoretical models associated with preventive health behaviours and the model contains three major elements:

1 A person's readiness to take action is determined by their perceived susceptibility to a particular illness and by their perceptions of the severity of the consequences.
2 An internal or external stimulus that triggers the appropriate health behaviour.
3 The person's evaluation of the advocated health behaviour in terms of its perceived benefits versus perceived barriers (physical, psychological, financial, etc.).

Several researchers have used the HBM in studies of exercise behaviours, where the third element, 'perceived barriers', has been found to be the most strongly related to compliance (Tirrell and Hart, 1980). At the same time, and contrary to the predictions of the model, Lindsay-Reid and Osborn (1980) found that perceptions of susceptibility to heart disease and to general illness were negatively associated with exercise participation. People, as already noted, engage in exercise for a host of reasons which may or may not include health. The HBM does not, and more importantly cannot, account for this diversity of motives.

The psychological model for physical activity participation (Sonstroem, 1978) is one of the rare theoretical contributions to have been developed specifically to address the question of participation in physical activity. Sonstroem's model is an attempt to identify mechanisms underlying participation in physical activity and the psychological benefits associated with involvement. Stated simply it is assumed that initial involvement in physical activity increases physical ability, which raises physical self-estimation and leads to higher levels of overall self-esteem. The continuance of physical activity then leads to increased perception of physical ability and heightened self-esteem, which results in even greater attraction to physical activity, and the cycle continues. Although the model has been successful in predicting adoption of physical activity, Sonstroem (1988) himself, in a critique of his own model, has acknowledged its inability to predict exercise adherence. Recent developments by Sonstroem and Morgan (1989) have led to a more complex model of self-esteem and exercise that may be more successful in attempting to explain prolonged exercise behaviour, but to date this model remains largely untested.

In its various forms, over the last 15 years cognitive theory has increasingly dominated the study of human motivation, and one approach derived from this tradition holds considerable promise for understanding exercise and physical activity. According to social cognitive theory, otherwise known as self-efficacy theory (Bandura, 1977; 1986), self-efficacy involves more than the possession of knowledge and skills; it also includes the perception that one is capable of performing effectively. Perceived efficacy is believed to affect both the initiation and persistence of behaviour; that is, people tend to involve themselves in activities and behave with confidence if they perceive these activities are within their ability to cope. Mastery expectations, in other words, influence both choice of activity and performance.

Bandura proposed four ways in which self-efficacy may be enhanced. These are past performance accomplishments, vicarious experience, social persuasion and physiological arousal (Bandura, 1977). Of these four factors, the most important for the development of self-efficacy is past performance accomplishment. When athletes repeatedly experience success they begin to expect to be successful and thereby develop feelings of self-efficacy. In other words a success circle is created in which success leads to belief in one's self which in turn leads to even greater success. Bandura has gone on to demonstrate that the most effective way to help individuals develop self-efficacy is through participatory modelling, where the coach shows the subject what to do and then helps him or her perform the task successfully a number of times.

The theory predicts that those who perceive themselves to be best able to reach their targets with respect to their physical capabilities are then more likely to adopt and maintain some form of physical activity. Sallis *et al.* (1986) found self-efficacy to be a significant predictor of both the adoption of vigorous exercise and the maintenance of moderate activity. Also, research with gymnasts has demonstrated that those exhibiting higher self-efficacy expectations are more successful than those with lower expectations (Weiss, Wiese and Klint, 1989). In addition, Feltz and Mugno (1983) and Kavanagh and Hausfeld (1986) have shown the effectiveness of participatory modelling in sports-related situations. Overall, studies that have examined the relationship between self-efficacy and sport performance have found a positive relationship but in most cases this relationship is weak (Feltz, 1982; McAuley, 1985). Once more, the general findings suggest that self-efficacy is a reliable, even if modest, predictor of sport performance, but other mechanisms can and do contribute to achievement behaviours (Bandura, 1986; Feltz, 1988).

In a very similar vein, cognitive evaluation theory argues that intrinsic motivation is maximised when individuals feel competent and self-determining in dealing with their environment (Deci, Cascio and Krusell, 1975; Deci and Ryan, 1985). Deci has argued that any activity which affects an individual's perceptions of competence and feelings of self-determination will ultimately have an impact on the individual's level of intrinsic motivation. Events, according to cognitive evaluation theory, consist of two functional parts, a controlling aspect and an informational aspect. The 'controlling aspect' relates to an individual's perceived locus of causality within any situation. For example, if an event or situation is seen as controlling one's behaviour, then an external locus of causality and a low level of self-determination will be enhanced and this will cause a decrease in intrinsic motivation. Conversely, if an event is seen as one that contributes to an 'internal locus of causality', that is the person feels they have control over their destiny, then intrinsic motivation will increase. The 'informational aspect' refers to the perceived competence of the individual. If an activity provides negative information about an individual's competence, then intrinsic motivation will decrease while activities that provide positive information about competence will result in higher perceived competence and intrinsic motivation.

Numerous research projects have substantiated these principles in the sport domain. For example, Orlick and Mosher (1978) examined the influence of type of reward on children's motivation. They concluded that external rewards for an inherently interesting activity may undermine children's interest in that activity and therefore jeopardise future participation. Likewise, Ryan (1980) studied the effects of college scholarships on athletes' intrinsic motivation. He hypothesised that athletes on scholarships, that is those receiving concrete, extrinsic rewards, would report less intrinsic motivation than non-scholarship athletes. His results supported this contention. Vallerand and Reid (1984) conducted a study to investigate the effects of feedback on perceived competence and intrinsic motivation. They found that subjects in a positive feedback condition scored higher on intrinsic motivation than subjects in a no-feedback condition. These results again offer support for cognitive evaluation theory, and the role which cognitive evaluation plays in relating rewards to motivation. However, this is once more unikely to be the whole picture but instead one component of the process which translates motive into action.

In contrast, the social role–social system model (Kenyon and McPherson, 1973) has identified a number of factors to be included in any analysis of participant motivation. These are:

- The psychological and physical attributes of the person 'being socialised'.
- The encouragement and rewards provided by others, especially significant others, and the opportunities for those 'being socialised' to 'rehearse' various sports roles.
- The social systems (such as family, peer group, school, community) in which those 'being socialised' are exposed to and influenced by general values, norms and orientations.

The social role–social system model has generated a number of studies which in turn have generated the following conclusions:

- Participation in sport roles is positively related to the amount of social support coming from significant others (Higginson, 1985; Furst, 1989).
- The relative influence of various significant others and the extent and type of encouragement received in particular social systems varies for 'athletes' and 'non-athletes' by gender (Fagot, 1984), socio-economic status (Hasbrook, 1986), race (Harris and Hunt, 1984), age (Rudman, 1989), and culture (Yamaguchi, 1984).
- Socialisation does involve reciprocity or bi-directional effects in the sense that children's involvement in sport creates responses among

adults who sponsor and encourage that involvement (Hasbrook, 1986).

However, in nearly all these studies, the percentage of variance explained by socialising agents is very low (Weiss and Knoppers, 1982), and there is considerable confusion about the relative influence of different socialising agents.

Yet another approach has been proposed by Smith (1986). His conceptual model of sport withdrawal contends that sport drop-out results largely from a change of interests or a logical cost–benefit analysis by the athlete, whereas sport burnout is withdrawal from sport due to chronic stress. Smith believes that social exchange theory (Thibaut and Kelly, 1959) best explains drop-out, while burnout is best explained by cognitive–affective theories of stress (for example, Lazarus, 1966).

The basic premise of social exchange theory is that social behaviour is driven by the desire to maximise positive experiences and minimise negative experiences, that is to accentuate the positive and eliminate the negative. Individuals will remain in relationships or activities so long as the outcome is favourable, which is itself said to be a function of costs and benefits. The decision to remain involved in a current activity is not merely a function of costs and benefits but rather includes two levels of satisfaction – satisfaction with the current activity and satisfaction with alternative activities. Thus an individual weighs the costs, benefits and satisfaction of a current situation with those of alternative activities and makes a decision accordingly. This explanation of sport drop-out is consistent with two patterns of findings in the participation motivation literature. First, the most frequently cited motive for sport drop-out, as we have seen above, is 'having other things to do'. Second, since most individuals cite multiple motives for both participation and drop-out, it seems apparent that behaviour is not the result of a single factor but is likely to be influenced by a weighting of the costs and benefits of continued participation.

While the notion of cost–benefit analysis is intuitively appealing only one study has used it in an investigation of participant motivation in sport and exercise. This was Petlichkoff's (1988) study of motivation among high school basketball players. However, while Petlichkoff's results supported the contentions of social exchange theory, more research needs to be conducted using this theory before its practical utility can be accurately gauged in the area of sport and exercise motivation.

Another theory which seems potentially relevant but has attracted little research is the theory of reasoned action (Fishbein and Ajzen, 1975), a theory which enjoys prominence within social psychology in relation to attitude change research. The theory argues that specific measures of attitude, in conjunction with social influences, will predict behavioural intention and subsequent behaviour. This theory is based on the assumption that intention is an immediate determinant of behaviour and that intention, in turn, is predicted from attitudinal and social (subjective) factors. Fishbein and Ajzen suggest that the attitude component of the model is a function of the beliefs held about the specific behaviour, as well as the evaluation (value) of the likely outcomes. The social norm component of the theory comprises of the beliefs of significant others and the extent that the individual wishes or is motivated to comply with these beliefs.

The theory of reasoned action has been recommended but used only occasionally in exercise research (Riddle, 1980; Godin and Shephard, 1990). For example, Riddle (1980) found a correlation of 0.82 between intention and sport behaviour. Additionally, attitude towards the behaviour and the subjective norm component combined to explain 55 per cent of the variance in intentions. At the same time the theory has not been without its critics, and it appears that perhaps certain parts of the model can be related to participation even if the total model works less well (Godin and Shephard, 1986a; 1986b). Since Riddle's (1980) study, reports on the common variance between intentions and exercise behaviour have been substantially lower, ranging from a low of 9 per cent (Wurtele and Maddux, 1987) to a high of 32 per cent (Valois, Desharnais and Godin, 1988). It would seem that intentions may be generally necessary but not sufficient to predict physical activity.

The theory of planned behaviour goes beyond the theory of reasoned action by considering perceived and actual control over behaviour. It recognises that intentions, however powerful, are often not implemented because of factors such as lack of ability, situational barriers, or even the instability of intentions (Ajzen, 1985). The theory of planned behaviour would seem to have considerable potential in relation to understanding exercise behaviours, particularly as physical activity in the real world is often impeded by many barriers, thus making it something that is only partly under volitional control. However, to date few studies testing the model have been reported (Dzewaltowski, Noble and Shaw, 1990).

Looking across these theories, each in its own way has helped to illuminate crucial mechanisms involved in participant motivation in sport and exercise, but in fairness each could be accused of failing to identify all the elements that energise, direct and sustain exercise behaviour. As is clear, no one theory has emerged as 'the single and sovereign approach'; each has its supporters, each its detractors. It can be argued that any single approach inevitably will be inadequate in attempting to explain something as complex as participation motivation. For example, competence theory cannot hope to explain why thousands of us continue to play football even though we are not very good at it; the HBM cannot explain why many continue to run or play sport, even though they are injured, and the activity can only make their injuries worse.

One of the most important lessons to be gleaned from the descriptive data, including the present data set, is that young people generally give several reasons for participating in sport and exercise, and fundamentally each of these single perspectives has been unable to take account of this complexity of purpose. For example, when asked to rate the reasons why they continued in their chosen sport, the majority of young people in the SCNI Survey spontaneously mentioned a great many factors, including getting better (78 per cent), enjoyment (69 per cent), feeling good (67 per cent), keeping fit (65 per cent), making friends (63 per cent) and the excitement of the sport (63 per cent). For the majority, all these factors, and not just a subgroup, were important reasons for their continued participation and any theory must be able to accommodate this sophistication of motivation and intent, alongside extrinsic motivators and inhibitors which govern our thoughts and actions.

At best each theory gives us a snapshot of why some participate at one point in time and some do not. For example, it could be argued that self-efficacy only becomes an important factor after the initial decision to, say, 'exercise to lose weight' has been made. After the initial decision the next question is: 'Am I confident of my ability to exercise, run, play squash, etc., or maybe I should, perhaps, try walking to and from my work for a while to see how that goes first?' Of course some people become involved in various forms of physical activity for health reasons or to demonstrate their physical competence but often these reasons may be insufficient to sustain interest. Once involved, some individuals may be 'bitten by the exercise bug' or they may come to enjoy the social contact associated with an exercise class. For example, the SCNI Survey revealed that school, family and friends were the three most important socialising influences on young people's decision to take up sport. However, as seen above, once involved in sport and exercise other factors become increasingly important in determining continued participation. In this way participation motivation must be conceptualised as an ongoing process with different motivating factors kicking in or vying for salience at different points during the course of an individual's life. Once more, any comprehensive model of participation must be capable of coping with and explaining the complicated dynamics of sport and exercise adherence over time.

The approaches briefly reviewed here have opened up important avenues of exploration and have offered insights into the process of motivation. Through these theories it is possible to see the importance of cognition, learning, socialisation, expectancies, values and affect (or mood) on whether individuals become involved in sport and then continue their interest. Current theories have shown that participation motivation is a highly complex phenomenon comprising individual, social and situational factors. Taking any of these factors or concepts in isolation makes us vulnerable to a myopic and static view of the motivation process. Instead it is how these variables interact which must be explored if our understanding of participation motivation is to progress further.

TOWARDS AN INTEGRATED PROCESS MODEL OF PARTICIPATION MOTIVATION

To reiterate, participation motivation in sport and exercise is a multidimensional construct that can be viewed from a variety of different theoretical perspectives. Alongside their unique theoretical contributions to the understanding of exercise participation, many perspectives share similarities with regard to the underlying processes used to explain and describe sport and exercise participation. The next logical step towards understanding participation motivation must therefore be the formulation of models which try to pull together common themes from various theories, incorporate findings from the empirical research, and initiate a process of thoughtful consideration of the relationship between factors affecting sport motivation.

Given the explosion of research in this area over the past 15 years it should come as no surprise to learn that a number of researchers have recently taken this step, and have attempted to integrate the common and unique components of a variety of theories in order to form a cohesive model which they hope will embrace all, or most, of the motivational influences on sport and exercise participation.

An early example was Gould who devised a model of youth sport withdrawal which addresses intrapersonal, motivational and situational influences. Gould found that factors affecting withdrawal included conflicts of interest, lack of playing time, lack of success, no skill improvement, stress, lack of fun, dislike of coach, boredom and injury (Gould and Horn, 1984; Gould, Feltz and Weiss, 1985). Gould incorporated these factors into his three-component attrition model, in order to explain the process of withdrawal (Gould, 1987; Gould and Petlichkoff, 1988). He first emphasised that an individual may withdraw from a particular activity rather than sport in general. He then proposed that individuals employ a cost–benefit analysis (based on social exchange) to gauge satisfaction with the activity (comparison level) and then weigh it up against alternative activities. The third component, motivation for withdrawal, is made up of two parts, explanations (derived from descriptive research) and theoretical constructs, which he drew from a number of theories, including achievement goals, Harter's competence motivation theory and Smith's cognitive affective model of stress (Kremer and Scully, 1994).

A second integrative model is the sport commitment model (Schmidt and Stein, 1991), which is based on an elaborated version of social exchange theory, emphasising the athlete's commitment to sport. The model focuses on the positive and non-positive factors that act over time to hold the athlete in a chosen sport, suggesting that people continue participation for one of two reasons. First, they may stay involved for reasons of enjoyment. These people would be characterised by 'increasing rewards, lower costs, increasing satisfaction, lower alternatives, and increasing investments'. The second type of person will continue their involvement for reasons unrelated to enjoyment and these people are more vulnerable to burn-out: 'Persons in danger of burn-out may experience a sharp increase in costs with no attendant rise in rewards, the perception of low or non-existent alternatives, and an increase in already high investments in sport' (Schmidt and Stein, 1991). It is a combination of alternatives and investments that distinguishes burn-out from drop-out. Drop-outs will leave sport because of lack of enjoyment. These people are characterised by steady or falling rewards, increasing costs, decreasing satisfaction, increasing alternatives and lowered investment. Burn-out is more likely to occur where an athlete has made large investments in an activity and therefore finds it difficult to quit before literally burning out.

Coming from a more sociological tradition, Greendorfer's (1992) research on sport socialisation cites three clusters of factors which influence participation. These are personal attributes (personality, achievement goals, competence, experience), significant others (parents, peers, coaches and role models) and socialisation situations (culture and opportunity). Through the combined influence of these factors, role learning occurs. Her model emphasises the importance of role models, gender (boys tend to have more positive physical experiences and encouragement than girls and are therefore more likely to participate, see Chapter 2), and experience (for example, bad school and coaching experiences may ultimately discourage some children from participating in sport) in determining participation and continuation, while adopting a more macro-perspective to understanding participation.

To date, each of these models remains to be tested in its entirety. It is Weiss and Chaumeton (1992), however, who have undoubtedly produced the most comprehensive integrated model. They have taken a social cognitive approach, concentrating on how personal, social and contextual factors interact to affect an individual's cognition about participation. Weiss and Chaumeton (1992) have integrated a number of major theories to form the motivational orientation model. The model begins with a consideration of the motivational orientation of the individual, and then proceeds to mastery attempts and performance outcomes, responses by significant others and the internalisation of a reward system and a standard of goals. The predominant use of internal criteria for reinforcement and mastery goals, versus dependence on external approval and goals defined by others, then influences the individual's perceptions of competence and control, positive and negative affective outcomes, and (ultimately) motivated behaviour in the form of levels of persistence in the physical achievement domain. In addition to these themes which work their way through the integrated motivation model, the model also takes account of individual differences and social contextual factors, previously shown by several of the motivational orientation theories to have the potential for mediating relationships between motivation and exercise. In the motivational model these factors are shown to the left and right of the 'core' of the model.

While the integrated model of sport motivation was proposed in an attempt to consolidate the findings derived from a range of theoretical approaches, it should be obvious from even this brief description that it draws most heavily on cognitive or motivational orientation approaches to sport and exercise participation. According to this approach the most salient element which affects whether individuals will persist or discontinue is their motivational orientation, that is whether they are intrinsic/mastery oriented or extrinsic/outcome oriented. An intrinsic-oriented individual embraces optimal challenges in which the individual can learn and improve skills and adopts a self-reward system and a standard of mastery goals. This results in enhanced perception of competence and internal control, positive affect and the probability that the individual will continue to participate. The extrinsic-oriented individual, in contrast, selects less than optimal challenges and focuses on the outcome (winning) as a means of judging personal capabilities. This individual may come to depend primarily upon external forms of information to judge physical ability. Perceptions of competence may be attenuated, and perceptions of external control and feelings of anxiety in mastery situations will be fostered. The result may be decrements in persistence behaviour or perhaps dropping out altogether from physical activity.

The integrated model has undoubtedly advanced our understanding of sport motivation. It can be argued, however, that its primary focus on the motivational orientation of the individual has detracted attention from other important factors. For example, social context and support, personality, activity history, self-efficacy, intrinsic and extrinsic rewards, competence, self-esteem and equity are all concepts derived from various theoretical perspectives which at one time or another have been implicated in the search for understanding sport and exercise motivation, and therefore deserve to be incorporated into any genuinely integrated model of participant motivation.

Existing integrated models of sport motivation have also failed to incorporate two of the most important and obvious findings from empirical research into motivation. First, that exercise behaviour is negatively affected by environmental and social barriers. For example, Slenker *et. al* (1984) reported in their study of joggers and non-exercisers that the single most powerful predictor of jogging was what they termed 'barriers', accounting for almost 40 per cent of behaviour. Similar results have been found in tests of several theoretical models (including the health belief model (Tirrell and Hart, 1980); social cognitive theory (Dzewaltowski, Noble and Shaw, 1990); the theory of reasoned action (Sonstroem, 1982) and also in descriptive research (Andrew and Parker, 1979).

Second, descriptive research has identified multiple reasons for initiating, continuing and discontinuing sport and exercise involvement (Gill, Gross and Huddleston, 1983; Gould and Horn, 1984; Ebbeck, Gibbons and Loken-Dahle, 1995). This research has also shown that several, rather that only a few, of these motives are salient as reasons for participation, and that their salience changes over time (Sidney and Shephard, 1976; Knapp *et al.*, 1983). The exercise process itself is dynamic, and the motives which individuals give for participation in the process are themselves dynamic, in that they are liable to change as the process develops. None of the integrated models looked at so far have been able to cope with the dynamics of this process.

The final point concerns the fact that motivational theories in common with any theory (as opposed to model) must address the 'Why question'. Why does someone suddenly take up or stop exercising? Why do they persist? Why do they change to a different sport? Because of its concentration on motivational orientation, the motivational orientation model cannot give an adequate explanation to at least some of these questions. The lens through which it views participation does not afford wide enough scope to deal adequately with these issues. It cannot explain, for example, why someone who has not trained for years suddenly starts again. It can be argued that a truly integrated theory of participant motivation should allow us insights into the variety of participant motives evidenced in sport and exercise contexts.

The failure of the motivational orientation model to incorporate findings such as these may have partially limited its ability to cope with the complexities of participant motivation in sport and exercise. While acknowledging these criticisms, it is imperative not to lose sight of the fact that process models *per se* are undoubtedly the way forward. The present work aims to build upon the concept of an integrated model, pulling together elements from social, cognitive and behavioural approaches to motivation.

Why a process model? Well it seems clear from past research that whichever concepts are more or less important, an individual's motivation to take up sport will be influenced by the reinforcement which is offered, the rewards which accrue and the feedback which is received. These are all terms commonly used in expectancy-value models of work motivation. In research on work motivation these models have been used to describe how personal and environmental variables play a role in determining the relationship between effort, performance, rewards and job satisfaction, and thus future motivation (Kremer and Scully, 1994). Roberts (1992) argues that most achievement motivation theories are couched in expectancy-value terms. It is therefore upon this simple process theory of work motivation that the present model is predicated.

The process model of participant motivation in sport and exercise is depicted in Figure 9.1. While initially the model may appear daunting in its complexity, the process underlying the model is actually straightforward. Stated simply, it is assumed that personal variables such as 'personality', 'experience' and 'role perceptions' interact with contextual variables, such as 'opportunity', 'awareness' and 'interac-

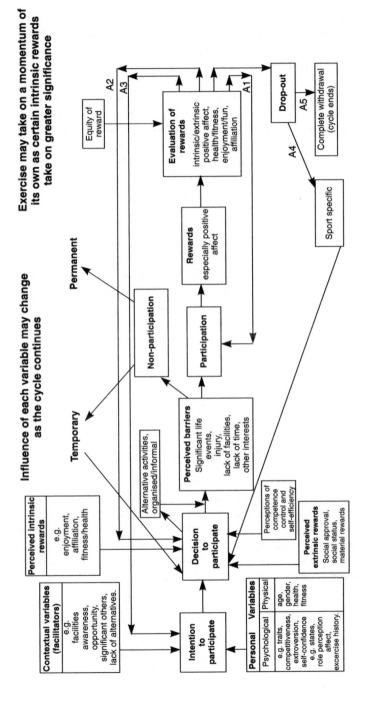

Figure 9.1 The process model of participation motivation in sport and exercise

tion with significant others', to produce an intention to participate. It is these factors which provide the gateway into the exercise process which in turn leads to a decision to participate in a particular physical activity, mediated by perceived intrinsic and extrinsic rewards.

Providing any barriers to participation can be overcome, this decision leads to performance of the activity and internalisation of the perceived rewards. The final step of the process is an evaluation of these rewards. It is this evaluation which provides the dynamic for the model, for as a result of this evaluation the person can choose to follow one of five paths. S/he may weigh up the costs/benefits of participation and choose to drop out, either (1) completely from all sports, in which case the cycle ends, or (2) from this activity in particular, in which case the cycle continues via one of the alternative routes. On the other hand, (3) s/he may intend to continue with the present activity, in which case s/he moves back to the start of the decision process and the cycle repeats itself. (4) The person may make a conscious decision to continue with participation. Alternatively (5), participation may become routine or non-conscious, that is something which takes place without having to think about it. In this case the person will only move back as far as participation in the model, and, as long as things are 'going well', will continue to move in this shortened cycle.

To elaborate on this structure, a brief discussion of each of the model's components along with a rationale for its inclusion is now presented, set in the context of some of the principal findings from the present data.

INTENTION TO PARTICIPATE

The model begins with the assumption that most social behaviours are voluntarily controlled and that intention is the immediate determinant of a decision to act. A number of studies have found intentions to be predictive of exercise behaviour (Riddle, 1980; Dzewaltowski, Noble and Shaw, 1990; Kimiecik, 1992). As shown in Figure 9.1, behavioural intentions are in turn the product of two broad sets of determinants, personal and contextual, and these are outlined below.

Previous experience

There is some suggestion in the literature that an individual's activity history is a significant determinant of participation motivation (Morgan *et al.*, 1984; Valois, Desharnais and Godin, 1988). Harris (1970), in one of the first studies to consider the influence of past involvement, found that physically active men were more likely to have been high school athletes than sedentary men. The active men were also more likely to have participated in physical activity programmes while in college. A further study of 376 college professors also found a relationship between prior experiences in high school and college sports and more extensive exercise involvement later in life (Krotee and La Point, 1979). In addition, past participation in an exercise programme has been found to be one of the most reliable predictors of current and future participation in such programmes (Dishman, 1985). Bearing this last study in mind it would seem logical to propose that the more recent an individual's involvement in an activity, the more likely it is that the individual will repeat that activity. It also seems likely that negative past experiences with sport or exercise will prove to be a factor in determining non-participation (Orlick, 1973). In both cases the more recent the previous experience the more valuable this construct is likely to prove in predicting behavioural intentions.

According to the present survey, over 99 per cent of those young people interviewed, regardless of age, recorded that they were active in sport at both primary and post-primary school. Of those who reported having a 'top sport', 91 per cent of boys and 83 per cent of girls recorded that they had experienced their 'top sport' by the age of 11 years, and 71 per cent of boys by the age of 8 years. Evidence of the importance of early involvement in sport comes from the fact that of those who were involved at an 'élite' level, 40 per cent had become involved in their chosen sport between the ages of 6 and 9 years and 27 per cent as early as 5 years of age.

One important question is: how can these high participation rates be maintained after these children have left the school system? Given the results of the research reported above, it should be possible to build upon this 'exercise experience' to encourage these individuals to maintain active lifestyles.

Personality

One approach to the study of exercise adherence has been to attempt to identify stable characteristics of the exerciser. Intuitively, it seems logical to suppose that certain personality attributes, for example competitiveness, self-confidence and extroversion, would be related to the intention to participate in physical activity.

In the present study, measures of self-worth and perceived self-competence were included (see Chapter 3), and it would appear that those who were active in sport had higher self-worth scores and elevated feelings of perceived self-competence, and especially in the physical domain. In addition, in response to a more general question, 'What standard would you like to have achieved?', 28 per cent said 'basic', 48 per cent 'competitive' and 20 per cent 'élite'. A further question asked what standard they felt they had the potential to achieve. Here 23 per cent said 'basic', 46 per cent 'competitive' and 26 per cent 'élite'. The answers to these questions suggest that a majority of those who took part in the SCNI survey were not only competitive in nature but also confident in their ability to achieve some measure of success in their chosen physical activity. Given that élite sport, by definition, can only be the preserve of a select few, it remains to be seen how the mismatch between high expectations and limited opportunities can be resolved. Certainly it would seem important that those involved in sport ensure that the coming together of expectations and experiences is not a painful process so as to maximise future participation.

Social context

Contextual variables such as 'opportunity to exercise', 'awareness of what is available' and 'location' will undoubtedly play a role in any decision to participate in physical activity. For example, even the size of an exercise class has been shown to affect exercise adherence, with adherence tending to be higher in smaller rather than in larger groups (Massie and Shephard, 1971; Andrew et al., 1981). Several studies have also shown that individuals are not willing to travel long distances to exercise (Andrew and Parker, 1979; Dishman, 1982).

Given that young people spend much of their time at school, it is likely that school will play a pivotal role in fostering an interest in sport. The SCNI survey supported this contention. 'Because of school' (31 per cent) was ranked as the most influential factor in their uptake of sport. Indeed 26 per cent noted that their school was responsible for kindling their interest in their 'top sport'. It is no accident, therefore, that the three most popular 'top sports' (soccer, swimming and netball) were also the sports most mentioned as being available at their present school – soccer (47 per cent), swimming (46 per cent) and netball (35 per cent). The school was in fact the most popular site for the practice of sport for both girls (34 per cent) and boys (48 per cent), followed by the home (29 per cent and 44 per cent), and then the street or park for boys (33 per cent) and the swimming pool for girls (17 per cent).

Further evidence of the importance of social context comes from the fact that the numbers of sports attempted by young people increased from, on average, three to 10 between primary and post-primary school. This increase in the number of attempted sports almost certainly reflects a change in the availability of school sports.

Sports, as well as other types of clubs, also provide opportunities for young people to participate in sport. A total of 588 clubs were mentioned in the SCNI survey, but, only 36 per cent of the entire sample were members of organised clubs and just over half of these were involved with clubs where the primary focus was sport.

Significant others

Adults who have the support of significant others are far more likely to adhere than are those who do not have this support (McCready and Long, 1985). For example, a survey by Wold and Anderssen (1992) found that children whose parents, siblings and best friends took part in sport were much more likely to take part in sport themselves than were children whose significant others were not involved in sport. Despite these findings, surprisingly little research has examined the role of significant others in the participation and attrition process even though it has frequently been suggested as a prime area of study by sociologists (Brown, 1985; Lewko and Greendorfer, 1988). Friends, neighbours and colleagues can all influence how people spend their discretionary time. Significant others probably influence behaviours in ways in which the individual is not even aware. Moreover, as participants in ongoing social systems, people tend to conform to behavioural norms (theory of reasoned action (Ajzen and Fishbein; 1980)). One of the most consistent findings to emerge from preliminary research testing of the model, away from the SCNI survey, has been not only the preference of most people to exercise with a friend, but also the fact that most subjects were encouraged to take up sport and exercise again by their friends and peers.

With regard to the SCNI survey, when asked what motivated them to take up a particular sport, 20 per cent said 'because of friends', 10 per cent replied 'because of father' and 7 per cent 'because of mother'. The young people in the sample were also asked to name their two closest friends and then to give some indication of what type of sports they were involved in. The replies indicated a close concordance between the sports chosen, particularly in relation to some of the major team sports. For example, of those who chose soccer as their 'top sport', 63 per cent also reported that their friends played, in Gaelic football the figure was 46 per cent, and for camogie it was 47 per cent. With very few exceptions young people had more friends associated with their own sport than any other sport.

The survey also demonstrated the importance of family support in initiating and maintaining involvement in sporting activities: 39 per cent of the sample mentioned family members as most important in maintaining their interest and involvement, with the father being the most influential figure (21 per cent). A further 65 per cent prioritised parental support in terms of finance, transport and encouragement as vital to their participation. When it came to reasons for joining a club, 48 per cent mentioned their family and 40 per cent their friends as the source of introduction to the club. Taken together the results of the survey demonstrate quite clearly the importance of family and friends in initiating and maintaining young people's active involvement in sport and exercise.

DECISION TO PARTICIPATE

The second step in the model is the decision to participate in a specific form of physical activity. This decision is mediated by the perception of various intrinsic and extrinsic rewards as well as the variables of self-efficacy and competence.

Intrinsic and extrinsic rewards

The earlier review of descriptive studies on participation motivation revealed that most individuals participate in sport and physical activity for reasons such as developing competence (improve skills), affiliation (social aspects), health and fitness (get stronger, stay in shape), and for enjoyment or the sheer fun of participating in sport (Gould and Horn, 1984; Gill *et al.*, 1983; Gould, Feltz and Weiss 1985; Weiss and Petlichkoff, 1989). These can be classified as intrinsic or internal motives for participation. There may also be extrinsic or external reasons for participation, such as gaining social approval from parents, peers, etc., material rewards (for example, money, trophies) and social status.

The majority of the literature argues that intrinsic motives are most salient when making a decision to participate, and the results obtained from the survey support this contention. For example, when asked to rate the importance of factors which encouraged their participation in sport, only 33 per cent said winning was very important, 25 per cent mentioned trophies and only 11 per cent cited perks such as money or equipment. On the other hand 78 per cent mentioned enjoyment, 67 per cent feeling good, 65 per cent keeping fit, 63 per cent making friends and 63 per cent excitement.

With reference to Chapter 3, when intrinsic or internal motivation was measured using five bi-polar scales ('Preference for challenge' vs. 'Preference for easy work', 'Curiosity vs. Pleasing the teacher', 'Succeed against oneself' vs. 'Compete against others', 'Independent mastery' vs. 'Dependence on others', 'Fitness for its own sake' vs, 'Fitness for appearance in the eyes of others') a significant difference was found in the scores of pupils participating in their 'top sport' at different levels. 'Basic' participants had the lowest mean score for 'Preference for challenge', 'Curiosity' and 'Fitness for its own sake', 'competitive' participants scored higher, with 'élite' participants scoring highest of all. These scores suggest a concordance between intrinsic motivation and level of participation, with 'basic' participants being markedly less intrinsically motivated in their sporting activities than their 'competitive' or 'élite' peers.

Self-efficacy

Most people are familiar with the adage 'You can do it if you just have a little faith/confidence in yourself'. Put very simply, self-efficacy represents a form of situation-specific self-confidence. The concept of self-efficacy has been one of the most extensively utilised concepts for investigating motivational issues in sport and exercise. Self-efficacy theory predicts that highly self-efficacious individuals, those who perceive themselves to be more efficacious with respect to their physical capabilities, are more likely to adopt and maintain a lifestyle in which exercise plays an important role. In a study of the behavioural epidemiology of physical activity, Sallis *et. al.* (1986) examined variables considered to be predictors of adoption and maintenance of physical activity. They found that self-efficacy was a significant predictor of the decision to participate in vigorous physical exercise. In addition, self-efficacy has been shown to be influential in the choice, effort and persistence of individuals in a variety of activities (Bandura, 1977) and therefore should be included in any comprehensive model of motivation. There was no specific measure of self-efficacy in the present survey, although Harter's work on perceived self-competence, as operationalised in Chapter 3, conceptually is closely related.

Perceptions of competence and control

The degree to which an individual feels that he or she is capable of succeeding at a task is a powerful predictor of participation. When interviewees were asked if they had the potential to play to a certain standard in their chosen top sport, 26 per cent of those naming a 'top sport' felt that they had the potential to perform at élite level. Harter (1978; 1981) views competence motivation as a multidimensional construct that influences the initiation of mastery attempts in particular achievement domains. If successful, these mastery experiences result in feelings of efficacy and positive affect, which in turn result in continued motivation to participate. The construct 'perceptions of control' refers to the degree to which individuals feel that they (internal) or others (external) are responsible for success or failure in certain achievement contexts. Those who perceive themselves to be in control are more likely to decide to participate in physical activities than those who do not. Harter's competence motivation theory has been the most frequently used theoretical framework for the study of participation motivation. In general the results of this research have supported the theory (Roberts, Kleiber and Duba, 1981; Feltz and Petlichkoff, 1983). In the present survey, statistically significant differences were found between the groups on perceptions of 'athletic competence' and 'physical appearance' (Chapter 3). The mean score for 'basic' participants being the lowest and 'élite' participants the highest. Hence, as one would expect, perception of athletic competence in a chosen sport correlates with actual levels of participation in that sport.

ALTERNATIVE ROUTES

Alternative routes or pathways are integral to the model in order to take account of the fact that individuals who discontinue with a particular sporting activity should not necessarily be classified as drop-outs. For example, Gould *et.al.* (1982) found that 68 per cent of adolescents who withdrew from competitive swimming programmes were active in other sports. The alternative routes also take account of the fact that individuals may attempt a number of different sports over any given period of time. For example, in this study it was found that the most common number of sports attempted per year at primary school was three, rising to 10 or more for post-primary age groups. With this number of sports being attempted each year it is little wonder that researchers have recorded high drop-out rates in particular sports. It is unlikely that any individual could sustain an interest in all these sports over a prolonged period of time. At this point in the decision making process the individual has a choice of route which he or she can take. The individual can either continue on a route previously chosen or choose a different route and use it to continue through the model.

BARRIERS

According to the model, the likelihood of implementing the decision to participate depends on overcoming any perceived barriers to the proposed activity. Barriers can be both personal and institutional. Personal barriers include such things as injury or illness, lack of time, or indeed any significant life event which interferes with an individual's intended behaviour. Institutional barriers are of particular importance in schools. These can be lack of facilities, for example one may wish to play a game which is not catered for, or other school commitments leaving less time for participation.

Of all the constructs in the model,'barriers' has probably received the most support through empirical research in relation to the health belief model, the theory of reasoned action and social cognitive theory. As anticipated, this research has demonstrated that exercise behaviour is negatively affected by environmental and social barriers, with subsequent non-participation being either permanent, where the individual drops out of a particular sport, or non-permanent, where the individual returns to the sport, for example after completing examinations.

The results of the survey show that only 17 per cent of those who had ever attempted a sport, and only 4 per cent of those who named a top sport, had discontinued that sport completely. Having established that young people do, albeit in small numbers, drop out of sport, the survey then went on to record the reasons why they were dropping out. The main reasons cited were 'lack of interest' (34 per cent), 'not available at school' (16 per cent), 'school commitments' (9 per cent), 'starting another sport' (6 per cent), 'too time consuming' (4 per cent) and 'because friends had stopped' (4 per cent). Therefore both intrinsic and extrinsic barriers had played a part in determining non-participation, although in contrast with previous research, rates of drop-out, even among those in mid- to late adolescence, were extremely low.

FACILITATORS

Facilitators are those factors, both personal or institutional, which enable the individual to overcome the barriers. Good health, the provision of good facilities within easy reach of the individual, are examples of facilitators. Interestingly the same significant life event can be either a barrier or a facilitator, depending on the individual. Some individuals will lose interest in training during holidays while others will use it as an excuse to double their efforts. Again, the SCNI survey highlighted the significance of facilitators, and particularly school availability of sports, as determinants of participation, where 'because of school' was the single most important factor determining the take-up of a sport across the sample.

PERCEIVED REWARDS

Completion of the activity takes us to the next step in the model, the perceived rewards. The perceived rewards deriving from participation are similar to the factors which mediated the decision to participate. For example, a participant may experience enjoyment which was one of the factors which mediated his or her decision to participate. However, as well as these anticipated rewards a participant may also gain a greater sense of social integration into his or her new environment, affiliation with those around him or her or may experience improved affect/mood state. The effects of exercise on affective state are likely to be one of the most important factors influencing an individual's decision to participate in sport and exercise. These unexpected rewards will then become incorporated, either consciously or unconsciously, into the motivating factors which provide the dynamic for the chosen physical activity.

EVALUATION OF PARTICIPATION REWARDS

The basic premise of social exchange theory is that social behaviour is motivated by the desire to maximise positive experiences and minimise negative experiences. For example, positive affect in the form of enjoyment, happiness, pride, excitement and pleasure will be likely to enhance motivation and future mastery attempts, whereas negative affect in the form of anxiety, embarrassment, shame, sadness and disappointment would be likely to attenuate future participation motivation. Individuals will remain in relationships or activities so long as the outcome is favourable. Furthermore, this probability is considered to be a function of benefits and costs. The decision to remain involved in a current activity is not merely a function of benefits and costs but rather includes two levels of satisfaction: satisfaction with the current activity and satisfaction with alternative activities. Thus, an individual weighs the costs, benefits and satisfaction of a current activity with those of alternative behaviours and makes a decision accordingly.

It is this evaluation which provides the dynamic for the model. If these concepts are applied to sport and exercise it can be seen how they may affect motivation. People will tend to participate in a physical activity if they expect to gain rewards, for example positive affect, health/fitness, enjoyment, etc., which they value. This is the expectancy-value component of the model, and it has to be assumed that when the young people indicated that they were still involved with a sport, then the balance of the cost–benefit equation fell in favour of continuation. The difficulty which respondents experienced in even thinking of ways in which clubs had hindered their development, or reasons why they had dropped out from certain sports (including because of other commitments and interests), coupled with numerous benefits which were cited in connection with sport, support a positive social exchange evaluation in favour of sport. In addition, when these young people were asked to evaluate their feelings towards their 'top sport' over the last year, 51 per cent maintained that they had become 'a lot more keen', and 26 per cent 'a bit more keen'. They were also asked whether they felt that the time spent on their chosen sport had been worthwhile: 77 per cent replied very worthwhile and 18 per cent said quite worthwhile. Together with low drop-out rates, these figures would indicate that the majority of young people value their experiences in sport, and expect to continue to participate in sport and exercise; 61 per cent said that they intended to continue with their top sport after leaving school.

When individuals are evaluating their rewards they are doing more than just looking for expected benefits, they are comparing these benefits with those they might expect to gain from alternative activities. That is, they are looking for equity of reward. Depending on the outcome of this evaluation, the participant may take one of five routes in the model.

- *Route 1*: After weighing up the costs/benefits of participation the individual may decide that the benefits accrued from exercise are not worth 'the pain', at least not to him or her. Thus the individual drops out of sport and exercise participation altogether and the cycle ends at this point. This is the 'domain-specific withdrawal' referred to by Gould and Petlichkoff (1988). In the survey this route was taken by few of the children interviewed, with only 4 per cent of those who named a top sport having discontinued that sport completely, and for most this was between the ages of 10 and

15. The two factors cited most often for drop-out by this age group were 'school commitment' (22 per cent) and 'lack of interest' (18 per cent).

- *Route 2*: Rather than giving up of all physical activity the individual may decide that even though this present activity was not quite what he or she had expected it to be, the individual would like either to drop out temporarily or try a different activity. In the survey, 'to start other sports' was one of the top five reasons (6 per cent) given for dropping out of a specific sport. This is the 'sport-specific withdrawal' referred to by Gould and Petlichkoff (1988) and in this case the participant re-enters the model via the 'alternative routes' path. The 'alternative routes' path is likely to be an important track back into the decision process, given that young people in post-primary education participate in over 10 sports per year and it is highly unlikely that they will be able to sustain the same motivation for all, all the time. This route may also incorporate an 'on hold' or 'time-out' strategy, where the intention may be to re-enter sport (either the same or an alternative activity) at a later date, but for one of a number of reasons (either intrinsic or extrinsic) the present activity has been curtailed temporarily but with an intention to resume.

- *Route 3*: After evaluating the participation rewards, the individual may intend to continue with this activity but may not yet be sure of his or her commitment to the exercise process. In this case the participant re-enters the model at a more conscious stage, the intention stage, and the cycle then continues as before.

- *Route 4*: After evaluating the rewards the individual may take, at this stage, a deliberate decision to repeat his or her present activity. In this case the individual will re-enter the model at the 'decision to participate' stage and the cycle continues from there.

- *Route 5*: Alternatively, as a consequence of the perceived rewards and in particular positive affect, the participant may 'fall into an exercise routine' where participation becomes automatic and no conscious intention or decision to participate is made; behaviour is non-conscious.

The final point to be made concerns the dynamic nature of the process model. As the participant proceeds from the evaluation of participant rewards back through the model to the intention to participate again (that is, as the cycle continues) the significance or value of each variable may change; for example, intrinsic motivating factors are liable to become more important than extrinsic motivators over time. The significance of the various concepts will also be different for different individuals. Indeed it is highly likely that the values and beliefs held by individuals concerning vigorous physical activity are subject to significant modification as a function of not only age but also recent activity history/experience. For example, the individual differences and the social environmental factors will probably change as the cycle continues.

The survey has shown that the most common number of sports attempted at primary school was three compared with 10 or more attempted by post-primary school children. This may simply reflect the availability of a wider variety of sports at post-primary schools but it also demonstrates quite clearly the impact of social environmental factors on the exercise process. The five routes described above also demonstrate the model's ability to adapt to the differing consequences of participation. The process model allows for these changes, and is able to cope with the dynamic nature of participation motivation in physical activity over time.

CONCLUSION

Understanding of participation motivation in sport and exercise has progressed from piecemeal observations of factors affecting participation towards the development of integrated theories. Through the myriad of theoretical perspectives, we can see the importance of cognition, learning, socialisation, expectancies, values and affect on whether or not individuals participate in sport. Current theories together reveal participation motivation to be a jigsaw of individual, social and situational factors working in concert. In this chapter, three such earlier models have been identified, and these have set the scene for the current formulation.

The process model of sport and exercise motivation was conceived to try to pull together the common themes and most useful concepts from the various theoretical approaches discussed above, incorporate the most important findings from empirical research, and initiate a process of thoughtful consideration of the factors affecting participation motivation in sport and exercise. It is to be hoped not only that the model outlined above will prove useful in answering the 'why', 'how' and 'what' questions of sport and exercise participation, but that it will also provide useful insights into the practical questions of 'how to enhance' participation, and the personal satisfaction associated with participation. At the end of the day, these are the practical issues to which all research into participant motivation should ultimately be

206   *Garnet J. Busby*

directed, not simply to understand, nor to manipulate or coerce, but to help, in this case to help young people enjoy their sport.

Ajzen, I. (1985). From intentions to actions. A theory of planned behaviour. In J. Kuhl and J. Beckman (eds), *Action Control: From Cognition to Behaviour*. Heidelberg: Springer.

Ajzen, I. and Fishbein, M. (1980). *Understanding Attitudes and Predicting Social Behaviour*. Englewood Cliffs, NJ: Prentice Hall.

Andrew, G.M. and Parker, J.O. (1979). Factors related to drop out of post myocardial infarction patients from exercise programs. *Medicine and Science in Sports and Exercise, 11*, 376–378.

Andrew, G.M., Oldridge, N.B., Parker, J.O., Cunningham, D.A., Rechnitzer, P.A., Jones, N.L., Buck, C., Kavanagh, T., Shephard, R.J., Sutton, J.R. and McDonald, W. (1981). Reasons for drop out from exercise programs in post-coronary patients. *Medicine and Science in Sport and Exercise, 13*, 164–168.

Bandura, A. (1977). Self-efficacy: Towards a unifying theory of behavioural change. *Psychological Review, 84*, 191-215.

Bandura, A. (1986). *Social Foundation of Thought and Action: A Social Cognitive Theory*. Englewood Cliffs, NJ: Prentice Hall.

Brown, B.A. (1985). Factors influencing the process of withdrawal by female adolescents from the role of competitive age group swimmer. *Sociology of Sport Journal, 2*, 111–129.

Buonamano, R., Cei, A. and Mussino, A. (1995). Participation motivation in Italian youth sport. *The Sport Psychologist, 9*, 265–281.

Deci, E.L. and Ryan, R.M. (1985). *Intrinsic Motivation and Self Determination in Human Behavior*. New York: Plenum.

Deci, E.L., Cascio, W.F. and Krusell, J. (1975). Cognitive evaluation theory and some comments on the Calder and Straw Critique. *Journal of Personality and Sport Psychology, 31*, 81–85.

Dishman, R.K. (1982). Compliance/adherence in health-related exercise. *Health Psychology, 1*, 237–267.

Dishman, R.K. (1985). Medical psychology in exercise and sport. *Medical Clinics of North America, 69*, 123–143.

Dzewaltowski, D.A., Noble, J.M. and Shaw, J.M. (1990). Physical activity participation. Social cognitive theory versus the theory of reasoned action and planned behaviour. *Journal of Sport and Exercise Psychology, 12*, 388–405.

Ebbeck, V., Gibbons, S.L. and Loken-Dahle, L.J. (1995). Reasons for adult participation in physical activity: An international approach. *International Journal of Sport Psychology, 26*, 262–275.

Fagot, B.I. (1984). Teacher and peer reactions to boys' and girls' play styles. *Sex Roles, 11*, 691–702.

Feltz, D.L. (1982). Path analysis of the causal elements of Bandura's theory of self-efficacy and an anxiety-based model of avoidance behaviour. *Journal of Personality and Social Psychology, 42*, 764–781.

Feltz, D.L. (1988). Self-confidence and sports performance. *Exercise and Sport Sciences Reviews, 16*, 423–458.

Feltz, D.L. and Brown, E. (1984). Perceived competence in soccer skills among young soccer players. *Journal of Sport Psychology, 6,* 385–394.

Feltz, D.L. and Mugno, D.A. (1983). A replication of the path analysis of the causal elements in Bandura's theory of self-efficacy and the influence of self perception. *Journal of Sport Psychology, 5,* 263–277.

Feltz, D.L. and Petlichkoff, L.M. (1983). Perceived competence among inter-scholastic sport participants and dropouts. *Canadian Journal of Applied Sport Sciences, 8,* 231-235.

Fishbein, M. and Ajzen, I. (1975). *Belief, Attitude, Intention and Behaviour: An Introduction to Theory and Research.* Reading, MA: Addison-Wesley.

Fishbein, M. and Middlestadt, S. (1987). Using the theory of reasoned action to develop educational interventions: Applications to illicit drug use. *Health Education Research, 2,* 361–371.

Furst, D.M. (1989). Sport role socialization: Initial entry into the subculture of officiating. *Journal of Sport Behaviour, 12,* 41–52.

Gettman, L.R., Pollock, M.L. and Ward, A. (1983). Adherence to unsuper-vised exercise. *The Physician and Sports Medicine, 11,* 56–66.

Gill, D.L. (1988). Gender differences in competitive orientation and sport participation. *International Journal of Sport Psychology, 19,* 145–159.

Gill, D.L. and Strom, E.H. (1985). The effect of attentional focus on perfor-mance of an endurance task. *International Journal of Sport Psychology, 16,* 217–223.

Gill, D.L., Ruder, M.K. and Gross, J.B. (1982). Open-ended attributions in team competition. *Journal of Sport Psychology, 4,* 159–169.

Gill, D.L., Gross, J.B. and Huddleston, S. (1983). Participation motivation in youth sport. *International Journal of Sport Psychology, 14,* 1–14.

Godin, G. and Shephard, R.J. (1986a). Importance of type of attitude to the study of exercise behaviour. *Psychological Reports, 58,* 991–1000.

Godin, G. and Shephard, R.J. (1986b). Psychosocial factors influencing inten-tions to exercise of young students from grades 7 to 9. *Research Quarterly for Exercise and Sport, 57,* 44–52.

Godin, G. and Shephard, R.J. (1990). Use of behavioural models in exercise promotion. *Sports Medicine, 10,* 103–121.

Gould, D. (1987). Understanding attrition in children's sport. In D. Gould and M.R. Weiss (eds), *Advances in Paediatric Sciences: Volume 2, Beha-vioral Issues.* Champaign, IL: Human Kinetics.

Gould, D. and Horn, T. (1984). Participation motivation in young athletes. In J.M. Silva and R.S. Weinberg (eds), *Psychological Foundations of Sport.* Champaign, IL: Human Kinetics.

Gould, D. and Petlichkoff, L.M. (1988). Participation motivation and attri-tion in young athletes. In F.A. Smoll, R.A. Magill and M.J. Ash (eds), *Children in Sport, 3rd Edition.* Champaign, IL: Human Kinetics.

Gould, D., Feltz, D., Horn, T. and Weiss, M. (1982). Reasons for attrition in competitive youth swimming. *Journal of Sport Behaviour, 5,* 155–165.

Gould, D., Feltz, D. and Weiss, M. (1985). Motives for participating in compe-titive youth swimmers. *International Journal of Sport Psychology, 16,* 126–140.

Greendorfer, S. (1992). Sport socialisation. In T. Horn (ed.) *Advances in Sport Psychology.* Champaign, IL: Human Kinetics.

Harris, D.V. (1970). Physical activity history and attitudes of middle-aged men. *Medicine and Science in Sports, 2,* 203–208.

208   *Garnet J. Busby*

Harris, O. and Hunt, L. (1984). Race and sports involvement: Some implications of sports for black and white youth. Paper presented at the meeting of the American Alliance for Health, Physical Education, Recreation, and Dance, Anaheim, CA.

Harter, S. (1978). Effectance motivation reconsidered: Towards a developmental model. *Human Development, 21*, 34–64.

Harter, S. (1981). The development of competence motivation in the mastery of cognitive and physical skills. Is there a place for joy? In G.C. Roberts and D.M. Landers (eds), *Psychology of Motor Behaviour and Sport – 1980*. Champaign, IL; Human Kinetics.

Hasbrook, C.H. (1986). Reciprocity and childhood socialization into sport. In L.Vander Velden and J.H. Humphrey (eds), *Psychology and Sociology of Sport: Current Selected Research*. New York: AMS Press.

Higginson, D.C. (1985). The influence of socializing agents in the female sport participation process. *Adolescence, 20*, 73–82.

Kavanagh, D. and Hausfeld, S. (1986). Physical performance and self-efficacy under happy and sad moods. *Journal of Sport Psychology, 8*, 112–123.

Kenyon, G. and McPherson, B.D. (1973). Becoming involved in physical activity and sports: A process of socialization. In G.L. Ranick (ed.) *Physical Activity: Human Growth and Development*. New York: Academic Press.

Kimiecik, J. (1992). Predicting vigorous physical activity of corporate employees: Comparing the theories of reasoned action and planned behaviour. *Journal of Sport and Exercise Psychology, 14*, 192–206.

Klint, K.A. and Weiss, M.R. (1987). Perceived competence and motives for participating in youth sports: A test of Harter's Competence Motivation Theory. *Journal of Sport Psychology, 9*, 55–65.

Knapp, D., Gutmann, M., Squires, R.A. and Pollock, M.L. (1983). Exercise adherence among coronary artery bypass surgery (CABS) patients. *Medicine and Science in Sports and Exercise (supplement), 15*, S120.

Kremer, J. and Scully, D. (1994). *Psychology in Sport*. London: Taylor and Francis.

Krotee, M.L. and La Point, J.O, (1979). Sociological perspectives underlying participation in physical activity. In M.L. Krotee (ed.) *Dimensions of Sport Sociology*. Champaign, IL: Leisure Press.

Lazarus, R.S. (1966). *Psychological Stress and the Coping Process*. New York: McGraw-Hill.

Lewko, J.H. and Greendorfer, S.L. (1988). Family influence in sport socialization of children and adolescents. In F.L. Smoll, R.A. Magill and M.J. Ash (eds), *Children in Sport, 3rd Edition*. Champaign, IL: Human Kinetics.

Lindsay-Reid, E. and Osborn, R. W. (1980). Readiness for exercise adoption. *Social Science Medicine, 14*, 139–146.

McAuley, E. (1985). Success and causality in sport: The influence of perception. *Journal of Sports Psychology, 7*, 13-22.

McCready, M.L. and Long, B.C. (1985). Locus of control, attitudes towards physical activity, and exercise adherence. *Journal of Sport Psychology, 7*, 346–359.

Massie, J.F. and Shephard, R.J. (1971). Physiological and psychological effects of training – A comparison of individual and gymnasium programs, with a characterization of the exercise 'drop out'. *Medicine and Science in Sports, 3*, 110-117.

Morgan, P.P., Shephard, R.J., Finucane, L., Schimmelfling, L. and Jazmaij, V. (1984). Health beliefs and exercise habits in an employee fitness programme. *Canadian Journal of Applied Sport Sciences*, *9*, 87–93.

Orlick, T.D. (1973). Children's sport – a revolution is coming. *Canadian Association for Health, Physical Education, and Recreation Journal, Jan/Feb*, 12–14.

Orlick, T.D. and Mosher, R. (1978). Extrinsic rewards and participation motivation in a sport related task. *International Journal of Sport Psychology*, *9*, 27–39.

Petlichkoff, L.M. (1988). Motivation for sport persistence: An empirical examination of underlying theoretical constructs. Unpublished Doctoral Dissertation, University of Illinois at Urbana–Champaign.

Riddle, P.K. (1980). Attitudes, beliefs, behavioural intentions, and behaviours of women and men toward regular jogging. *Research Quarterly for Exercise and Sport*, *51*, 663–674.

Roberts, G.C. (1992). *Motivation in Sport and Exercise*. Champaign, IL: Human Kinetics.

Roberts, G.C., Kleiber, D.A. and Duda, J.L. (1981). An analysis of motivation in children's sport. The role of perceived competence in participation. *Journal of Sport Psychology*, *3*, 206–216.

Rosenstock, I.M. (1974). Historical origins of the Health Belief Model. *Health Education Monographs*, *2*, 1–9.

Rudman, W. (1989). Age and involvement in sport and physical activity. *Sociology of Sport Journal*, *6*, 228–246.

Ryan, E.D. (1980). Attribution, intrinsic motivation and athletics: A replication and extension. In C.H. Nadeau, W.R. Halliwell, K.M. Newell and G.C. Roberts (eds), *Psychology of Motor Behavior and Sport – 1979*. Champaign, IL: Human Kinetics.

Sallis, J.F., Haskell, W.L., Fortmann, S.P., Vranizan, M.S., Taylor, C.B. and Solomon, D.S. (1986). Predictors of adoption and maintenance of physical activity in a community sample. *Preventative Medicine*, *15*, 331–341.

Sapp, M. and Haubenstricker, J. (1978). Motivation for joining and reasons for not continuing in youth sport programs in Michigan. Paper presented at the Meeting of the American Alliance for Health, Physical Education, Recreation, and Dance, Kansas City, MO.

Schmidt, G.W. and Stein, G.L. (1991). Sport commitment: A model integrating enjoyment, drop out and burn-out. *Journal of Sport and Exercise Psychology*, *13*, (*3*), 254–265.

Sidney, K.H. and Shephard, R.J. (1976). Attitudes toward health and physical activity in the elderly. Effects of a physical training program. *Medicine and Science in Sports and Exercise*, *8*, 246–252.

Slenker, S.E., Price, J.H., Roberts, S.M. and Jurs, S.G. (1984). Joggers versus nonexercisers: An analysis of knowledge, attitudes and beliefs about jogging. *Research Quarterly for Exercise and Sport*, *55*, 371–378.

Smith, R.E. (1986). Towards a cognitive-affective model of athletic burn-out. *Journal of Sport Psychology*, *8*, 36–50.

Sonstroem, R.J. (1978). Physical estimation and attraction scales: Rationale and research. *Medicine and Science in Sports and Exercise*, *10*, 97–102.

Sonstroem, R.J. (1982). Attitudes and beliefs in the prediction of exercise participation. In R.C. Cantu and W.J. Gillespie (eds) *Sports Medicine,*

Sports Science: Bridging the Gap. Lexington, MA: The Collamore Press.

Sonstroem, R.J. (1988). Psychological models. In R.K. Dishman (ed.) *Exercise Adherence: Its Impact on Public Health.* Champaign, IL: Human Kinetics.

Sonstroem, R.J. and Morgan, W.P. (1989). Exercise and self-esteem: Rationale and model. *Medicine and Science in Sports and Exercise, 21,* 329–337.

Thibaut, J.W. and Kelly, H.H. (1959). *The Social Psychology of Groups.* New York: Wiley.

Thuot, S.M. (1995). College-students attitudes towards anticipated sport participation. *Perceptual and Motor Skills, 80, (1),* 155–160.

Tirrell, B.E. and Hart, L.K. (1980). The relationship of health beliefs and knowledge to exercise compliance in patients after coronary by pass. *Heart & Lung, 9,* 487–493.

Ulrich, B.D. (1987). Perception of physical competence, motor competence, and participation in organized sport: Their interrelationships in young children. *Research Quarterly for Exercise and Sport, 58,* 57–67.

Vallerand, R.T. and Reid, G. (1984). On the causal effects of perceived competence in intrinsic motivation: A test of cognitive evaluation theory. *Journal of Sport Psychology, 6,* 94–102.

Valois, P., Desharnais, R. and Godin, G. (1988). A comparison of the Fishbein and Ajzen and the Triandis Attitudinal models for the prediction of exercise intention and behaviour. *Journal of Behavioural Medican, 11,* 459–472.

Weingarten, G., Frust, D., Tenendaum, G. and Schaefer, U. (1984). Motives of Israeli youth for participation in sport. In J.L. Callaghan (ed.) *Proceedings of the International Symposium "Children to Champions".* Los Angeles: University of Southern California.

Weiss, M.R. and Chaumeton, N. (1992). Motivational orientations in sport. In T.S. Horn (ed.) *Advances in Sport Psychology.* Champaign, IL: Human Kinetics.

Weiss, M. and Knoppers, A. (1982). The influence of socializing agents on female collegiate volleyball players. *Journal of Sport Psychology, 4,* 267–279.

Weiss, M.R. and Petlichkoff, L.M. (1989). Children's motivation for participation in and withdrawal from sport: Identifying the missing links. *Pediatric Exercise Science, 1,* 195-211.

Weiss, M.R., Wiese, D.M. and Klint, K.A. (1989). Head over heels with success: The relationship between self-efficacy and performance in competitive youth gymnastics. *Journal of Sport and Exercise Psychology, 11,* 444–451.

Willis, J.D. and Campbell, L.F. (1992). *Exercise Psychology.* Champaign, IL: Human Kinetics.

Wold, B. and Anderssen, N. (1992). Health promotion aspects of family and peer influences on sport participation. *International Journal of Sport Psychology, 23,* 343-359.

Wurtele, S.K. and Maddux, J.E. (1987). Relative contributions of protection motivation theory components in predicting exercise intentions and behaviour. *Health Psychology, 6,* 453–466.

Yamaguchi, Y. (1984). A comparative study of adolescent socialization into sport. The case of Japan and Canada. *International Review for Sociology of Sport, 19,* 63–82.

10 International perspectives on public policy and the development of sport for young people

Shaun Ogle

INTRODUCTION

During the last 20 years, public policy addressing the development of sport has increasingly assigned priority to policies and programmes associated with the provision of opportunities for all young people to take part in sport. Every major government strategic plan for sport, or that of its sponsored public sector sports development organisations, has placed an explicit emphasis on young people. Some of the leading exponents of this policy are set out in Table 10.1.

In general, sports development policies for young people centre on three areas of activity. First, strengthening physical education and sport within schools (and particularly after-school sport); second, creating sustainable links between sport played in school and sport played outside of school in the community (and especially through school–club links and by giving the community access to sporting facilities within schools); and third, developing means to ensure that all participants, and those with talent, can progress (whether through an appropriate club setting, coaching or competition). All three areas of activity are interrelated and achieving success in one will almost certainly have knock-on benefits for the others.

As has been pointed out in Chapter 1, this survey represents a contribution to a relatively small body of existing research on young people's involvement with sport. Within Northern Ireland, and the UK in general, most survey-based research has included young people's participation in sport as a secondary concern, the effects on health from such involvement being the primary emphasis. As such, the SCNI survey represents an attempt to redress the balance away from research in which sport is seen as one variable among others influencing health outcomes, and towards sport itself as the explicit research objective.

Table 10.1 Government-backed sports policies and programmes for young people

Public Sector Sport Development Organisation	Policies and Programmes for Young People
Hillary Commission, New Zealand	Kiwisport – modified games for children aged 5–13 years Sportfit – post-primary students aged 13–19 years
Australian Sports Commission	National Junior Sports Policy Aussie Sports Programme Sports Start – infants/play 1–4 years Sport It – 4–11 years Ready, Set, Go – modified games Sports Search – help young people to choose sports
Department of Sport and Recreation, Republic of South Africa	Protea Sport Super Kids – aged up to 6 years Sports Pioneers – 6–15 years Isizwe Stars – 15–21 years
Scottish Sports Council	Team Sport Scotland – school-aged children; centred on sports' governing bodies; strategies for youth in governing bodies
Sports Council (Great Britain)	National Junior Sports Programme Top Play – 4–9 years Top Sport – 7–11 years Champion Coaching – 11–14 years Top Club – 11 upwards Sportsmark and Gold Star Awards – post-primary schools
Sports Council Northern Ireland	Youth Sport Policy Top Play Top Sport Champion Coaching City Sport Sportsmark – primary and post-primary schools

The rationale for the survey lay in a concern by the Sports Council for Northern Ireland that more needed to be done to improve opportunities for children to become involved, keep going and improve at sport. This chapter aims to place the survey, on which contributions to this book are based, in a broader context of sport policy. It examines, briefly, rationales for government investment in sport and goes on to suggest that while research which demonstrates the benefits of sport in economic, health and social terms may be a useful political persuader, without research which examines how sport itself is developing then the ability to continue to expound the broader benefits accruing from sport will be greatly reduced.

The priority assigned to young people is examined in the context of this rationale and it is suggested that the shift in focus to young people by government organisations is a partial recognition of the failure of the ideal or shibboleth of 'Sport for All'. This policy shift has its most explicit expression in the change from largely remedial or curative policies, designed to put right previous wrongs, towards preventive strategies which encourage a healthy and active lifestyle from an early age. The chapter also contains a comparative overview of policies and programmes, and suggests these too are an expression of new thinking in sports development. The chapter concludes by examining some of the challenges for a new public policy supporting the development of sport for young people.

GOVERNMENT INVESTMENT IN SPORT

Broadly speaking, governments invest public monies in sport not only to assist the development of sport itself but also to achieve improvements to the quality of life of their citizens. Both objectives are interlinked but internationally during the 1980s and 1990s the race was on to justify investment in sport primarily for economic, social and health or well-being reasons. For example, The Australian Sports Commission, Hillary Commission (New Zealand) and Sports Councils in Northern Ireland, Scotland, Wales and Great Britain have all published research demonstrating the economic, social and health benefits associated with sport (cf. Australian Sports Commission, 1993; Hillary Commission, 1993; Sports Council (GB), 1992b; Sports Council Northern Ireland, 1992a; 1992b; MacAuley *et al.*, 1994).

The governments in Northern Ireland and the Republic of South Africa (RSA) have explicitly emphasised social objectives underlying sport policies, often aimed directly at the resolution of fundamental socio-political conflicts. In the RSA, sport has been adopted by government as a means to promote 'a new democratic ethos', as a 'unifier and healer of wounds' and 'redeemer of marginalised youth' (Department of Sport and Recreation RSA, 1995). In Northern Ireland, investment channelled through the education service reflects wider strategic priorities concerned with fostering mutual esteem and equality (Department of Education for Northern Ireland (DENI), 1996).

These principal justifications for investment in sport have recently received further endorsement from the First World Forum on Physical Activity and Sport (1995); 101 countries reached consensus on these and other benefits, most notably including sport's ability to foster a 'culture of peace'. The forum went even further by recommending that sport can be used as 'an effective means to reduce poverty, economic disparity and health problems' (World Forum, 1995).

Certainly, at the level of the individual, there is strong evidence that sport can alleviate health problems, and significant relationships have been established between past participation in sport and a reduced prevalence of health problems, most commonly heart disease, angina or breathlessness (Ogle and Kelly, 1994; Sports Council (GB), 1992a). In countries demonstrating this association, however, only a minority of the adult population are actually engaging in physical activities sufficient to produce sustained cardiovascular benefits; hence such claims must be kept in perspective. In terms of the 'macro' aspirations, of reducing poverty and economic disparity, there is little existing unequivocal evidence supporting the efficacy of sport. Indeed, evidence from throughout the world shows a marked association between higher education qualifications, higher socio-economic status, male hegemony and participation in sport (Ogle, 1994). Therefore, in broad terms, sporting participation would appear to reflect and perhaps even exaggerate disparities within societies rather than being in itself an effective means of reducing such disparities. It is one matter to promote the overall economic and personal health benefits which can in part result from participation in sport, but an entirely different matter to make claims for sport's ability to reduce socio-economic inequalities across entire cultures.

The picture of the typical sporting participant in the 1990s suggests that the ideal of 'Sport for All', which has been the dominant policy for active leisure since the late 1950s (Ravenscroft, 1996), has not been realised, at least among adults. Moreover, in terms of adult motivation to participate in physical activity, including sport, increasingly evidence suggests that both women and men rate 'improved health' as their most important motive rather than fundamental enjoyment of the activity itself. In Northern Ireland, women considered health benefits a more important reason than males (MacAuley *et al.*, 1994). Eight out of 10 men and women, in Northern Ireland, believed that physical activity, including sport, is important in determining health but, at the same time, only half of all adults exercised at a level likely to confer cardiovascular benefit (Ogle and Kelly, 1994).

A widespread awareness of the health benefits derived from sport may be 'common knowledge', but, 'participation is lagging behind the received wisdom about its benefits' (Clarke, 1994). For example, in spite of a higher level of belief among women than men concerning the health benefits of sport, women's participation lags far behind that of men's. When coupled with a strong association between education and high social class, the continued failure to achieve 'Sport for All' is one probable reason why most sports development organisations have been forced to refocus their policies and programmes on a more limited form of the same ideal, only this time among young people.

It was almost as if so much energy had been invested in justifying sport, or showing how good sport was in meeting grandiose social objectives, that problems actually occurring on the ground within sport itself had become obscured. For example, and very obviously, not everyone was participating in sport, and among young people opportunities to participate were very uneven, being especially poor for young women. At the same time, the policy shift towards young people reinforced the movement from the curative or remedial to the preventive role to be played by sport in health promotion. As with adults, however, there is seemingly a continued emphasis on *all* young people, as opposed to those who genuinely want to take part.

The Council of Europe, through its European Sports Charter (1992) which was endorsed by all government-sponsored member organisations, reinforced the theme of sport for all young people. The Charter states 'that all young people should have the opportunity to receive physical education ... and acquire basic sports skills' and 'that everyone should have the opportunity to take part in sport and physical recreation'. The assertion implicit in these statements is that everyone has a 'right to sport'. Similar forceful statements were made in 1995 by the North American Regional Forum Committee on behalf of the World Forum on Physical Activity and Sport in their *'Global Vision for School Physical Education'*. The committee stated their belief 'that all students ... should have the right and the opportunity to experience sustained, vigorous physical activity ... '. This policy finds a regional expression in policies designed for young people by the Sports Councils in Great Britain and Northern Ireland. Both emphasise that the aspirations of all young people should be met 'irrespective of gender, class, race or ability' (Sports Council (GB), 1993; SCNI, 1993).

On closer examination these statements fail to make the crucial distinction between having an 'opportunity to participate' and having 'the right to participate'. Where is this extension of rights to end?

Should all young people have a right to go to the cinema, to paint pictures or watch television? Would policies not be more equitable if, rather then giving *all* the opportunity to participate, the focus for policy was on targeting those disadvantaged young people who, despite their desire to do so, could not become involved in sport?

As evidenced by the findings from this survey, and a National Survey of Young People and Sport in England (Mason, 1995), among young people there is already a limited form of 'Sport for All'. That is, among young children aged up to 14 years, nine out 10 boys and girls participate in a wide variety of sports both in and out of school. Away from school boys and girls are involved in different sports and the English study found that higher percentages of boys participated than in school. These broad brush strokes outlining involvement, however, mask important differences in levels of participation and choice of sports, including the amount of time spent on sport, the influence of significant others, and expectations of what can be achieved from participation in sport. The SCNI survey confirms that while the 'right' to unlimited access to sport is, justifiably, unattainable, in the real world the lowlier aspiration of 'opportunity' to continue to maintain an interest in a particular physical activity remains limited for a great many young people, and this lack of opportunity for translating aspiration into reality has to be a matter of considerable concern.

SHIFTING POLICY PRIORITIES: PREVENTION IS BETTER THAN CURE

The work with young people of public-sponsored sports development organisations, particularly in the UK in the 1980s, was characterised by, first, a target group approach; second, partnerships of coincidence rather than commitment to agreed objectives; and third, concentration on young people aged 13–24 (Sports Council (GB), 1993; SCNI, 1993). Each of these characteristics of development had weaknesses which militated against success, not the least of which were the Councils' attempts to deliver and resource entire schemes directly, rather than facilitating their delivery in the community. By and large, policies and programmes were conceived at national level and were then delivered by people operating at this same level. There is evidence to suggest that, prior to the creation of the Aussie Sports Programme in 1986, the development of sport for young people in Australia suffered from similar weaknesses, and especially in attempts to resource and deliver development directly (Australian Sports Commission, 1995).

Looking at each of the three development processes outlined above, it can be seen that the target group approach, in the case of young people, was based on a belief that young people dropped out of sport on leaving school. By focusing on 13–24-year-olds, remedial action was directed towards the 'at risk' groups themselves. 'Taster Days' or 'Come and Try It' sessions were established to tempt ex-participants back into sport, yet success in encouraging people to remain partici- pants was negligible. Other curative programmes included the appoint- ment of Sports Development Officers who set up a variety of schemes to attract people back to sport. Subsequently, young people became dependent on these officers who did everything, and, not surprisingly, on their withdrawal schemes collapsed. Basically, opportunities fell away as appropriate structures had not been put in place, and in this vacuum local people were simply unable to carry on with the same job.

Difficulties therefore arose with this 13–24 target age group. By the age of 13 years many young people were already frustrated with the inability of existing sporting structures, and primarily local clubs, to meet their needs. This inflexibility in structures, coupled with pres- sures on volunteers, meant that young people, although still interested in sport, dropped out, took up other leisure activities or swelled the ranks of those participating outside of formal sporting structures, for example in recreational cycling, swimming or aerobics. At this stage, the idea of partnerships providing sport for young people were nor- mally based on coincidence rather than on clear objectives from which partners and sport could both benefit; clearly these experiments served as a vivid illustration that cure could not remedy what had failed to be avoided by adequate prevention.

Through this painful learning process there emerged a policy shift from cure to prevention. Increasingly, this shift to preventive policies has encouraged policy makers to place a premium on facilitating or enabling development initiatives, rather than on direct provision of initiatives. The emphasis has shifted, and so although policies and programmes can still be conceived nationally, it is now felt that they must be owned and delivered locally. In order to be successful, it is recognised that programmes have to be the responsibility of locally based people who are trained first to deliver and then to nurture these programmes over time. Inevitably, simply imposing solutions without giving empowerment through ownership means that development will be difficult to sustain. Throughout the world evidence suggests that public sector policy is now firmly focused on, first, improving partner- ships and structures enabling better opportunities for after-school sport, and sport in primary schools; and second, in offering support for volunteers, including teachers, to deliver programmes. The emphasis now lies with cementing relationships and establishing connections between agreed strategies and partnerships, two elements which were previously regarded as separate parts of the sports system.

By way of example, the Aussie Sports Programme, introduced in Australia in 1989, has centred on working with 'local communities in order to establish the most appropriate environment for the delivery of quality junior sport...supported and complemented by similar strategies at regional, state and national level, and...effective partnerships' (Australian Sports Commission, 1993). In Scotland, Team Sport Scotland's general remit has been to, 'foster and develop team sports by establishing a network of links between existing agencies, in particular between schools and communities' (Team Sport Scotland, 1994). In England, the National Junior Sport policy, which began operating in primary schools in 1996, is consistent with Australian and Scottish policies. It is designed to provide a framework within which schools, local government, governing bodies of sports, clubs and youth organisations can work together to provide opportunities for 4–18-year-olds in a planned and co-ordinated manner. These same principles are being implemented in Northern Ireland through the Sports Council designing programmes together with local communities and implementing them using locally based development officers, who in turn skill others in local areas. This new thinking suggests policy has shifted from direct remedial action towards enabling people to own and undertake developments in their localities, should they wish to do so.

OVERVIEW OF PROGRAMMES

Table 10.1 highlights the significance which public sector organisations currently attach to helping young people achieve an appropriate start in sport. Australia and New Zealand are often the pace setters or innovators in much of this thinking, with other countries following similar paths – perhaps a case of new wine being decanted into old antipodean bottles? For example, five of the organisations listed in Table 10.1 are currently implementing programmes using similar core ingredients. Scotland is the exception, concentrating on children aged 11 years and over, and on team sports. The five are all focusing on primary-aged children and equipping schools with resource materials to play games (Australia and New Zealand also give parents and/or carers books to introduce children to sport through play). Modified games or mini-sports have an almost universal acceptance in New

Zealand and Australia with 90 per cent of primary schools delivering modified games. The Aussie Sports Programme has also pioneered programmes aimed at involving students from post-primary and tertiary education in roles and responsibilities, other than as participants. Post-primary pupils have been trained to provide supervised sports-based leadership, and have learned a variety of sport-related skills. Together these programmes come under the umbrella of the Australian National Junior Sport Policy, launched in 1994.

The English National Junior Sports Programme similarly comprises packages of core skills and fun activities for 4–9-year-olds, based on equipment bags and activity cards, and 7–11-year-olds are introduced to specific sports through the use of adapted kit and games, while a Champion Coaching Scheme is designed to improve the sporting performance of 11–14-year-olds in a range of 17 sports.

In all, six organisations listed in Table 10.1 recognise that forging working partnerships between schools and clubs is of the utmost importance. In England, recognition will be given to post-primary schools who demonstrate a commitment to developing sport in partnership with local communities, and in Northern Ireland recognition schemes rewarding good junior development practice in clubs are being implemented.

In general, although the particular socio-cultural context differs for each organisation, all are working with broadly similar programmes based on putting young people at the centre of the development programme rather than on developing the sport itself. Such programmes are designed to overcome failings in previous initiatives, as outlined above. For example, the rationale for partnerships is now based on explicit objectives benefiting both organisations and young people. Together with national policy statements, and local ownership and delivery based on the needs of communities, public policy for the development of sport for young people is attempting to overcome strong centrifugal tendencies. Specialisms within the sporting system – physical education, coaching, sport development officers, sports scientists – are now being linked through agreed frameworks for development. For research, the challenge lies in showing the extent to which this policy shift is being, or has been, successful.

PUBLIC POLICY AND THE DEVELOPMENT OF SPORT FOR YOUNG PEOPLE IN NORTHERN IRELAND

This chapter has ranged widely in attempting to show the broad similarities in international policies and programmes for the development of sport for young people. Young people within Northern Ireland, between 1993 and 1996, have been the subject, in whole or in part, of four government policy statements directly related to sport. These are:

- A Strategy for the Development of Sporting Opportunities for Young People (SCNI, 1993)
- A Strategy for the Development of Performance and Excellence (SCNI, 1994)
- The Future of Sport for Young People in Northern Ireland (DENI, 1995)
- Strategic Plan for Education (DENI, 1996)

All have in common the desire to strengthen links between different providers within the sports system, namely schools, clubs, youth organisations and local government, and to enable young people to have access to a wide range of facilities and expertise, thus enhancing both their experience of sport and enabling those who wish to do so to improve. Above all, development is designed to enable participation in sport to be sustained into adult life.

All the policies implicitly contain a shift towards recognising the need to invest in people. Whether recommending the appointment of sports development officers, sports–specific coaches, or training for teachers and others in the provision of sport, including parents, each of the policies proposed is people centred. Northern Ireland in the 1970s and early 1980s witnessed a huge expansion in the provision of leisure centres provided by the public sector. One rationale offered for this growth was to keep young people off the streets and out of trouble (Sugden and Bairner, 1986). While there is limited evidence suggesting Northern Ireland has some of the highest usage of indoor facilities by young people (Roberts *et al.*, 1989), the high level of subsidy per user also suggests that more than simply providing facilities is required to develop sporting opportunities for young people.

The simplistic belief that bricks and mortar are sufficient to sustain sports development – building blocks for a better society (*sic*) – is being replaced by a view, perhaps unpalatable to some in government, that sustaining participation requires partnerships and people, not just facilities. New facilities are a factor but not a sufficient factor in themselves.

Other public policies are also influencing the development of sport, particularly within the education service. The introduction of a revised Northern Ireland curriculum in 1990, ensuring that physical education is mandatory for all children throughout their years of compulsory schooling, is now well established within schools. The Northern Ireland Health Promotion Agency, in its Strategy for Physical Activity, assigns a crucial role for public policy makers in designing policies which reduce the prevalence of inactivity. The strategy emphasises that 'schools and the youth sector have an important role to play in ensuring young people adopt healthy habits which will lead to lifelong activity' (Health Promotion Agency, 1996). The forthcoming Children's Order will also directly affect those in sport working with young people in schools and the wider community; organisations will have a responsibility for safeguarding young people from possible exploitation.

Consequently, both directly and indirectly young people's experiences of sport are being subject to unprecedented influence from a range of public policies in education, health and sport itself. In order to be able to show the impact of change on sporting opportunities for young people a picture of their current involvement in sport is essential, and this survey was designed to provide this broad picture of involvement. It builds on work previously undertaken in 1991 which examined the management and delivery of physical education and games in post-primary schools in Northern Ireland (Sutherland, 1992), which in turn drew on work carried out in Wales in 1991/1992 (Sports Council (Wales), 1993). The 1991 Northern Ireland survey was undertaken prior to education reforms, and the 1994 survey prior to the implementation of development programmes based on new thinking for sports development. The present survey has the potential to inform the development of these policy initiatives, and to provide hard evidence against which suppositions and speculations can be tested.

PREVIOUS RESEARCH: REDRESSING THE BALANCE FROM HEALTH TO SPORT

As previously stated, across the UK, and indeed internationally, large-scale surveys yielding broad pictures of young people's involvement in sport are rare. Moreover, existing studies have largely examined physical activity, including sport, as one variable among many others influencing lifestyle (Hendry *et al.*, 1993), or in terms of its effects on young people's health (Armstrong et al., 1990), or indeed in terms of the specifics of physical education within the curriculum (Armstrong and Biddle, 1992).

The influence of the health rationale has been strongly present in research undertaken with young people in Northern Ireland. The

Northern Ireland Fitness Survey in 1989, although producing much material on children aged 11–18 years, had as its primary objectives measures of fitness and health. Again, a survey of the health behaviour of school children aged 11–17 (Health Promotion Agency, 1994) and a study detecting early signs of coronary risk factors in school children aged between 12 and 15 years (Boreham *et al.*, 1993) underline the dominance of the health rationale. In Ireland, a survey of post-primary school children's involvement in sport was one measure used to record the state of health of children (O'Reilly and Shelley, 1987). In turn, these studies have drawn heavily on research into the fitness of American youth (Corbin and Pangrazi, 1992; Freedson and Rowland, 1992; Kuntzleman and Reiff, 1992).

The key variable for measurement in all these studies has been the intensity of exercise, and follows a similar search to measure the intensity of physical activity among adults. In Northern Ireland, since 1983 six out of seven different survey instruments used to measure physical activity among adults have included measures of intensity as part of questions on sporting involvement (Ogle, 1994). Only limited data have been collected on a range of indicators of sports development.

As one of its three overall policy objectives, the Sports Council for Northern Ireland has: 'To increase committed participation in sport ... amongst the population with particular emphasis on young people'. An ultimate outcome from this objective is the extent to which voluntary participation by the population increases in both frequency and quality, where voluntary participation is a specific reference to sport undertaken outside of the compulsory physical education curriculum.

As regards measuring the (hopefully) increasing commitment of young people, SCNI required a picture of young people's involvement in sport and in particular their voluntary participation in after-school sport and community-based sport. A series of measures indicating the 'extent of commitment' was devised, namely the percentage of young people participating in sport after school and away from school in the community, the percentage who were members of clubs, the percentage who received instruction and who practised, and finally, the percentage of those involved in competitions.

Frequency or regularity of participation is the most commonly found measure in all surveys of young people, and is normally measured in terms of the number of occasions of participation per week or in a four-week period. Quality of participation is much less frequently measured. The behavioural proxy indicators used in the SCNI survey assume that participants who have found a club, and are playing members, have through this action explicitly indicated an intention to invest and to 'improve' at their particular sport. Club membership can also open access to coaching and competitions, two important means of improving.

These measures have only recently been derived from the new thinking currently informing sports development, and their recency, together with the dominance of the 'medical model', may be one reason why there is still such a dearth of data on participation. Involvement in sport outside of school hours and school terms was touched on in the 1989 Northern Ireland Fitness Survey, but measures of the extent of instruction, practice, club membership or competition were not included. A study of children's sport participation in Wales in 1991/1992, while sharing with the 1989 Northern Ireland survey a strong focus on physical education and games, did provide some information on club membership (that is, 47 per cent of young people were members of clubs that offered sport although only 23 per cent were members of sport-only clubs), but once more the extent of information on participation was limited.

In 1990 the Australian Sports Commission conducted a large-scale survey of young people aged 13–18 years. The survey was designed to examine the importance of sport in the lives of young Australians and asked a range of questions about lifestyle, indeed questions often unconnected with sport at all. The survey did, however, ask about membership of clubs and found that 26 per cent of young people were members of both school- and community-based sports clubs, while just 9 per cent played solely for community-based clubs. Information was also collected on young people's experience of coaching: 80 per cent of young people who were members of clubs had received coaching, and nearly all (90 per cent) felt it had been helpful.

The 1989 Northern Ireland, 1991/92 Welsh and 1990 Australian surveys were all conducted among older children, aged 11 years and upwards. The 1994 English National Survey of Young People and Sport, and the 1994 Northern Ireland survey, collected information from children aged from 7 years upwards. Nearly four-fifths (77 per cent) of young people in England were members of clubs playing sport, with 56 per cent members of sports clubs only, compared with 36 per cent who were members of clubs in Northern Ireland, and 18 per cent who were in sport-only clubs. Further comparisons on the key indicators of commitment are not possible owing to differences in surveying techniques and phraseology. However, it would be fair to say that these surveys represent the first significant attempts to gather large amounts of data on the participation of young people in sport, and the shortage of previous research stands as stark testimony to the agendas which have dominated sport policy during the last 20 years, but which look set to face radical change.

POLICY CHALLENGES: DEVELOPING QUALITY SPORTING OPPORTUNITIES

In terms of an indication of the extent of commitment to sport by young people, the SCNI survey provides the Northern Ireland Sports Council with baseline data against which the broad impact of policies and programmes can be assessed. As the next century approaches rising expectations for improved or higher-quality sporting experiences for young people will pose difficult challenges for those responsible for policies and their implementation. Some, but certainly not all, of these challenges are discussed below. As mentioned earlier, the ethos of 'Sport for All' may now be recognised as unsustainable. In its place, and bearing in mind issues of ownership, partnership and preventive treatment raised earlier, a replacement but less catchy philosophy could be enshrined as 'Sport for Those Who Genuinely Want It'. Two very important yet simple messages to emerge from this project are, first, that children continue to enjoy sport for its own sake, and, second, that there is a considerable market demand for sport among young people of whatever age and whatever gender. The demand for sport shines through the data powerfully, but for primarily structural reasons, demand at present seems to outstrip supply or opportunity. One role of the policy maker must be to co-ordinate supply and demand, and it is with this sentiment in mind that the following specific issues are highlighted.

First, as several authors explicitly or even implicitly indicate, there is a need to look closely at the delivery of sport within the primary school curriculum, together with after-school sporting opportunities for children attending primary schools. The UK has belatedly recognised the importance of this age group, yet almost seven out of 10 young people in Northern Ireland (68 per cent) maintained that they had their first and all-important experience of their top sport before the age of 9, that is while still at primary school. For some sports the influence of school was of crucial importance in beginning sport, for example netball (88 per cent), basketball (57 per cent) and swimming (30 per cent). When asked why they had attempted sports, 'because of school' was mentioned most frequently, yet despite the importance of school to a child's initial experience of sport, most primary schools appear only to be offering limited opportunities for practice, instruction or competition.

Certainly, policies and programmes are beginning to be introduced in an effort to improve the situation but Northern Ireland still has a very long way to go to come close to the Australian and New Zealand penetration of the primary school sector. For example, only 1 per cent of children in Northern Ireland had any experience of mini-sport, and fewer than one-quarter received practice, instruction or competition in their 'top sport' from their primary school.

Second, the links between sport in primary and post-primary schools would appear to be weak and must be looked at closely. There is no guarantee that sparks of sporting interest which may have been generated before the age of 11 years will continue to burn after the transfer procedure. Instead, it is only that small number of children who have been fortunate enough to foster links outside school, or who have committed parents, who are likely to see their sporting careers continue uninterrupted throughout childhood. The advent of the Sportsmark scheme may act as an incentive for some schools to begin building sustainable links, and the appointment of school co-ordinators from the post-primary sector may also assist in forging links. Without these links the discontinuity between primary and post-primary school is likely to continue to inhibit sporting development.

Third, Northern Ireland's post-primary school sector is not homogeneous and this creates obvious problems in terms of imbalance of opportunity. A selective system of schooling and segregated schooling for Protestants and Catholics significantly affect the school-based sporting experiences of young people. Although differences have been found between Protestant and Catholic schools in terms of time devoted to curriculum physical education, and the range of sports offered, far more significant differences were found between schools in the grammar and secondary sectors. For example, previous research has shown grammar schools to be involved in three and a half times more weekend interschool and intraschool competitions than secondary schools, and grammar school sports clubs to be over four times more likely to be involved in weekend sport than secondary school sports clubs (Sutherland, 1992). The present study has largely confirmed this picture. In terms of assistance available to deliver after-school sport, 21 per cent of grammar schools were using coaches in comparison with just 3 per cent of secondary schools. Parents help out in 16 per cent of grammar schools but in only 4 per cent of secondary schools, and whereas senior pupils helped with extra-curricular sport in 43 per cent of grammar schools, only 14 per cent did so in second-ary schools (Sutherland, 1992).

The present data point to imbalances within schools in terms of the amount of competition and instruction young people receive. There is a clear challenge to help secondary schools to provide competition and instruction even to levels found in grammar schools, and a broader challenge to establish improved links between schools, clubs and local government as outlets for competition and a source of instruction. Catholic schools appear to lead the way in terms of their links with sports clubs, often at a local community level, and there may be examples of good practice here which could inform the wider Northern Ireland school and club system.

Certainly, the survey has highlighted the small number of young people who have experience of competition, even in their chosen or 'top' sport. This is a problem which is most acute for girls, and is a problem which becomes worse with age, highlighted by the small number of sixth form girls who have associations with clubs outside school. A great many of the 'top sports' chosen by these young people are by their very nature competitive. Leaving aside the ongoing debate concerning the role of competitive sport in schools, for these young people to be denied the opportunity to compete, at whatever level and in whatever context, seems perverse and would seem guaranteed to dampen enthusiasm for that activity, given that one vital component, healthy competition, remains absent.

Instruction naturally raises the issue of coaching, and the provision of coaches remains a complex matter for resolution. Not all coaches, for example, are trained to work with young people and consequently cannot meet the expectations of schools or pupils. As regards local government, in 1991 it was found that only 4 per cent of local government personnel regularly assisted in after-school sport in post-primary schools (Sutherland, 1992). When coupled with evidence from this survey, for example showing that only 28 per cent of young people used leisure centres with their school, and 44 per cent not with school, there would appear to be enormous potential for expansion. Given that only 43 per cent of pupils in post-primary schools could participate in their 'top sport' in school, the use of a local leisure centre could considerably enhance the opportunity to take part, and even perhaps compete in their favoured activities.

The use of facilities outside school highlights another key concern, namely the use of sports clubs. In 1992 there were around 6,500 sports clubs in Northern Ireland (Ogle, 1995), and yet this survey has revealed that only 18 per cent of young people were members of sport-only clubs (36 per cent belonged to clubs which offered sport as one activity among others, for example youth clubs and church groups). Only just over a quarter (26 per cent) of members received any form of instruction in sports clubs, with 18 per cent receiving instruction as members of youth clubs. While the survey shows that young people are busier participants in their 'top sport' away from school, in terms of being able to improve or 'get better' (which for four out of five young people was the most frequently mentioned factor making them more keen about sport), opportunities in the community are very uneven. Low club membership levels, coupled with low levels of instruction away from school and limited competitive opportunities, suggest that the current gap between participation rates for young people and adults (40 per cent), excluding walking (unpublished data from Continuous Household Survey (1991/92), Northern Ireland Statistics Research Agency), will be maintained unless opportunities to 'get better' are available. In terms of gender, the problem is amplified. Young people represent only around three out of 10 members of sports clubs, but among under 18-year-old members, it is estimated that in Northern Ireland there are four and a half times as many young male members as female members (Ogle, 1995). Once more there is a clear signal here that bridges need to be built to ensure that the road from sporting promise to the realisation of sporting potential is as smooth as possible.

In Chapter 2, gender differences in competitive sporting participation are highlighted, with males having a much higher overall proportion of participants at the competitive level (64 per cent) than females (36 per cent). Again, the picture from clubs supports this survey, in that female membership, and by implication access to competition, lags far behind that for males. A 1994 survey of social attitudes towards sport in Northern Ireland found that more people agreed with the statement that 'sports clubs in general are run by men for men' (49 per cent) than disagreed (36 per cent). A breakdown by gender is not available, but in response to the statement that 'women have no place in sports clubs', 80 per cent of respondents disagreed with only 9 per cent in agreement (SCNI, 1995). What this 'place' might be was not questioned, but the response at least suggests support for greater involvement of women in sports clubs, and was certainly less equivocal than attitudes towards the manner in which clubs are run. Nevertheless a considerable challenge remains in order to reduce the male ethos within clubs if more women are to participate, and at the same time to recognise that the type of clubs and activities which may be attractive to women are not the same as those for men.

CONCLUSION

In terms of a great many structural indices of young people's 'commitment' to sport (including experience of instruction, club membership and competition), as the contributors to this book amply testify, a great many policy challenges remain. Fortunately there is international evidence that change is occurring within sport itself in an attempt to address these challenges (Australian Sports Commission, 1991; Department of National Heritage, 1995; Ofsted, 1995). Over recent years there has emerged a convergence in thinking and practice across public sector sports development organisations worldwide. This convergence reflects on the energy currently being generated within sport to assist young people's sporting development. However, enthusiasm and energy alone, without the necessary material resources, may be insufficient either to initiate change or to sustain opportunities for young people. At the same time, the experience of 'Sport for All' policies and programmes serves to remind those involved in the administration of sport of the dangers associated with pursuing grandiose and perhaps ill-defined ideals embracing all young people. 'Sport for All' may be Utopian but it is undeniable that young people regularly engage in high levels of voluntary sporting activity, and, as the survey reveals, this is maintained by high levels of interest and motivation towards sport, sometimes helped by schools, less frequently by clubs, but quite often maintained 'against all odds'. Policy makers may have to come to terms not with an 'all or nothing' approach to involvement, but with how they may be able to shorten these odds and balance the probability that involvement and enthusiasm for sport is sustained.

On the one hand, the strong associations noted between sport participation and high educational attainment and self-esteem may be gratifying. On the other hand these findings may act as a powerful reminder that, in its present form, sport in itself does not represent an agent capable of generating a more equal or equitable society. In Northern Ireland, which 'has...long term unemployment three and a half times higher than that for the UK as a whole [and] has...the second lowest number of young people involved in education and training across the whole of Europe' (SCNI, 1993), aspiring towards ideals of universal involvement in sport, almost on demand, would appear to be unrealistic. At the same time, however, this survey has demonstrated that a number of demographic and structural factors may conspire together to dampen an appetite for sport, and that this appetite does not appear to be quite as dependent on personal or demographic background as may commonly be believed.

At both an ideological and a pragmatic level, the task ahead should not be labelled as remedial action, targeting 'at risk' adult populations, or rekindling lost enthusiasms, or providing opportunities for those who have left behind formal education. Instead, a more manageable goal, and one which tallies comfortably with current thinking on preventive sport strategies, should be to explore practical strategies for lowering barriers and removing structural obstacles which stand in the way of those who show a desire to maintain their interest and involvement in sport. This is not a renewed clarion call for 'Sport for All' but a call to try to enable those young people who have shown interest and involvement to at least see a way forward for their sporting careers. As developmentalists tell us, the span from childhood to adulthood is not great but in terms of sport participation it can present itself as a yawning chasm. With energy and with resource, our task remains to span that chasm.

REFERENCES

Armstrong, N. and Biddle, S. (1992). *Health Related Physical Activity in the National Curriculum; New Directions in Physical Education, Volume 2: Towards a National Curriculum.* Leeds: Human Kinetics (UK).

Armstrong, N., Balding, J., Gentle, P. and Kirby, B. (1990). Peak oxygen uptake and physical activity in 11–16 year olds. *Paediatric Exercise Science,* 2, 349–358.

Australian Sports Commission (1991). *Sport for Young Australians: Widening the Gateways to Participation.* Canberra: Australian Sports Commission.

Australian Sports Commission (1993). *Sport: A Great Investment.* Canberra: Australian Sports Commission.

Australian Sports Commission (1995). *Evaluation of The Australian Sports Commission's Impact on Sports Performances and Participation in Australia 1994.* Canberra: Australian Sports Commission.

Boreham, C., Savage, J., Primrose, D., Cran, G. and Strain, J. (1993). Coronary risk factors in school children. *Archives of Disease in Childhood, 68,* 182–186.

Clarke, A. (1994). Farewell to welfare? The changing rationales for leisure and tourism policies in Europe. In D. Leslie (ed.) *Tourism and Leisure: Towards the Millenium, Volume 2: Perspectives on Provision.* Eastbourne: LSA Publications.

Corbin, C. and Pangrazi, R. (1992). Are American children and youth fit? *Research Quarterly for Exercise and Sport, 63, (2),* 96–106.

Department of Education Northern Ireland (1995). *The Future of Sport for Young People in Northern Ireland.* Belfast: HMSO.

Department of Education for Northern Ireland (1996). *Strategic Plan for Education, 1994–2000.* Belfast: HMSO.

Department of National Heritage (1995). *Sport: Raising the Game.* London: HMSO.

Department of Sport and Recreation, Republic of South Africa. (1995). *Getting the Nation to Play.* Pretoria: RSA Government.

Division of Physical and Health Education, The Queen's University of Belfast (1989). *Northern Ireland Health and Fitness Survey: The Fitness, Physical Activity, Attitudes of Lifestyles of Northern Ireland Post-Primary School Children.* Belfast: The Queen's University of Belfast.

Freedson, P. and Rowland, T. (1992). Youth activity versus youth fitness: Let's redirect our efforts. *Research Quarterly for Exercise and Sport, 63, (2),* 133–136.

Health Promotion Agency (1994). *The Health Behaviour of School Children in Northern Ireland (1994).* Belfast: Health Promotion Agency for Northern Ireland.

Health Promotion Agency (1996). *Be Active, Be Healthy: 1996 Northern Ireland Physical Activity Strategy 1996–2002.* Belfast: Health Promotion Agency for Northern Ireland.

Hendry, L.B., Shucksmith, J., Love, J.G. and Glendenning, A. (1993). *Young People's Leisure Lifestyles.* London: Routledge.

Hillary Commission (1993). *The Business of Sport and Leisure.* Auckland: Hillary Commission.

Kuntzleman, C. and Reiff, C. (1992). The decline in American children's fitness levels. *Research Quarterly for Exercise and Sport, 63, (2),* 107–111.

MacAuley, D., McCrum, E., Scott, G., Evans, A., Sweeney, K., Trinick, T. and Boreham, C. (1994). *The Northern Ireland Health and Activity Survey (1994).* Belfast: HMSO.

Mason, V. (1995). *Young People and Sport in England, 1994: A National Survey.* London: Sports Council.

North American Regional Forum Committee for the World Forum on Physical Activity and Sport (1995). A global vision for school physical education. Unpublished conference paper, Quebec.

Office for Standards in Education (1995). *Physical Education and Sport in Schools: A Survey of Good Practice. A Report from the Office for Her Majesty's Chief Inspector of Schools.* London: HMSO.

Ogle, S. (1994). *The Assessment of Adult Participation in Sport and Physical Recreation in Northern Ireland 1983-1993 using Physical Activity Questionnaires.* Belfast: Sports Council Northern Ireland.

Ogle, S. (1995). *Membership. Realised and Potential, of the Voluntary Sporting Sector in Northern Ireland.* Belfast: Sports Council Northern Ireland.

Ogle, S. and Kelly, F. (1994). *Northern Ireland Health and Activity Survey: Main Findings.*Belfast: HMSO.

O'Reilly, O. and Shelley, E. (1987). *The Kilkenny Post-Primary Schools Survey.* Unpublished report, Kilkenny, Ireland.

Ravenscroft, N. (1996). Leisure, consumerism and active citizenship in the UK. *Managing Leisure, An International Journal, 1, (3),* 163–174.

Roberts, K., Dench, S., Minten, J. and York, C. (1989). *Community Response to Leisure Centre Provision.* London: Sports Council (GB).

Sports Council (GB) (1993). *Young People and Sport: Policy Frameworks for Action.* London: Sports Council (GB).

Sports Council (GB)/Health Education Authority (1992a). *Allied Dunbar National Fitness Survey: Main Findings*. London: Sports Council (GB).

Sports Council (GB)/Henley Centre (1992b). *The Economic Impact of Sport in the United Kingdom*. London: Sports Council (GB).

Sports Council Northern Ireland (1992a). *The Economic Impact of Sport in Northern Ireland*. Belfast: Sports Council Northern Ireland.

Sports Council Northern Ireland (1992b). *European Sports Charter, Council of Europe*. Belfast: Sports Council Northern Ireland.

Sports Council Northern Ireland (1993). *Sport for Young People: A Strategy on the Development of Sporting Opportunities for Young People in Northern Ireland*. Belfast: Sports Council Northern Ireland.

Sports Council Northern Ireland/Coopers and Lybrand Ltd (1995). *Public Attitudes to Sport in Northern Ireland*. Belfast: Sports Council Northern Ireland.

Sports Council (Wales) (1993). *Children's Sport Participation, 1991/1992*. Cardiff: Sports Council (Wales).

Sugden, J. and Bairner, A. (1986). Northern Ireland: The politics of leisure in a divided society. *Leisure Studies*, 5, 341–352.

Sutherland, A. (1992). *Physical Education and Games in Post-Primary Schools in 1991*. Belfast: Sports Council Northern Ireland.

Team Sport Scotland (1994). *Monitoring and Evaluation Study*. Edinburgh: Centre for Leisure Research.

World Forum on Physical Activity and Sport (1995). *International recommendations*. Unpublished conference paper, Quebec.

11 Technical report

Peter Ward

The SCNI survey was commissioned by the Sports Council for Northern Ireland (SCNI) in November 1992, the aim of the research being to establish baseline information on young people's degree of involvement in sport and physical recreation, and to improve understanding of the processes and factors affecting that involvement. The definition of sport adopted by the SCNI was inclusive and consistent with that set out in the Council of Europe 'Sport for All' Charter which identifies four categories:

1 Competitive games and sports (for example, netball, hockey, soccer)
2 Outdoor and adventure activities (for example climbing)
3 Aesthetic movement (for example dance, figure skating)
4 Conditioning activity (for example weight training, aerobics)

RESEARCH INSTRUMENTS

Following preliminary consultation between the client and the researchers, and after a review of the relevant literature, it was decided that the research would comprise three elements:

1 A survey of a sample of 7–18-year-olds in schools in Northern Ireland using a customised questionnaire.
2 A 'Harter' personal identity questionnaire among all post-primary children in the sample.
3 A four-day diary to be maintained by a subset (50 per cent) of the post-primary sample.

QUESTIONNAIRE DEVELOPMENT

In accordance with the objectives of the SCNI, a three-part interview schedule was developed to identify basic information, experience of all attempted sports, and involvement with named 'top sport' for the individual. John Kremer and Karen Trew from the School of Psychology at Queen's University were responsible for designing the content and layout of the questionnaire while Research and Evaluation Services (RES) was responsible for providing technical advice on its various drafts.

The questionnaire sought to make a clear distinction between those having a 'top sport', that is a sport, either currently or previously, with which the person was especially involved, and those who could not identify a preferred activity. The questionnaire development was mindful too that what was being measured was 'sport' *per se*, and that 'physical activities' engaged in by young people did not necessarily equate with sporting involvement. The final version of the questionnaire was subsequently broken down into the following sections:

- Demographic and background information on the respondent
- Sports which had been tried out at any time by the respondent, including sports available at school
- Sports which respondent would like to try if given the opportunity
- Sporting involvement of other family members
- Sporting involvement of two closest friends
- 'Top sport' – details of the sport with which the respondent was most closely associated, including details of times, places, practice, instruction, availability if this sport at primary school, and future intentions as regards this sport

One limitation of the survey was the inability to ask for parental occupation in order to derive social class. Although social class may be related to sporting involvement, schools were not happy about the occupation question being asked of children.

A showcard listing all the sports recognised by the SCNI, with individual code numbers, was carried by the interviewer. The interviewer referred to this card for the appropriate code to be entered for unprompted mentions of sport and was handed to the respondents at those parts of the questionnaire where prompted answers were accepted.

The questionnaire was found to take an average of 40 minutes to complete (see the appendix).

THE HARTER PERSONAL IDENTITY QUESTIONNAIRE

This scale was developed in the USA by Susan Harter as a means of measuring self-perception and personal identity (see Chapter 3). It contains 66 pairs of statements and respondents must choose whether they most identify with the statement on the left side or the right side and indicate the strength of their agreement by choosing 'Sort of true for me' or 'Really true for me'. The response to each item on the inventory is then scored to produce a personal profile. The Harter scale must be completed by the respondent.

DIARY

A four-day diary was produced on a pro forma basis (see Chapter 7). This set a framework for each day starting with time of getting up and culminating with time of going to bed. Subjects were asked to detail their activities into broadly structured phases of the day, such as before going to school, during school break times, immediately after school and after tea time. Prevailing weather conditions on each day were also recorded. The diary covered a period of four consecutive days: two school days and two non-school days. The sections of the diary relating to each of these types of day were colour coded for emphasis.

PILOT SURVEY

Owing to the complexity of the concept, structure and administration of the survey instruments, a pilot survey was conducted using the agreed draft questionnaire. Six schools were chosen arbitrarily for the pilot study to take account of different school types (namely, primary, post-primary, Catholic, Protestant, single sex and mixed sex). Interviews were achieved with all designated children ($n = 50$) at five of the six schools. Exam schedules in the sixth school prevented interviews with pupils. The pilot survey was principally seeking to test:

- the procedure for obtaining access to children at school
- the questionnaire with regard to its duration, coverage of the wide range of experiences encountered, respondent reaction, relevance to children of various ages
- respondents' understanding of terminology associated with consideration of sport

The principal lessons derived from the pilot were as follows.

Main survey

- The interview schedule took an excessive time to complete (up to 90 minutes).

- There were 'flow problems' associated with the use of complicated matrix structures .
- Emerging sports were not covered in the SCNI lists, for example variations in martial arts.
- There was a need for show cards to improve the quality of responses on items with long lists of options.
- There was a need to adapt the final instrument to exclude those items not considered appropriate to the younger respondents.

The diary

- There was variable quality of completion and adherence to guidelines.
- Some pupils failed to maintain the diary day by day and reconstructed their activities prior to handing it in.
- Some diaries were lost, therefore necessitiating a reconstruction of the period with the interviewer's assistance.
- The assessment of diaries and assistance with reconstruction, in addition to interviewing, proved time consuming.

All these issues were subsequently addressed prior to the launch of the survey.

FIELDWORK

Fieldwork was carried out between March 1993 and October 1994. To reduce response bias towards seasonal sport, 427 interviews were conducted during the summer term, 867 were conducted during the autumn term and 995 took place during the winter term. The interviewing was carried out by 12 experienced interviewers employed by RES.

INTERVIEWER BRIEFING

All interviewers attended a half-day briefing session run by the principal researchers and staff of RES, which focused on:

- the approach to the schools and how to select children from the register
- the arrangements for being in the school
- briefing children on the completion of the questionnaire and how to maintain the diary
- the content and structure of the main survey questionnaire and how to code and interpret responses

One month after commencing fieldwork, the interviewers were recalled to evaluate the procedure. No significant difficulties were noted at that time.

THE SAMPLE

It was recognised that, as regards the age range of 7–16 years, the school population was almost entirely congruous with the same age group in the population as a whole, while for the 17–18 age range only a minority were still attending school. Despite this, a decision was taken to include this upper age band in the sampling frame. The sampling objective was therefore to achieve a representative sample of all school pupils aged 7–18 years across the following range of variables.

- Age bands (corresponding to key stages in the curriculum)
- School type (single sex and mixed sex)
- Location (Education and Library Board, population density)
- School management type (Catholic maintained, controlled, integrated, other)

In adopting a sampling strategy for the project it was considered that to control for all four strata in the sample would lead to some very small cell sizes and accordingly the sample scheme was defined by two variables: Education and Library Board area and school type.

SAMPLING FRAME

The sampling frame was considered to consist of 15 strata, defined by the combinations of the five Area Education and Library Boards which operate in Northern Ireland (Belfast, Western, North Eastern, South Eastern and Southern) and three school types (primary, secondary intermediate and grammar). Children aged 7–11 years were further deemed to be in Primary forms P4 to P7. (The Department of Education for Northern Ireland (DENI) determines the appropriate class/form by the age of child on 1st July prior to the start of the school year.) Pupils in forms P4 to P7 in grammar school preparatory departments were deemed to be 'primary'.

Table 11.1 shows the actual school populations in the 15 strata (data supplied by DENI). The secondary intermediate (SI) and grammar school populations are based on 1992 enrolments (ENROL92), and P4 to P7 populations (P4–P7) are believed to be based on 1993 enrolments. (In Northern Ireland, only a minority of pupils are given

Table 11.1 The populations (school numbers in bold; pupil numbers in light face)

Area Board	P4–P7	SI	Grammar	Totals
Belfast	**98**	**24**	**15**	**137**
	18,146	14,744	14,200	47,090
Western	**204**	**35**	**13**	**252**
	20,435	17,007	10,022	47,464
North Eastern	**233**	**39**	**17**	**289**
	22,161	19,171	12,631	53,963
South Eastern	**168**	**29**	**10**	**207**
	20,168	15,270	9,307	44,745
Southern	**273**	**38**	**15**	**326**
	23,248	21,203	9,610	54,061
Totals	**976**	**165**	**70**	**1,211**
	104,158	87,395	55,770	247,323

access to grammar school places, allocation depending on performance in the transfer procedure which is completed during P7.)

SAMPLING DESIGN

Sampling proceeded in two stages. The primary sampling units (PSUs) were the schools within each stratum, and the secondary sampling units (SSUs) were the pupils within each sampled school. Schools within each stratum were selected with probability proportional to size (PPS). With size taken as enrolment, PPS provided a 'self-balancing' sample across all strata, that is different weights were not required.

A target sample of 2,400 pupils was selected from a total of approximately 120 schools. Therefore the schools' sampling fraction was:

$$F = 120/1,211 = 0.09909$$

The pupils' sampling fraction was:

$$F = 2,400/247,323 = 0.009704$$

The sampling fraction was applied to Table 11.1 and rounded to the nearest integer, yielding the sample sizes as shown in Table 11.2.

PPS requires a fixed number of pupils to be selected from each school, implying, for example, 17.6 pupils from each of the 10 Belfast primary schools. Fractional numbers of pupils were avoided by selecting 17 pupils from four schools and 18 from the remaining six schools ((4 × 17) + (6 × 18) = 176). The four schools with the smallest

Table 11.2 The sample sizes (school numbers in bold; pupil numbers in light face)

Area Board	P4–P7	SI	Grammar	Totals
Belfast	**10**	**2**	**1**	**13**
	176	143	138	457
Western	**20**	**3**	**1**	**24**
	198	165	97	460
North Eastern	**23**	**4**	**2**	**29**
	215	186	123	524
South Eastern	**17**	**3**	**1**	**21**
	196	148	90	434
Southern	**27**	**4**	**1**	**32**
	226	206	93	525
Totals	**97**	**16**	**6**	**119**
	1,011	848	541	2,400

enrolments were those allocated 17 pupils each. Three grammar schools with preparatory departments were included in the P4–P7 strata.

IDENTIFICATION OF SAMPLED SCHOOLS

The methodology is illustrated here using the South Eastern SIS stratum, but was identical for all strata.

The 29 schools in this stratum were first sorted into ascending order of school reference number, and then the order was randomised using a random permutation of the numbers 1 to 29. (All randomisations were obtained with Microsoft FORTRAN random number subroutines from the associated Subroutine Library; arithmetic was performed to 32 bit accuracy.) Random ordering of the list was employed to minimise or remove any potential (and unknown) ordering effect that may be relevant to the survey. For example, school reference numbers tend to correlate with the age of the school.

The values of ENROL92 were then accumulated down the list (see Table 11.3). This effectively produced a sequence list of all 15,270 pupils in this stratum.

The three schools to be selected were identified by those pupils containing every 5,090th pupil in the sequence (5,090 = 15,270/3). The random starting point among the first 5,090 pupils was determined by generation of a random number in the range 1–5,090, in this case 450. Thus the first school was that containing the 450th pupil in the sequence (School no. 4210201), the second the 5,540th (450 + 5,090) pupil in the sequence (School no. 4260266), and the third the

Table 11.3 South Eastern secondary intermediate stratum

School ref number.	ENROL92	Cumulative ENROL92	Selection
4210201	777	777	450
4210046	515	1,292	
4210012	645	1,937	
4210031	297	2,234	
4210194	447	2,681	
4210029	402	3,083	
4230211	952	4,035	
4210215	1,048	5,083	
4210095	396	5,479	
4260255	730	6,209	5,540
4210214	754	6,963	
4210063	266	7,229	
4210183	809	8,038	
4230224	500	8,538	
4210045	523	9,061	
4230165	379	9,440	
4210272	213	9,653	
4230102	430	10,083	
4230223	350	10,433	
4230023	477	10,910	10,630
4230067	380	11,290	
4210024	273	11,563	
4210051	430	11,993	
4210072	738	12,731	
4230161	444	13,175	
4210262	613	13,788	
4210030	473	14,261	
4210086	626	14,887	
4230107	383	15,270	

10,630th (5,540 + 5,090) pupil in the sequence (School no. 4230023). Those strata that required only one school were obtained in the same way. For example, in the case of 'Belfast; Grammar', the random starting point was simply a random number in the range 1–14,200.

SELECTING CHILDREN WITHIN THE SCHOOL

The selection of individual pupils from within the school was based on a random start/fixed increment scheme applied to the total of form registers. The registers were arrayed in the general order of ascending pupil age/class order to provide representative coverage of age. A random selection interval was calculated by dividing the number of pupils to be interviewed in that school into the number of pupils currently on the school roll. If a selected child was absent a substitution was made by selecting the next name on the class register.

APPROACHING SCHOOLS

A letter outlining the objectives and methods of the survey was sent to the principal in each of the selected schools, after permission had been sought and obtained from the relevant Education and Library Board. The designated interviewer then telephoned the principal seeking an appointment to discuss arrangements for carrying out the survey. In many cases, having granted permission, the principal delegated liaison with the interviewer to another member of staff, in many cases from the PE department. Interviewers were instructed to be extremely flexible regarding dates for being in the school in order to cause minimum disruption to normal school routine. This was an especially important consideration in schools where the sample included children from classes engaged in or preparing for external examinations such as GCSE or 'A' levels. In some of the larger schools, where a significant number of pupils had to be interviewed, these interviews were spread across three terms at the request of the schools. Of the 120 schools originally selected only 10 (8 per cent) refused or were otherwise unable to take part. In such cases the school was replaced by another of the same type and from within the same Education and Library Board area.

INTERVIEW PROCEDURE IN SCHOOL

Within primary schools, the co-ordinating teacher was asked to make arrangements for the selected pupils to come along in consecutive order to the room in the school assigned to the interviewer. Children were then interviewed in private. In post-primary schools, because of the use of the Harter questionnaire and the diaries in addition to the main questionnaire, a different procedure was used. Co-ordinating teachers were asked to bring all selected children together (if the sample was very large this would have been in two or three groups). At this session the interviewer explained the Harter questionnaire before asking all pupils to fill one in individually. Next the interviewer randomly selected half the assembled children as those who would maintain the diary of activities over a four-day period. These children were then given instructions on how to complete the diaries. These were to be returned to the interviewer when he or she came back to the school to conduct the main survey interview. Individual interviews were conducted in the secondary and grammar schools in the same way as primary schools.

DATA PREPARATION

Main Survey

Returned questionnaires were manually checked and edited prior to coding. For open-ended questions, codes were developed on a continuous basis and accorded unique code numbers. Entry onto computer was via the SPSS data entry module and primary analysis was carried out in the SPSS PC programme. For ease of analysis, those respondents having a 'top sport' were decanted onto a secondary data file, while the principal file contained all cases and all variables from the main survey, as well as the variables contained in the Harter questionnaire where appropriate (post-primary respondents only).

Diaries

To facilitate analysis of the information contained on the returned diaries, these were first checked manually for completeness before being fully coded. The coding scheme recorded the following key variables:

- time of getting up in the morning
- time of going to bed
- day of the week
- whether this was a typical/untypical day

Within these parameters individual periods of activity were identified and coded on a 24 hour clock basis. Although respondents were instructed to ignore routine items such as washing, eating or dressing, this was not always the case. Owing to this, and the prevalence of certain non-specific activities such as 'hanging around with friends', only those activities which were either sporting in nature or considered purposeful were recorded for analysis. For sporting activities, code numbers corresponding to the codes used in the main survey were used. For other activities, codes were developed on a continuous basis with a prefix to distinguish them from the sport codes.

SAMPLING ERROR AND CONFIDENCE INTERVALS

Table 11.4 sets out sample errors and confidence intervals at the 95 per cent confidence level, based on a sample of 2,400 respondents. The

Table 11.4 Standard errors and 95 per cent confidence intervals ($N = 2,400$)

$N = 2,400$	%p									
	5	10	15	20	25	30	35	40	45	50
	95	90	85	80	75	70	65	60	55	50
Standard error	0.44	0.61	0.73	0.82	0.88	0.93	0.97	1	1	1
95 % confidence Interval (+ or −)	0.9	1.2	1.4	1.6	1.7	1.8	1.9	2	2	2

sample errors assume a simple random sample (SRS) design. It is acknowledged that the stratified nature of the sample has produced a design effect (DEFT) although the magnitude of the DEFT on sample error is likely to be negligible.

EXAMPLE OF SAMPLING ERROR

The use of sampling errors and confidence intervals is best illustrated by means of an example from the survey. The sample estimated that 40 per cent of young people are introduced to clubs by their friends. Therefore assuming a simple random sample, the margin of error at the 95 per cent confidence level is ±2 per cent. In other words we can be 95 per cent confident that the true proportion of young people introduced to clubs by their friends in Northern Ireland is within the range 38 per cent to 42 per cent. Indeed the margin of error for all sample estimates is within the parameters of ±2 per cent.

Appendix: SCNI survey

SECTION A: GENERAL INFORMATION

SERIAL NUMBER (**leave blank**)

PUPIL'S NAME: (first) _____ (last) _____

CODE NUMBER (to tally with your name sheet)

Interviewer code:

Date of interview:

Date of birth:

Sex: (Male = 1; Female = 2)

School: _____

Local Govt Dist: _____

Board:	Belfast	1
	North Eastern	2
CODE ONE	South Eastern	3
	Western	4
	Southern	5

Form/class: _____
(YEAR AND
CLASS e.g. P6G)

Educational attainment (estimated in terms of year average):

	Upper 25%	1
	Mid 50%	2
	Lower 25%	3

School type:	Protestant	1
	Catholic	2
	Integrated	3
	Grammar	1
	Secondary	2
	Comprehensive	3
	Primary	4
	Mixed sex	1
	Girls only	2
	Boys only	3

SECTION B: ATTEMPTED SPORTS

(Questions to be used in conjunction with MATRIX ONE)

1. *Sport code (see SCNI list)*

2. *At what age did you first try this sport?*

4 or under	1
5–7 years	2
8–9 years	3
10–11 years	4
12 or older	5

3. *What was the most important reason why you took up this sport?*

Something to do	1
Because of my friends	2
Because of my father	3
Because of my mother	4
Because of elder brother/sister	5
To keep fit	6
Because of school	7
Seemed interesting	8
Seemed a challenge	9
To practise skills	10
To learn new skills	11
Because I thought I would be good	12
Saw it on the TV/video etc.	13
Saw a game competition live	14
Don't know/can't remember	15
Other _____	16

4. *What is/was your involvement?*
    Active participant   1
    Administrator   2
    Coach   3
    Official (e.g. referee, judge)   4

Active participant – playing, performing or practising the sport/activity
Administrator – involved in the organisation of the sport/activity
Coach – provider of instruction/supervision/advice to active
    participants
Official – referee, judge (e.g. linesman) etc.

4i. *If active participant, what is/was the highest standard that you achieved?*
    Basic (family recreation; play; school clubs open to all;
        recreational; largely non-competitive; informal)   1
    Competitive (competitive club level; selected school teams) 2
    Elite (county, regional and nationally recognised standard;
        black belt)   3

4ii. *If active participant, what do you think is/was your potential level of achievement?*
    Basic (family recreation; play; school clubs open to all;
        recreational; largely non-competitive; informal)   1
    Competitive (competitive club level; selected school teams) 2
    Elite (county, regional and nationally recognised standard) 3

5. *Is/Was your involvement with this activity?*
    School based   1
    Outside school   2
    Both   3

6. *Have you ever received formal instruction/coaching in this sport?*
    No   0
    Yes, in school   1
    Yes, parent   2
    Yes, coach outside school   3
    Yes, both in school and outside   4

7. *If you are no longer involved, at what age did you finish?*
    4 or under   1
    5–7 years   2
    8–9 years   3
    10–11 years   4
    12 or older   5

8. *If you have finished, what was the most important reason for stopping?*

Injury	1
Lack of interest	2
Other commitments (school)	3
Other commitments (part-time job, boy/girl friend)	4
Not good enough	5
No encouragement from family	6
Not big/strong enough	7
Too expensive	8
Lack of resources (e.g. equipment)	9
Took up too much time	10
Coaches were unfriendly	11
Other players my age were unfriendly	12
Older players were unfriendly	13
Started another sport	14
My friends had stopped	15
Training was boring	16
Mainly for boys/girls	17
Wasn't allowed	18
Not played at school	19
Other _____	20

9. *At which times of the year are/were you normally involved?*

All year round	1
Mainly winter months	2
Mainly summer months	3

10. *On average, how often are/were you involved with this sport?*

Twice a week or more	1
Once a week	2
Once a month	3
Can't remember	4

11. *Where do/did you most often take part in this sport?*

Informal/various settings	1
In school (between 9.00 and 3.30)	2
In school (outside 9.00 and 3.30, Mon–Fri)	3
In school (both of above)	4
Sport club or clubs	5
Private gym/leisure centre	6
Multi-user public leisure centre (with a club)	7
Multi-user public leisure centre (other)	8
Swimming pool	9
Outdoors	10

SECTION B: ATTEMPTED SPORTS

At some time or another most young people have tried various sports, hobbies, outdoor pursuits and games. Could I find out which you have ever tried, when you started, what you did, what level you achieved and if you are still involved?

Allow respondents to spontaneously mention sports, then show SCNI list and ask if there are any others which they have tried. Draw a line separating the 2 sets of sports. For each, please ask the following series of questions in turn and code-entry a column at a time for each sport.

For Sport code refer to SCNI list.

For sports with "mini" versions (see list), please use specific key questions to identify whether full or junior version, and code appropriately as either full or junior.

MATRIX 1: ATTEMPTED SPORTS

Spontaneous and Cued mention (Separate with a bold line)

	spt 1	spt 2	spt 3	spt 4	spt 5	spt 6	spt 7	spt 8	spt 9	spt 10
1. Sport code										
2. Age started?										
3. Why started?										
4. Involvement?										
4i. Highest level?										
4ii. Potential?										
5. School based?										
6. Instruction?										
7. Age finish?										
8. Why finish?										
9. When?										
10. How often?										
11. Where?										

SECTION B: SPORTS WISH LIST

The following questions to be coded in MATRIX 2. For each, please ask the following series of questions in turn and code-entry a column at a time for each sport.

Allow respondents to spontaneously mention sports, then show SCNI list and ask if there are any others which they have tried. (Draw a line separating the 2 sets of sports.)

Sport code (see SCNI list)

For sports with "mini" versions (see list), please use specific key questions to identify whether full or junior version, and code appropriately as either full or junior.

Of the sports which you have never tried, which would you like to be able to try and why?

1. *Why do you want to try this sport?*
(Code two most important)

It looks like fun	1
I have seen it on the TV/films/video	2
I have read about it in books/magazines	3
My father is interested	4
My mother is interested	5
My brother/sister is interested	6
I have another relative who is interested	7
I have a friend who is interested	8
It looks exciting	9
It looks like a challenge	10
I like to learn new skills	11
I like to compete	12
Other	13

2. *Why have you not tried this sport before?*
(Code two most important)

I don't know how to start	1
It is too dangerous	2
It costs too much	3
I don't know anyone who is involved	4
I don't have the equipment	5
I'm not good enough	6

I'm too young	7
I'm not allowed by family	8
I'm not strong enough	9
My friends don't like it	10
Other	11

MATRIX 2: SPORTS WISH LIST

Spontaneous and Cued mention (Separate with a bold line)

	spt 1	spt 2	spt 3	spt 4	spt 5	spt 6	spt 7	spt 8	spt 9	spt 10
Sport code										
2 reasons for trying										
2 reasons not tried										

SECTION B: SCHOOL SPORTS

Sport code (see SCNI list)

For sports with "mini" versions (see list), please use specific key questions to identify whether full or junior version, and code appropriately as either full or junior (separate codes for each if both played).

1. *Which sports are available for you at your current school?*

Sport code (see SCNI list)

For sports with "mini" versions (see list), please use specific key questions to identify whether full or junior version, and code appropriately as either full or junior (separate codes for each if both played).

2. *Which other sports would you like to be available at your present school?*

Sport code (see SCNI list; instructions as above)

3. *For Post-Primary Only Which sports were available to you at your primary school?*

Sport code (see SCNI list; instructions as above)

SECTION B: WATCHING SPORTS

Which sports have you been to see live (not on television)?

1. Sport code (3 digits) _____
How often?	Once	1
	2–3	2
	4–9	3
	10+	4

2. Sport code (3 digits) _____
How often?	Once	1
	2–3	2
	4–9	3
	10+	4

3. Sport code (3 digits) _____
How often?	Once	1
	2–3	2
	4–9	3
	10+	4

SECTION B: YOUR FAMILY'S SPORTS

The following questions concern your relations and their involvement with sport.

Which relatives do you know to have been involved with a particular sport?

Indicate their involvement in terms of the following questions.

Named sport (up to 2 per relative; see SCNI Sports List)

Type of involvement:

Active participant (basic)	1
Active participant (competitive)	2
Active participant (elite)	3
Administrator	4
Coach	5
Spectator (see games live)	6
Official (e.g. referee)	7

When involved?

Presently involved	1
Past, but within five years	2
Past, more than five years ago	3

How often? (for seasonal sports, code as for most active period)

Once a month	1
Once a week	2
Twice a week or more	3
Can't remember/don't know	4

(Specify relation in first column, i.e. father, mother, brother, sister, uncle, aunt, cousin, grandmother, grandfather; Specify sport by 3 digit code)

	Relative	*Sport 1*	*type*	*when*	*freq*	*Sport 2*	*type*	*when*	*freq*
1									
2									
3									
4									
5									
6									
7									
8									
9									
10									

SECTION B: YOUR FRIENDS' SPORTS

Who are your two closest friends?
    Friend 1 _____
    Friend 2 _____

FRIEND 1:

As far as you know, does he/she take part in any sport?

	YES	NO
	1	2

IF NO, go to next friend. If YES, continue

Which sports or hobbies is/was s/he involved with (include the two most significant), *to what standard, and how often is s/he usually involved?*

Type of activity (i.e. Sport code; 3 digit code):
    Sport 1   **Sport 2**

Type of involvement

	Active participant	1
CODE	Administrator	2
ONE	Coach	3
	Spectator	4
	Official	5

If 1, to what standard?

Basic (family recreation; play; school clubs open to all; recreational; largely non-competitive; informal)	1
Competitive (competitive club level)	2
Elite (county, regional and nationally recognised standard)	3
Don't know	4

How often? (for seasonal sports, code as for most active period)

Once a month	1
Once a week	2
Twice a week or more	3
Can't remember/don't know	4

FRIEND 2:

As far as you know, does he/she take part in any sport?

	YES	NO
	1	2

IF NO, go to next section. If YES, which sports or hobbies is/was s/he involved with (include the two most significant), **to what standard, and how often is s/he usually involved?**

Type of activity (i.e. Sport code; 3 digit code):
    Sport 1   **Sport 2**

Type of involvement

	Active participant	1
CODE	Administrator	2
ONE	Coach	3
	Spectator	4
	Official	5

IF 1, to what standard?
    Basic (family recreation; play; school clubs open to all;
      recreational; largely non-competitive; informal)   1
    Competitive (competitive club level)   2
    Elite (county, regional and nationally recognised standard) 3
    Don't know   4

How often? (for seasonal sports, code as for most active period)
                Once a month   1
                Once a week   2
                Twice a week or more 3
                Can't remember/don't know 4

SECTION B: GENERAL QUESTIONS

Do you have any form of paid part-time work?

	YES	NO
	1	2

If YES, apart from holidays, when do you normally work?

		YES	NO
	Before school, weekdays	1	2
CIRCLE ALL	After school, weekdays	1	2
	Saturdays	1	2

How far away is the nearest public leisure centre to your house?

Less than a kilometre	1
One-two kilometres	2
More than two kilometres	3
Don't know	4

How often would you go to a leisure centre?
a) With school?

	More than once a week	1
	Once a week	2
CODE	Twice a month	3
ONE	Once a month	4
	Not very often	5
	Never	6

b) Not with school?

	More than once a week	1
	Once a week	2
CODE	More than once a month	3
ONE	Once a month	4
	Not very often	5
	Never	6

If you visit outside school time, how do you travel to the leisure centre?

		YES	NO
	Walk	1	2
	Bicycle	1	2
	Car	1	2
CIRCLE ALL	Taxi	1	2
	Train	1	2
	Bus	1	2
	Varies a lot	1	2

Do your parents own a car?

	YES	NO
CIRCLE ONE	1	2

Your height (in centimetres) _____ cm
Your weight (in kilograms) _____ kg

SECTION C: YOUR TOP SPORT

This section is only to be completed by those who have had, or presently have, an active involvement in a particular sport, whether as participant, coach or official.

Now we would like to ask you about the sport or activity which you have been especially involved with. This can be but is not necessarily a competitive or team sport. It can be any sort of physical activity which has been important to you. It may also be a sport which you aren't playing right now but have played or will play at certain times of the year.

C1. *What is the sport?* _____
(Refer to sport list for code)

C2. *What is/was your involvement with the sport?*

	Active participant	1
CODE	Administrator	2
MOST	Coach/instructor etc.	3
IMPORTANT	Official (referee, judge, etc.)	4

Active participant – playing, performing or practising the sport/ activity
Administrator – involved in the organisation of the sport/activity
Coach – provider of instruction/supervision/advice to active participants
Official – referee, judge (e.g. linesman) etc.

If 1, *what is your current level of achievement?*

Basic (family recreation; play; school clubs open to all; recreational; largely non-competitive; informal)	1
Competitive (competitive club level; selected school teams; all belts except black)	2
Elite (county, regional and nationally recognised standard; black belt)	3
Retired	4

GETTING STARTED (and finishing)

C3. *At what age did you become involved with the sport?*
Age in years _____ years

C4. *How did you become involved?*

	School	1
	Father	2
	Mother	3
	Brother/sister	4
CODE MOST	Other relative(s)	5
IMPORTANT	By yourself	6
	Through youth/church club	7
	Tried it on holiday	8
	Through friends	9
	Other	10

C5. *Which person do you think has been most important to you in maintaining your interest and involvement in this sport?*

	Father	1
	Mother	2
	Brother/sister	3
CODE MOST	Other relative	4
IMPORTANT	Your PE teacher	5
	Other teacher/principal	6
	Your coach	7
	Nobody	8
	Other	9

C6. *If you are no longer actively involved in the sport, at what age did you finish?*

CODE ONLY IF   Age in years end _____ yrs
APPLICABLE

C7. *What were the two most important reasons for no longer being involved?*

	Injury	1
	Lack of interest	2
	Other commitments (school)	3
	Other commitments (part-time job, boy/girl friend)	4
CODE	Not good enough	5
TWO	No encouragement from family	6
	Not big/strong enough	7
	Too expensive	8
	Lack of resources (e.g. equipment)	9
	Took up too much time	10
	Coaches were unfriendly	11
	Other players my age were unfriendly	12

	Older players were unfriendly	13
	Started another sport	14
CODE	My friends had stopped	15
TWO	Training was boring	16
	Mainly for boys/girls	17
	Wasn't allowed	18
	Not played at school	19
	Other	20

YOUR INVOLVEMENT

C8. *Would you prefer/have preferred to spend more or less time on this sport?*

	YES, much more time	1
	YES, a bit more time	2
CODE ONE	The same time	3
	NO, a bit less time	4
	NO, a lot less time	5

C9. *Over the last year or the last year in which you were involved, in which months of the year were you actively involved in this sport?*
(1 = involvement; 2 = not involved)

		Involved	Not inv.
	January	1	2
	February	1	2
	March	1	2
	April	1	2
	May	1	2
CIRCLE	June	1	2
ALL	July	1	2
	August	1	2
	September	1	2
	October	1	2
	November	1	2
	December	1	2

C10. *During the months in which you were actively involved, in an average week, how many hours would you spend on this sport?*

	With the school (9.00–3.30, Mon–Fri)	_____ hrs
CODE EACH	With the school (outside this time)	_____ hrs
	Not with the school	_____ hrs

If Active participant (past or present), continue. All others, go to Question C.19.

PRACTICE

This section deals not with the times when you formally compete against others in organised games, tournaments or competitions but with practice (and practice may include practice games or matches either in or out of school).

C11. *Thinking of your sport in general, at the times of the year when you are/were involved, overall how often do/did you practise, including informal practices?*

At least twice a week	1
At least once a week	2
At least once a month	3
Very occasionally	4
Never	5

If 3 or 4, go to C.12. If 5, go to C.13. If 1 or 2, continue.

If 1 or 2, *when you say you practise this often, how regular is/was this pattern of attendance?*

I always/almost always attend	1
I miss an occasional session (1 or 2 per month)	2
I miss quite a few sessions (3+ per month)	3

C12. *Where do/did you normally practise?*

	YES	NO
School (between 9.00 and 3.30, Mon–Fri)	1	2
School (other times)	1	2
Home	1	2
Youth club	1	2
Sport club (own premises)	1	2
Sport club (in leisure centre)	1	2
CIRCLE ALL Sport club (elsewhere)	1	2
Swimming pool (in leisure centre)	1	2
Swimming pool (elsewhere)	1	2
Leisure centre (general use of facilities)	1	2
Outdoors (e.g. sea; mountains)	1	2
Public park/street	1	2

COMPETING

C13. *As opposed to practices and informal games etc. in practice, training or with friends, where do/did you normally compete/play in organised games, competitions or tournaments?*

		YES	NO
	School (between 9.00 and 3.30, Mon–Fri)	1	2
	School (other times)	1	2
	Home	1	2
	Youth club	1	2
	Sport club (own premises)	1	2
	Sport club (in leisure centre)	1	2
CIRCLE ALL	Sport club (elsewhere)	1	2
	Swimming pool (in leisure centre)	1	2
	Swimming pool (elsewhere)	1	2
	Leisure centre (general use of facilities)	1	2
	Outdoors (e.g. sea; mountains)	1	2
	Public park/street	1	2

C14. *During the playing season, how often do/did you play/perform competitively?*

At least twice a week	1
At least once a week	2
At least once a month	3
Very occasionally	4
Never	5

If 1 or 2, *when you say you played this often, how regular is/was this pattern?*

I always/almost always attend(ed)	1
I miss(ed) an occasional game (1 or 2 per month)	2
I miss(ed) quite a few games (3 + per month)	3

INSTRUCTION

C15. *Has anyone ever either given you instruction, coached you, supervised practices or generally shown you what to do or how to play/perform?*

Yes, at least twice a week	1
Yes, at least once a week	2
Yes, at least once a month	3
Very occasionally	4
Never	5

If 5, go to C.19. If 3 or 4, go to C.16. If 1 or 2, continue.

When you say you were instructed this often, how regular was this person in attendance?

Always/almost always	1
Missed an occasional session (1 or 2 per month)	2
Missed quite a few sessions (3 + per month)	3

C16. *Who has given you instruction in this sport?*

		YES	NO
	Your mother	1	2
	Your father	1	2
	PE teacher	1	2
CODE ALL	Other teacher, principal, etc.	1	2
	Qualified coach	1	2
	Friends	1	2
	Brother/sister	1	2
	Other relative	1	2
	Other _____	1	2

Which of these has given you the most help with your sport?

	Your mother	1
	Your father	2
	PE teacher	3
CODE MOST	Other teacher, principal, etc.	4
IMPORTANT	Qualified/club coach	5
	Friends	6
	Brother/sister	7
	Other relative	8
	Other _____	9

C17. *What sorts of things did this person do?*
CODE _____

TWO _____

C18. *Where do/did you normally get instruction?*

	YES	NO
School (between 9.00 and 3.30, Mon–Fri)	1	2
School (other times)	1	2
Home	1	2
Youth club	1	2
Sport club (own premises)	1	2
Sport club (in leisure centre)	1	2

CIRCLE ALL	Sport club (elsewhere)	1	2
	Swimming pool (in leisure centre)	1	2
	Swimming pool (elsewhere)	1	2
	Leisure centre (general use of facilities)	1	2
	Outdoors (e.g. sea; mountains)	1	2
	Public park/street	1	2

SCHOOL

C19. *Was this sport available at your primary school?*

	YES	NO
CIRCLE ONE	1	2

C20. *Is this sport available at your secondary school or was it available when you were involved?*

	YES	NO
CIRCLE ONE	1	2

If YES, which of the following apply?

		YES	NO
	Compulsory as part of PE/games lessons	1	2
	Optional as part of PE/games lessons	1	2
CIRCLE ALL	Available after school for anyone interested	1	2
	Available after school for those selected	1	2
	Played informally at lunchtime/break	1	2
	Available on request only	1	2

C21. *In which TWO ways do you think your school has most helped you with this sport?*

1. _____
2. _____

C22. *In which TWO ways do you think your school has been least helpful or has hindered you with this sport?*

1. _____
2. _____

CLUBS

C23. *If you play, train or attend a club of any sort (e.g. sport club, church group, youth club) associated with this sport, what is the name and address of the club?*
(If none, go to C.37 – Your Family)

Club Name: _____

Address: _____

C24. *How far from your home is the club?*

_____ kilometres

C25. *At what age did you join?*

_____ years

C26. *How much are the club fees for you?* (Work out total cost per week)

_____ pounds per week

C27. *Which of the following pays?*

		YES	NO
	Yourself	1	2
CIRCLE	Parents	1	2
ALL	School	1	2
	Other	1	2

C28. *Who introduced you to the club?*

	School/teacher	1
	Friend	2
CODE MOST	Parent	3
IMPORTANT	Brother/sister	4
	Other relative	5
	Neighbour	6
	Other	7

C29. *Who most often takes you to the club?*

	Both parents equally	1
	Mainly father	2
	Mainly mother	3
CODE MOST	Brother/sister	4
IMPORTANT	Other relative	5
	Neighbour	6
	Club member	7
	No-one	8
	Varies considerably	9
	Other	10

C30. *Who stays/is usually with you at the club?*

		YES	NO
	Father	1	2
CIRCLE ALL	Mother	1	2

CIRCLE ALL	Brother/sister	1	2
	Other relative	1	2
	Neighbour	1	2
	Friend(s)	1	2
	Club members	1	2
	No-one	1	2
	Other	1	2

C31. *Who normally looks after club training, practice, etc., sessions?*

		YES	NO
	Your mother	1	2
	Your father	1	2
	An interested parent	1	2
CIRCLE ALL	A coach	1	2
	Teacher	1	2
	Youth leader	1	2
	Club member	1	2
	No-one	1	2
	Other	1	2

C32. *How would you describe what this instruction usually involves?*

		YES	NO
	Generally looks after practice games	1	2
	Offers help with individual skills	1	2
CIRCLE ALL	Manages the team (e.g. organises kit, travel)	1	2
	Talks tactics	1	2
	Organises transport	1	2
	Other (specify)	1	2

C33. *How often do you attend other functions at the club (e.g. discos)?*

	Regularly at least once a week	1
	Regularly at least once a month	2
CODE ONE	Varies but often once a week	3
	Varies but often once a month	4
	Very occasionally	5
	Never	6

C34. *How would you describe the atmosphere at the club?*

	Very friendly	1
	Quite friendly	2
CODE ONE	Neither friendly nor unfriendly	3
	Quite unfriendly	4
	Very unfriendly	5

C35. *In which TWO ways do you think your club has most helped you with this sport?*

    1. _____

    2. _____

C36. *In which TWO ways do you think your club has been least helpful or has hindered you with this sport?*

    1. _____

    2. _____

YOUR FAMILY

C37. *How often do these people watch you play/perform?*

		Never	Rarely	Often	Always	N/A
	Mother	1	2	3	4	5
	Father	1	2	3	4	5
CIRCLE ALL	Brother/s	1	2	3	4	5
	Sister/s	1	2	3	4	5
	Grandparents	1	2	3	4	5
	Other relatives	1	2	3	4	5

C38. *Have your parents ever given you any instruction in this sport?*

	Yes, all the time	1
CODE	Yes, quite often	2
ONE	Yes, sometimes	3
	Yes, very occasionally	4
	Never	5

C39. *In which TWO ways do you think your family has most helped you with this sport?*

    1. _____

    2. _____

C40. *In which TWO ways do you think your family has been least helpful or has hindered you with this sport?*

    1. _____

    2. _____

ATTAINMENTS, OBSTACLES AND GOALS

To be completed by all.

C41. As a player, when do you think that you achieved your highest standard?

	At present/within last year	1
CODE	One–two years ago	2
ONE	More than two years ago	3
	Can't remember	4
	Not applicable	5

C42. *As a player, what standard would you like to have achieved?*

Basic (family recreation; play; school clubs open to all;
recreational; largely non-competitive; informal)   1

Competitive (competitive club level; selected school
teams; all belts except black)   2

Elite (county, regional and nationally recognised standard;
black belt)   3

C43. *As a player, what standard do you think you have the ability to achieve?*

Basic (family recreation; play; school clubs open to all;
recreational; largely non-competitive; informal)   1

Competitive (competitive club level; selected school
teams; all belts except black)   2

Elite (county, regional and nationally recognised standard;
black belt)   3

C44. *Over the last year, have you*

	Become a lot more keen	1
CODE	Become a bit more keen	2
ONE	Not changed	3
	Become a bit less keen	4
	Become a lot less keen	5

C45. *Over time, what things have made you become more keen?*
(1 = not important; 2 = quite important; 3 = very important)

		Not imp.	Quite imp.	Very imp.
	Winning	1	2	3
	Enjoying taking part	1	2	3
	Being with friends	1	2	3
	Keeping fit	1	2	3
CIRCLE ALL	Support from older players	1	2	3
	Winning trophies and medals	1	2	3
	Excitement of the sport	1	2	3
	Feeling good about performing well	1	2	3
	Getting better as a player/performer	1	2	3

		Not imp.	Quite imp.	Very imp.
	Meeting people	1	2	3
	Travelling	1	2	3
CIRCLE ALL	Encouragement from family	1	2	3
	Encouragement from school	1	2	3
	Financial reward/equipment	1	2	3
	Other	1	2	3

C46. *Over time, what things have made you become less keen?*
(1 = not important; 2 = quite important; 3 = very important)

		Not imp.	Quite imp.	Very imp.
	Losing	1	2	3
	Not enjoying taking part	1	2	3
	Not seeing friends	1	2	3
	Costs too much	1	2	3
	Takes up too much time	1	2	3
	Not good enough	1	2	3
	Coaches etc. are unfriendly	1	2	3
CIRCLE ALL	Lack of support from older competitors	1	2	3
	Weather/getting cold	1	2	3
	Injuries/getting hurt	1	2	3
	Not fit enough	1	2	3
	Not big/strong enough	1	2	3
	Lack of support from school	1	2	3
	Lack of support from family	1	2	3
	Other	1	2	3

C47. *Do you think that your time and effort on this sport has been worthwhile?*

	Yes, very worthwhile	1
CODE	Yes, quite worthwhile	2
ONE	No, not usually worthwhile	3
	Not at all worthwhile	4

C48. *How easy or difficult have you found it to find time for this sport?*

	Very easy	1
CODE	Quite easy	2
ONE	Neither easy nor difficult	3
	Quite difficult	4
	Very difficult	5

C49. *Do you think you will still play after you leave school?*

	Yes, definitely	1
CODE	Yes, probably	2
ONE	Yes, possibly	3
	No	4

C50. *What are the TWO most important things that you think you have gained from this sport?*

1. _____

2. _____

Index